MW01140006

THE EARLY WORKS OF
NIELS W. GADE

For my good friend
and colleague for
many years!

Enjoy,

Anne

Frontispiece : Portrait of Niels W. Gade. (Author's Private Collection)

The Early Works of Niels W. Gade

In search of the poetic

ANNA HARWELL CELENZA
Assistant Professor of Music
Michigan State University, USA

Ashgate

Aldershot • Burlington USA • Singapore • Sydney

Published by
Ashgate Publishing Limited
Gower House
Croft Road
Aldershot
Hants GU11 3HR
England

Ashgate Publishing Company
131 Main Street
Burlington, VT 05401-5600 USA

Ashgate website: http://www.ashgate.com

British Library Cataloguing in Publication Data
Celenza, Anna Harwell
    The early works of Niels W. Gade : in search of the poetic
    1.Gade, Niels W. (Niels Wilhelm), 1817-1890 - Criticism and
    interpretation 2.Music - Denmark - 19th century
    I.Title
    780.9'2

Library of Congress Cataloging-in-Publication Data
Celenza, Anna Harwell.
    The early works of Niels W. Gade : in search of the poetic / Anna Harwell Celenza.
        p. cm.
    Includes bibliographical references.
    ISBN 0-7546-0401-2 (alk. paper)
    1. Gade, Niels W. (Niels Wilhelm), 1817-1890–Criticism and interpretation. I. Title.

ML410.G12 C35 2001
780'.92–dc21   2001022814

ISBN 0 7546 0401 2

Printed and bound in Great Britain by Biddles Ltd, *www.biddles.co.uk*

For Aubrey S. Garlington

Only through the poetic can a human being expand his existence into the existence of humanity. Only in the poetic do all means serve one end.

– Friedrich Schlegel, *Kritische Schriften und Fragmente*, vol. 5, 256.

Contents

Appendices

Preface

Niels W. Gade (1817–90) was undoubtedly the most influential musical figure in nineteenth-century Denmark. Since the centennial of his death, appreciation for his music has been growing steadily in Europe and the United States. Over fifty recordings of his works are currently available on CD, and the inaugural volumes of *The Complete Works of Niels W. Gade*, published by Bärenreiter, have just started to appear. This book presents the first in-depth study in English of Gade's life and works. Its purpose is two-fold: to describe the evolution of Gade's compositional style as reflected in his early orchestral and chamber works and to re-evaluate his role as a nationalist composer.

Until now musicological investigations of Gade's life and music have been undertaken exclusively by Danish and German scholars. Given Gade's biography this is unsurprising: In addition to being the undisputed leader of Denmark's musical life during the second half of the nineteenth century, Gade enjoyed a brilliant career in the 1840s at the Gewandhaus in Leipzig and was one of the few Danes blessed with international success. This Danish/German duality has led to two distinct views of the composer. The first, given by most Danish scholars, categorizes Gade as a national composer who, through the creation of a 'national tone,' attempted to strengthen international recognition of Denmark's musical culture. The second, supported primarily by German scholars, stresses Gade's attachment to German Romanticism and stresses his allegiance to figures such as Felix Mendelssohn and Robert Schumann. Both viewpoints have much to recommend them, but neither fully clarifies what motivated Gade as a composer.

In this study I investigate Gade's musical roots. Rather than characterizing Gade's oeuvre in terms of purely Danish or German musical traditions, I offer a more complex, multivalent explanation. Among other things, I address the limited musical education available in Denmark during the first half of the nineteenth century; the creative confines imposed by Denmark's music societies and publishers of music; the sudden influx of German aesthetical thought into Danish artistic circles in the 1830s and 40s; the influence of Danish and German literature on Gade's creative identity; and the ideals of Danish nationalism (which differed substantially from those of German nationalism) and their effect on the reception of Gade's music.

Gade's early works are a valuable lens through which to view the evolution of his compositional style, and his composition diary, written between July 1839 and

October 1841, serves as a useful point of departure. The diary contains the programmatic origins for seven of Gade's early compositions: the published *Echoes of Ossian* Overture (Op. 1); Symphony No. 1 in C minor (Op. 5); Piano Sonata in E minor (Op. 28); and *Agnete and the Merman* songs (Op. 3); and the unpublished Trio in B-flat major for Violin, Cello, and Piano; String Quartet in F major; and *St. Hans' Evening Play* Overture. Tracing the evolution of these compositions from their literary origins to their final form, I describe the development of Gade's compositional style, especially in relation to his early struggles with large, symphonic forms, and examine his commitment to both German fashion and Danish folk culture.

Throughout his life, Gade looked to literature as a source of musical inspiration. In part one of this study, I explore Gade's literary and musical roots. Chapter one discusses Gade's formative years and his first exposure to literature from Denmark and abroad. Chapter two traces Gade's first experiments as a composer. Here special attention is given to the influence of Schumann's aesthetics in Copenhagen through the *Neue Zeitschrift für Musik* and the formation of what is perhaps best described as a 'Copenhagen Davidsbund' in the late 1830s.

Part two of this study traces Gade's 'Search for the Poetic' by presenting in-depth descriptions of the seven works represented in his composition diary. As chapter three explains, the first three works mentioned in Gade's diary – the Piano Trio, Piano Sonata, and String Quartet – all made use of a similar literary topic, the departure and return of a loved one. Gade's attempt to capture a single concept in various genres reveals his commitment to a poetic ideal. In the case of the Piano Trio and String Quartet, discussed in chapter four, Gade's immediate programmatic sources were excerpts of German poetry, namely Wilhelm Müller's 'Thränenregen' and Goethe's 'Wilkommen und Abschied.' The program for his Piano Sonata, discussed in chapter five, was based on excerpts of German and Danish texts written by his friends in the Copenhagen Davidsbund.

The fourth program in Gade's composition diary, a five-movement symphony entitled *Agnete and the Merman*, reveals Gade's interest in Danish literary sources. In addition to quoting Jens Baggesen's *Agnete from Holmegaard*, Gade takes excerpts from Hans Christian Andersen's *Agnete and the Merman* and quotes lines from several Danish chorales. Unfortunately, no musical realization of this program exists. But as chapter six explains, we can surmise from details in Gade's program and evidence in his correspondence that he was influenced by at least two musical works: Berlioz's *Symphonie fantastique* and Mendelssohn's *The Fair Melusine* Overture.

Gade's program for the famous *Echoes of Ossian* Overture is the fifth entry in his composition diary. Here we finally encounter the composer's successful integration of his Danish and German roots. Gade used excerpts of Steen Steensen Blicher's translation of the *Poems of Ossian* as the source for his program, and the thematic material in the overture shows an indebtedness to Danish folk music.

Twentieth-century scholars have looked to this work as the first of Gade's 'nationalistic' compositions. But as chapter seven explains, this assumption is misguided. The *Poems of Ossian* never served as part of Denmark's folk heritage, and a study of Danish literature shows no link between Ossian and Danish nationalism.[1] Gade did not choose Ossian for nationalistic reasons – such a connection never would have been understood in Denmark. Instead, he chose Ossian for a more pragmatic reason, the acquisition of international recognition.

The next work mentioned in Gade's composition diary is an overture entitled *St. Hans' Evening Play*. Inspired by Adam Oehlenschläger's text and Mendelssohn's overture, *A Midsummer Night's Dream*, this work, once again, shows Gade's successful integration of German and Danish influences. When *St. Hans' Evening Play* was premiered in Copenhagen in 1842, it received glowing reviews but, unfortunately, was never published. The second half of chapter seven explains how Gade's choice of Oehlenschläger's *St. Hans' Evening Play* restricted his audience and, consequently, offered music publishers little hope for financial gain.

Perhaps the fate of *St. Hans' Evening Play* influenced the creation of the final work in Gade's composition diary, the C-minor Symphony, Op. 5. On the whole, Gade's first symphony reflects a tension between Danish and German elements. Gade based his program on Danish ballad texts, but the music itself verifies the influence of German romantic models, i.e. Beethoven, Mendelssohn and Schubert. Gade's Danish colleagues were certainly aware of the symphony's Germanic leanings; when Gade first attempted, in 1842, to have his symphony premiered in Denmark, it was rejected by the Music Society – 'too German' being the reason for refusal. Chapter eight traces the unique reception history of Gade's first symphony, undoubtedly one of his most inimitable compositions.

No discussion of Gade's early works would be complete without an examination of their current status as Danish national monuments. Until now most twentieth-century scholars have maintained that Gade intentionally created a 'national tone' in his early works. They describe these pieces (especially *Echoes of Ossian* and the C-minor Symphony) as cornerstones of Danish nationalism, symbols of Denmark's independence from German dominance. The conclusions of my study presented in chapter nine differ from this picture substantially and suggest that Gade's status as a nationalist composer has to do less with his own aspirations and more with a late-nineteenth- and early-twentieth-century search for Danish national identity. I shed new critical light on the debate by focusing on four basic issues: Gade's original musical intentions; the discernable presence, if any, of a 'national tone' in Gade's music; the social, cultural, and political climate surrounding Gade during his formative years; and the reception history of Gade's

---

[1] See my article, '*Efterklange af Ossian*: The Reception of James MacPherson's *Poems of Ossian* in Denmark's Literature, Art and Music,' *Scandinavian Studies* 70 (1998): 359–96.

early compositions. My conclusions are simple: Gade's nationalistic status is not the result of his musical output, but rather the consequence of nineteenth-century German criticism and twentieth-century scholarship. Gade did not write his early works for an exclusively Danish audience, rather he composed with an international audience in mind; and by crossing the Danish/German cultural divide, he effectively established himself, with his early compositions, as Denmark's most famous composer and Leipzig's most promising prodigy.

Due to the amount of unpublished source material used for this study, I have included a number of appendices. Appendix one contains a transcription of Gade's composition diary. Appendix two contains personalia of Danish figures unfamiliar to non-Danish readers. Appendix three contains transcriptions of Gade's autobiographical sketch and the letters to and from the composer that appear in chapters one, two, and eight. Appendix four contains the unpublished correspondence between Felix Mendelssohn and the Musikforeningen in Copenhagen. And appendix five contains the rejected second movement to the Piano Sonata in E Minor, Op. 28.

The present study draws in varying degrees on some of my already published work and on my Ph.D. dissertation. Still, I would hesitate to describe this book as a mere 'reworking' of the dissertation. Rather, I hope that it might be viewed as an outgrowth of my earlier work, a fresh look at the topic from various scholarly perspectives.

At the risk of making omissions, I would like to acknowledge some of the individuals who have supported this project. To Niels Martin Jensen, Jan Maegaard, and Niels Krabbe, I offer 'mange tak' for their encouragement and guidance. They opened my eyes to Denmark's literary and musical culture when I was a graduate student and served as mentors during my time in Copenhagen. Also deserving thanks are Niels Bo Foltmann (Gade Edition and Carl Nielsen Edition), Anne Ørbæk Jensen (Gade Edition), and Claus Røllum-Larsen (Carl Nielsen Edition) for the long discussions we shared concerning Gade's life and music in the cafeteria of the Royal Library. This study would have never come to fruition without those collegial 'brainstorming' lunches. To Finn Egeland Hansen and Thorkil Hørlyk (Gade Edition and Aalborg University) I owe a debt of gratitude for their valuable criticism concerning my work on Gade's chamber music; and I thank David Birchler (A-R Editions) for his comments concerning *St. Hans' Evening Play*. Also deserving appreciation are Suzanne Thorbæk (Music Division – Royal Library) and Bendt Viinholt Nielsen (Danish Music Information Centre) for their help in tracking down invaluable sources and obscure recordings.

Thanks to the Royal Library in Copenhagen and the Fredriksborg Museum for allowing me to reproduce items from their collections, and a special thank you to Lynn Latham of Latham Enterprises and Paul Schreiber for their invaluable assistance with the music examples. Mary Black and the staff at the Michigan State University Library offered much help in the final stages of this project; I appreciate their patient assistance. I should also like to mention my indebtedness to James Forger, the director of the School of Music, for his support and guidance during my first years at Michigan State University. To the Fulbright Foundation, the Queen Margrethe and Prince Henrik Foundation (Denmark), and the Idella Foundation (Liechtenstein) I offer heart-felt thanks for their generous financial support.

The insight provided by the members of my dissertation committee during my early investigation of Gade's life and music laid the foundation for this study. Special thanks to R. Larry Todd, Bryan Gilliam, James Haar, John Nádas, Thomas Brothers and especially Aubrey Garlington. It was Aubrey Garlington who first encouraged me to embark on a career in musicology. Through the years he has been a constant source of inspiration and support. He has read numerous versions of this study and, by his careful scrutiny, has helped me to sharpen the argument considerably. I shall never be able to thank him adequately, but I hope that at least a small portion of my appreciation might be expressed through the dedication of this book.

East Lansing, Michigan   Anna Harwell Celenza
November 2000

Part One

The Formative Years
(1817–38)

Chapter One

Childhood and Early Musical Training

The only first-hand account of Gade's early childhood was written by the composer himself on 16 August 1885:

On 17 April 1812, a young carpenter and his bride were joined in holy matrimony in Trinity Church. His name was Søren Nielsen Gade, a twenty-two year old descended from a family of Jutland peasants who had taken the name Gade from a little town between Kolding and Frederits. Her name was Marie Sophie Hansdatter Arentzen, a twenty year old whose parents were originally from Bornholm. The year 1812 and the time that followed was very stormy [for Denmark]; the only peace and well being to be found was within the calm idyll of home life. Europe's destroyer of peace, Napoleon, had been conquered; but poverty and unrest still prevailed in most countries. This period was one of the most distressful for Denmark's people: Norway had been lost; and the treasury department was in the greatest confusion, causing want, despondency, and a standstill in trade everywhere. All of this subdued the population and covered everything with a cloud of philistinism. One lived simply for one's daily, very frugal, bread.

Nonetheless, the young couple's modest home was an idyll, illuminated with the sunshine of love. They did not hear the storms of their age, and their modest food became the most wonderful fare.

In this quiet home I first saw light, on 22 February 1817, and was baptized: Niels Wilhelm Gade. I was the only child, and because I had already left them waiting for five years, I was naturally greeted with great joy and tended with the most loving care by my parents.

One of my earliest memories from childhood involves a minor event from my fourth year. One summer night my parents gave me a few coins for a cake from the baker's across the way. With glad expectations I crossed the street, went into the boutique, and bought my box of cakes without misfortune. On the way home, however, I was not so lucky. I tripped and fell, and the box of cakes rolled down into the gutter. I was very frightened by this unexpected and sudden change in events. I broke down in heavy sobs and ran quickly home where both mother and father comforted me over the mistake. But even though I was forgiven, I could not stop my sobbing. I had to be taken to bed, and I can still remember quite clearly the mood I was in: It was as if my life's happiness – by my own fault – had sunken deep into Lethe's dark water and was being imprisoned there, permanently, without hope of ever seeing light again.

It was around this time that my father and his older brother, Jens Nielsen Gade, began to manufacture instruments. Together they set up a shop for musical instruments, namely guitar and violin. This shop did very well, and the brothers decided to divide the business, each establishing a shop for himself. My father moved from the joint home on Borgergade to the corner of Nygade and Skoubogade, in the middle of the city. I clearly remember sitting on the floor of the corner room, playing with [a newspaper], *Adressavisen*, while the sun shined through the windows, creating squares of light on the floor and walls and spreading a sense of comfort.

I was around six years old when I first began practicing music; namely I strummed on a little children's guitar that my father had given me as a present. Around the same time I studied ABC books under my mother's guidance. During this period the guitar, flute, and occasionally the harp were the instruments most fancied by amateurs. Men and women sang romantic and sentimental romances by Rudolph Bay, Plantade, etc. to the accompaniment of guitars, which hung from their shoulders on light-blue bands, – such was the fashion in the early twenties. My father had a certain fame for constructing guitars based on Spanish models that looked good and had a nice sound. His business was very profitable. Later on the guitar was supplanted by the piano. He wasn't very lucky in the fabrication of this instrument. Other manufacturers soon came into existence (Richter, Uldahl, Bechmann, Marschall, and others), which is why his business suffered a little. Nonetheless, peace and joy continued to bloom in our home, my father's sanguine temperament and jovial thoughts always provided sunshine and good humor when my mother's pensive and profound nature saw dark clouds approaching on the horizon.

Both [my parents] had a sense for poetry and reading, and in the twenties, when Oehlenschläger, Heiberg, Grundtvig, Schack-Staffeldt and Ingemann lived and wrote their best works, poetry blossomed in Denmark. My father had musical talent, and although he had never studied a particular instrument, he could play a little on almost all of them. My mother was also fond of music, but her greatest passion was the theater and especially tragedies, of which the talents at that time were first rate. The hero and the nordic virgin in Oehlenschläger's tragedies were performed excellently by Nielsen and Madam Wexschall (later Madam Nielsen). Dr. Ryge was outstanding in roles such as Hakon Jarl, Planatoke, etc. Comical roles were performed by similarly excellent artists: Frydendahl, Lindgreen, Stage, and others. It was as if all these excellent poets and dramatic artists were given to us [Denmark] as compensation for our political insignificance. We had artistic and scientific greats such as Thorvaldsen and H.C. Ørsted, who awakened the attention of all Europe and cast a splendor back over little Denmark. That is why the people of Denmark are drawn to the world of the poet, to art, and to theater, and why their sense for politics is so poor.[1]

---

[1] Dagmar Gade, *Niels W. Gade, Optegnelser og Breve*, (Copenhagen: Gyldendalsk Boghandels Forlag, 1892), 5–7. See appendix three for original Danish. All translations are my own unless otherwise indicated.

Figure 1. 17 Borgergade – The second floor was Neils W. Gade's first home.
(DkB: Photograph Collection)

Gade was sixty-eight years old when he recorded these memories, and hindsight undoubtedly colored his recollections. Nonetheless, this first-hand account serves as a valuable introduction to the cultural conditions that affected Gade's personality and his evolution as a composer.

Copenhagen was a provincial music center during Gade's formative years. Between 1780 and 1820 a number of social clubs served as the central source of Copenhagen's music life.[2] Eager to appeal to the demands of its members, these clubs offered a wide variety of concerts at reasonable prices.[3] But in the early 1820s, troubled financial times began to affect the capital's cultural climate, and concerts became an expensive luxury that many clubs discontinued. As an editorial from 1822 reveals, the dissolution of the club scene left Copenhagen's musicians with few performance opportunities:

> No capital in Europe has more lovers and performers of music than Copenhagen; but unfortunately the effect of recent circumstances has made the opportunity to hear good music more and more rare. The Musical Academy was terminated as early as several years ago, ... The King's Club and Harmony Club have almost cut their concerts out completely. This despite the fact that the latter, the most impressive society in Copenhagen, was originally founded as a club intended for the pursuit of music.[4]

---

[2] According to V.C. Ravn, vol. 1: *Koncerter og musikalske Selskaber i ældre Tid* in *Festschrift i anledning af Musikforeningens Halvhundredaarsdag*, (Copenhagen, Musik-foreningen, 1886), 99–148, the most popular clubs sponsoring concerts included Kongens Klub (with Claus Schall as concertmaster), Det harmoniske Selskab, Enigheds-Selskabet (also with Claus Schall as concertmaster), Det venskabelige Selskab, Det danske og norske Selskab, Musikselskabet ved gammel Strand Nr. 12, Musikens Dyrkerers og Elskeres Selskab, Det militære Selskab, Det forenede musikalske Selskab, Kronprinsens Klub, Det kgl. musikalske Akademi, Det holstenske Selskab, Den nye Harmoni, Det venskabelige musikalske Selskab, Det harmonerende musikalske Selskab, Euphonien, Coalitionen, Recreationen, Venne-selskabet, Polyhymnia, Selskabet den musikalske Forening, Det forenede musikalske Øvelsesselskab, Panphonia, and Det musikalske Selskab Foreningen.

[3] In an article appearing in *Allgemeine musikalische Zeitung* 39 (23 September 1812): 646, Frederik Kuhlau commented on Copenhagen's unique musical atmosphere: 'Am besuchtesten sind hier immer die sogenannten Clubb-Concerte, und zwar wol meistens des geringen Preises wegen, auf welchen allerdings Rucksicht zu nehmen die Zeitverhältnisse auch wohlhabende Musikfreunde nöthigen. Die bedeutendsten dieser sind: die kön. musikal. Academie, und die, der harmonischen Geselleschaft.' Chamber works for strings were often included on these concerts – on 22 February 1823, a concert in the Musical Academy's concert hall featured a quartet by Pechatschek (performed by Wexschall, C.F. Mohr, I.F. Bredal and Søren Kuhlau) and a quintet by Ries (performed by by C.F. Mohr and his son, Frøhlich, Bredal and Kuhlau). In March 1843 a Mayseder quartet was presented by Wexschall at another club-sponsored event.

[4] *Kjøbenhavn Skilderi* 19 February 1822. 'I ingen Hovedstad i Europa har Musiken flere Yndere og Dyrkere end i Kjøbenhavn; men Lejligheden til at høre god Musik er desværre som Virkning af Tidsomstændighederne i den nyere Tid bleven sjældnere og sjældnere. Det musikalske Akademi er allerede for adskillige Aar siden ganske ophørt,... Kongens Klub og

By the early 1820s musical life in Copenhagen centered around the simple salon repertoire mentioned in Gade's memoire.

As a child, Gade showed an interest in music but received little training. Neither of his parents were accomplished musicians, and the family's strained finances precluded Gade from receiving even the most basic education before age twelve. By the time Gade was able to begin formal music lessons on the violin, at age thirteen, he showed little interest in the instrument. The theater had become his first passion, and as an adolescent any interest in music was quickly overshadowed by an obsession with the dramatic arts.

Gade's unflagging interest in the theater was probably the result of his friendship with a neighborhood friend named Frederik Høedt (1820–85). Høedt came from a rather affluent family, and unlike Gade, he was a student at the Gymnasium. Høedt had an uncanny gift for languages, which undoubtedly led to his early interest in contemporary literature. Gade first met Høedt in 1830, and his life-long love of literature was largely due to Høedt's influence. The friends spent countless hours reading poetry and memorizing plays. Oehlenschläger and Shakespeare held the most honored positions in the young men's repertoire, but the works of Heiberg, Wieland, Schiller, and Goethe were included as well.

Gade's commitment to the theater was formally declared in 1831, when he approached his father and asked for permission to pursue a career in acting. Believing the livelihood of an actor to be insecure at best, Gade's father refused his son's request and suggested instead an apprenticeship in carpentry. Gade complied with his father's wishes and began to learn the trade of instrument construction, but this career was short-lived. His creative yearnings soon caused him to turn his attention to formal music studies once again. After promising to dedicate himself completely to the violin, Gade was given a second chance. In October 1832 he began lessons with the best teacher Denmark had to offer – Frederik Thorkildson Wexschall.

Gade made extraordinary progress on the violin. His first public concert took place at the Hotel Angleterre on 22 May 1833 when, together with the Hamburg pianist Karl Evers, he performed a Polonaise by Joseph Mayseder (1789–1863). Later that year Gade made his debut at the Royal Theater with a promising violinist named Fritz Schram.[5] Together they played John Wenzel Kalliwoda's Double Fantasy for two violins, and local papers praised the performers for their 'rare talent,' 'error-free playing' and 'clean technique.'[6]

Harmonien have næsten ganske indskrænket deres Koncerter, uagtet den sidste ikke alene er det anseligste Selskab i Kjøbenhavn, men ogsaa oprindeligen fra dets Stiftelse af har været bestemt til et Selskab for Musikøvelse.'

[5] Charles Kjerulf, *Niels W. Gade: Til Belysning af Hans Liv og Kunst* (Copenhagen: Gyldendalske Boghandel, 1917), 21.

[6] Dagmar Gade, 16.

In February 1834 Gade was admitted into the Royal Chapel's violin school. As a student he continued his private instruction with Wexschall and played in the Chapel orchestra. Although 'the honor of membership' was the only payment Gade received for his services in the Chapel, the position was invaluable, for it enabled him to play in an orchestral setting and augment his ever-expanding repertoire.

It is difficult to determine what music Gade was exposed to during his early years at the Royal Chapel. Cantatas and Singspiele were performed on a regular basis, and Rossini's operas were introduced as early as the 1820s. As a member of the Chapel, Gade was exposed to a relatively small amount of symphonic music. The works of Beethoven had not yet been introduced on a regular basis, and no school of symphonists like those in Paris, Vienna, London, or Berlin existed in Denmark. Consequently, symphonies from the south, most notably Germany, formed the most important part of the repertoire.

The provincial character of Copenhagen's musical culture is recorded in the pages of the *Allgemeine musicalishe Zeitung*. During the 1820s and 30s the journal periodically lamented the state of Copenhagen's concert activities. Critics found the programming conservative and uninteresting, and good performances were nonexistent outside the Royal Theater. They complained that orchestral works were given little attention and noted that when a symphony did appear on the program, it was rarely performed in its entirety.[7]

The Royal Chapel was not, however, Gade's only source for orchestral music. In the early decades of the nineteenth century, a number of subscription libraries were established in Copenhagen. For a modest payment members could borrow sheet music from a large selection of pieces carefully registered in the catalogues of various publishing firms. The music in these catalogues was both foreign and domestic, and ten thousand titles per catalogue was not unusual; some even contained as many as twenty thousand titles. The target of these lending libraries was largely the homes of music-making bourgeoisie. Consequently, the majority of the items available to lenders was for piano, either works written specifically for the instrument or arrangements of pieces for two, four, six, and even eight hands.[8] Vocal music and salon pieces were also popular. Some chamber music was available, along with scores of a few orchestral works. Unfortunately, no statistics concerning circulation at these libraries still exist. But it appears that Gade was a

---

[7] *Allgemeine Musikalische Zeitung* XIV: 645 f.; XV: 463 ff.; XXXII: 192 f. See also Niels Krabbe, 'The Reception of Beethoven in Copenhagen in the 19th Century,' *Music in Copenhagen: Studies in the Musical Life of Copenhagen in the 19th and 20th Centuries* (Viborg: C.A. Reitzel, 1996), 166–67.

[8] Krabbe, 166–67.

regular subscriber. His transcriptions of works by Handel, Mozart, Haydn and Beethoven were likely made from music he borrowed during the 1830s and 40s.[9]

In 1833 Gade began studying theory and composition with A.P. Berggreen (1801–80), a native composer who had recently secured a notable reputation with his cantatas and theater music.[10] Berggreen established his career with compositions for Denmark's royal family, but his preoccupation with music for the church and school dominated his aesthetic outlook. Berggreen was only sixteen years Gade's senior, but his philosophical outlook was more in tune with an older generation. He belonged to the circle of C.E.F. Weyse (1774–1842) and Friedrich Kuhlau (1786–1832), and his ideas concerning aesthetics and music's purpose were decidedly those of the Enlightenment. A staunch patriot, Berggreen believed in the educational value of music. Through the establishment of a firm system of music education in the church and schools, he believed that Denmark's society could regain the cultural traditions destroyed by the political and economic troubles of the past. Berggreen valued music for its edifying uses. For him music served as a tool for education, a medium for the enlightenment of the masses.[11]

When Gade first began studying with Berggreen, he showed little interest in his teacher's preoccupation with music's prosaic purposes. Headstrong and ambitious, Gade was eager to compose works on a grander scale. His earliest sketches reveal an interest in orchestral genres, but Berggreen soon took the upper hand and guided his student through an intensive study of counterpoint.[12] By the middle of 1835 Gade was focusing on works of a slightly smaller scale, namely an *Introduction and Duet* for voice and chamber orchestra and a setting of Goethe's *An Minna* for tenor and orchestra.[13] Invigorated by the completion of these projects, Gade returned to large orchestral genres at the end of the year and began work on an overture called *Socrates*. The story of this work is a popular one in late-nineteenth and early twentieth-century biographies of Gade. Berggreen had been commissioned to compose the incidental music for a play called *Socrates* written by Adam Oehlenschläger, and apparently Gade was given the task of

---

[9] These transcriptions are now held in Copenhagen's Royal Library (Det kongelige Bibliotek, hereafter referred to as DkB) Ny kgl. Saml. 1716, 4°, Gade's efterladte papirer.

[10] Berggreen's first success, a cantata for the 200th anniversary of Regensen (a well-known students' college in Copenhagen), earned him great favor with Denmark's royal family, and in 1829 he was commissioned to write a cantata for the wedding of Prince Ferdinand and Princess Caroline.

[11] Many of these beliefs were fueled by the writings of N.F.S. Grundtvig. These will be discussed further in chapter nine.

[12] Gade's earliest sketches (dated 1834) contain a transcription of an overture (perhaps by Romberg) entitled *Die Kindermörderin von Schiller* (DkB:Gade Saml. CII, 6.) A collection of Gade's counterpoint exercises are preserved in the Royal Library (DkB: Gade Saml. CII, 6). They are dated 2 August 1835 and 14 February 1836. On the first page Gade wrote: 'Hele min dobb. Contrap. Andel.'

[13] Both manuscripts are found in DkB: Gade Saml. C II, 6.

composing the overture. Gade completed the piece, but no trace of the work now exists. After hearing the overture in rehearsal at the Royal Theater, Gade supposedly collected the parts and burned them in disgust. When asked about this incident years later he replied: 'I needed to sit in the orchestra for a long time and listen to the instruments before I attempted to compose again for orchestra.'[14]

After the disappointment of *Socrates*, Gade turned his attention once again to smaller works, namely songs for voice and piano. Encouraged by Gade's change of heart, Berggreen published his student's setting of 'Lebet Wohl' in the periodical *Musikalsk Tidene* along with the following accolade:

> The public already knows Herr N.W. Gade as an excellent violinist trained at Concertmaster Wexschall's School. But this young musician, with his continual diligence and attentiveness, has also acquired a thorough knowledge in music theory. It is an absolute joy to remark on young musicians' eager attempts to become acquainted with a segment of musical resources which previously have been an unknown land to many.[15]

Berggreen's interest in vocal works blossomed into a preoccupation with folk music in the mid 1830s. For Berggreen, as for many others interested in the edifying value of music, folk tunes served as the foundation for a new era of art music. In 1842 he wrote:

> Within the movement that in this century has found its place among the arts and sciences, attention has been given to the treasures owned by nations in their folk songs and melodies. As direct expressions of a nation's spiritual nature, they [folk songs] attract, at the highest level, every single poetic disposition. They enrich the imagination and allow us to look deeply into each nation's distinctive soul. And since the strong characteristic differences [of folk songs and melodies] refresh the mind and prevent one-sidedness in taste, we learn to conceive of ideal beauty through the greatest variety of forms. In addition they [folk songs and melodies] furnish the most reliable touchstone for the truth of that which, in the arts, presents itself as being characteristic of a certain people...[16]

---

[14] Dagmar Gade, 20. 'Jeg maatte sidde længe nede i Orchestret og lytte efter Instrumenternes Klang, før jeg igjen prøvede at komponere for Orchester.'

[15] *Musikalsk Tidene* 2 (1836). 'Hr. N.W. Gade, der allerede er Publikum bekendt som en fortrinlig Violinspiller, uddanet i Koncertmester Wexschalls Skole. Ogsaa i den musikalske Teori har denne unge Musiker ved sin stadige Flid og Tænksomhed erhvervet sig grundige Kundskaber. Det er overhovedet glædigt at bemærke, med hvilken Iver de ynge Musikere søge at trænge in i en Del af Tonekunstens Rige, der før har været mange et ubekendt Land.'

[16] A.P. Berggreen, *Folke-Sange og Melodier, fædrelandske og fremmede*, (Copenhagen, 1842), vol. 1, 1. Herder expressed a similar idea in *Ideen zur Philosophie der Geschichte der Menschheit* (1785): '...die Musik einer Nation auch in ihren unvollkommensten Gängen und Lieblingstönen zeigt den innern Charakter derselben d.i. die eigentliche Stimmung ihres

Convinced that folk music provided a wealth of possibilities for Danish musicians, Berggreen offered advice to composers concerning the proper use of this valuable resource:

> Musicians have not yet fully recognized, as poets have with regard to folk poetry, the wholesome material for musical composition found in folk melodies. The employment of this element in art should not merely be to enclose these melodies in a musical work; instead these melodies must be recast according to the composer's style, which when filled with their [the folk melodies'] spirit will give the composer's work an individual, national character that, before all else, gives meaning to a work of art.[17]

Berggreen was an excellent teacher, but a romantic he was not. As Charles Kjerulf once noted, he was 'more a bourgeois than an artist,'[18] and Schumann undoubtedly would have classified him a philistine. Berggreen had a strict set of musical principles, and he 'fought like a lion' for the conservative values he inherited from composers such as Friedrich Kuhlau and C.E.F. Weyse.[19] Gade respected Berggreen's guidance and concern, but he did not share his teacher's interest in music's prosaic purposes.[20] Inspired by the music of Beethoven, Mendelssohn, and Spohr, Gade rebelled against his teacher's generation and sought artistic refuge in the company of his peers. In 1834 he became part of a close-knit circle of friends whose shared interests in music and literature eventually led to a fascination for the critical writings of Robert Schumann and his fictional community of artists, the Davidsbund.

The originality of Schumann's critical writings and the influence of his *Neue Zeitschrift für Musik* on German musical life is a topic that has been thoroughly explored by various scholars. But little has been said of the journal's influence on foreign, provincial communities. In the nineteenth century, the printed word was a powerful tool used in the establishment of intellectual communities. Continuous publications such as daily newspapers and weekly magazines proliferated in all parts of Europe and created a sense of ritualized community among readers of

---

empfindenden Organs tiefer und wahrer, als ihn die längste Beschreibung äußerer Zufälligkeiten zu schildern vermöchte.' *Herders sämmtliche Werke* XIII, B. Suphan, ed. (Berlin, 1887), 298.

[17] Berggreen, *Folke-Sange og Melodier*, vol. 1, 1.

[18] Kjerulf, 36.

[19] Ibid. A conservative by nature, Weyse was rooted in eighteenth-century music ideals from Handel and Bach to Haydn and Mozart, and he scarcely accepted the new trends in Beethoven's later works and Mendelssohn's programmatic pieces. Gade was no doubt familiar with Weyse's sentiments, beginning in 1839 he served as Weyse's assistant organist at Frue Kirke in Copenhagen. Berggreen's devotion to Weyse is affirmed by his publication of a Weyse biography: *C.E.F. Weyses biographie* (Copenhagen, 1876).

[20] Gade composed several folk-song arrangements for Berggreen's *Sange til Skolebrug* in 1837, but he generally showed little interest in his teacher's folk song projects.

various nationalities.[21] Schumann was fully aware of the power of the printed word, and in the 1830s he was eager to create a new intellectual community, a community of professional musicians who would join together in a 'fight against the Philistines.' The instrument for Schumann's new community was the *Neue Zeitschrift für Musik*, a journal unlike any other. It was created, in large part, as a reaction to the *Allgemeine musikalische Zeitung* and the intellectual community associated with that journal.[22]

Whereas the *Allgemeine musikalische Zeitung* was written for laymen interested in recent musical events, the *Neue Zeitschrift für Musik* was for a more select group of readers. It was established by professional musicians who had special interests to promote, and it was addressed primarily to people who might be expected to share its point of view, namely a new generation of composers, teachers and performers. The *Neue Zeitschrift für Musik* was far less committed than the *Allgemeine musikalische Zeitung* to reporting the events of Leipzig's musical scene. It had far fewer concert reviews, and those that were printed tended to focus on the music, rather than the performances.

Although the seriousness and professional standards of the *Neue Zeitschrift für Musik* restricted its audience in one sense, its subject matter had the opposite effect: the journal included reports from places as far away as the United States and South America. And the various articles often showed a keen interest in literature and the visual arts. As Schumann himself explained in the inaugural issue: 'We do not mean to share with our fellow art lovers only that having to do immediately with music. We also wish to provide them enjoyment and spiritual nourishment with things that would interest them as connoisseurs of the arts in general.'[23]

Among musical journals of the time the *Neue Zeitschrift für Musik* was unique. Partisan but progressive, it sought to inspire rather than to educate. Like several of the best-known literary journals in Germany, the *Neue Zeitschrift für Musik* quickly established itself as the organ for a special movement, a new school of

---

[21] In his book *Imagined Communities* (originally published in 1983; revised edition, London: Verso, 1991), Benedict Anderson examined the power of the printed word in the establishment of intellectual communities and showed how continuous publications such as daily newspapers and weekly magazines create a sense of ritualized community among readers. Anderson employed this concept of ritualized reading in an examination of the origins of nationalism, but I have found that it serves equally well, if not better, in discussions of nineteenth-century criticism and the establishment of intellectual circles.

[22] On the surface the *Allgemeine musikalische Zeitung* and the *Neue Zeitschrift für Musik* were quite similar: both were published in Leipzig, both were made up of general articles on various topics, both included reviews of recently published music and books, both gave reports of noted concerts and recitals, and both included correspondence articles from other cities. In fact, we know that Schumann studied the *Allgemeine musikalische Zeitung* extensively before he began formulating his ideas for the layout of the *Neue Zeitschrift für Musik*.

[23] *Neue Zeitschrift für Musik*, 1 (1834): 36.

opinion. It was the voice of musical Romanticism, and during its first decade it was stamped indelibly with the personality of Schumann.

Schumann wrote many of the articles that appeared in the *Neue Zeitschrift für Musik*, and his style of music criticism was a personal variation of the literary type associated with the music reviews of E.T.A. Hoffmann. Schumann used language rich in images and figures, and he strained to communicate in words the aesthetic qualities of musical experience. The result was the use of one artistic medium to explicate another. Schumann's earliest journal articles were fantasies in ornate prose. His music reviews were often cast as narratives, complete with descriptions of characters, dialogue, and even some action. They looked like fragments of novels, and they engaged the reader in intellectual discourse. The most noticeable aspect of Schumann's critical style was his creation of an imaginary community, the Davidsbund. In the Introduction to the 1854 edition of his collected writings, Schumann provided a succinct rationale for his creation of the Davidsbund:

> In order to express different points of view on artistic matters, it seemed appropriate to invent contrasting artist-characters, of whom Florestan and Eusebius were the most important, with Master Raro occupying a mediating position between them.[24]

By allowing various members of the Davidsbund to speak in his articles, Schumann presented the reader with a discourse on the topic of interest instead of the usual one-sided point of view. In short, he created an imaginary community that invited the participation of the journal's readers.

Schumann did not create his extravagant and fanciful style of music criticism for idiosyncratic reasons; the Davidsbund did not reflect a detachment from reality. Instead, the creation of the Davidsbund showed Schumann's never-failing presence of mind. Realizing that the creation of an 'imaginary' community would be appealing to readers both in and outside of Germany, Schumann effectively established an active, intellectual community unhampered by national borders. Subscriptions to the *Neue Zeitschrift für Musik* came from all corners of Europe, and in provincial capitals like Copenhagen the journal had an especially profound effect. Here the Davidsbund of Schumann's imagination eventually inspired the creation of a 'real' Davidsbund that included the city's most promising musicians, actors, and dancers.

The Copenhagen Davidsbund appears to have been founded several months after the appearance of the first issues of *Neue Zeitschrift für Musik* in 1834.

---

[24] R. Schuman, *Gesammelte Schriften über Musik un Musiker* (Leipzig, 1854), 8. 'Es schein, verschiedene Ansichten der Kunstanschauung zur Aussprache zu bringen, nicht unpassend, gegenfäßliche Künstlercharaktere zu erfinden, von denen Florestan und Eusebius die bedeutendesten waren, zwischen denen vermittelnd Meister Raro stand.'

Berggreen was one of the first in Copenhagen to subscribe to the journal. He was planning a new music journal of his own, and he hoped to use Schumann's publication as a model. But Berggreen drew little from Schumann's musings and quickly passed his copies of the journal on to Gade and his friends.[25] Berggreen viewed music criticism as a practical, concrete activity aimed at the educational benefit of the general public. Schumann's approach was quite different. He did not see criticism as a way to make art useful or instructive. Instead he adopted an esoteric definition of criticism as a creative way to interact with a work of art. This new philosophical approach captured the imagination of Gade and his friends. Enthralled by Schumann's unique writing style, the group of young artists read the *Neue Zeitschrift für Musik* on a regular basis and soon came to view themselves as the living embodiment of Schumann's imaginary community – a Copenhagen Davidsbund.

Membership in the Copenhagen Davidsbund appears to have fluctuated from year to year, but from 1835 on its nucleus remained constant: Niels W. Gade, Frederik Høedt (1820–85), Michael Wiehe (1820–64), Fritz Schram (1818–87), and the brothers Carl (1818–1904) and Edvard Helsted (1816–1900). A contemporary description of the group elucidates the personalities of the Davidsbund's nucleus members. As in Schumann's imaginary community, each member of the Copenhagen Davidsbund had his own distinct set of characteristics:

> Høedt, with his clever head and academic training often ... said the final word for 'the group,' and the other members were accustomed to acknowledging his superiority. Edvard Helsted was a quiet man, and his brother had, for all practical purposes, a well-developed and more powerful sense for things. Wiehe was taciturn until someone piqued his artistic interest. Then, whether for or against the topic under discussion, he would rise up with opinions and points of view that were often so personal and specific that they took off on their own into subjects that were completely outside the original discussion.[26]

Frederik Høedt was the group's initial intellectual leader. Fluent in Danish, French, German and English, he introduced his friends to the masterpieces of

---

[25] Niels Martin Jensen, 'Niels W. Gade og den nationale tone,' *Dansk Identitetshistorie III, Folkets Danmark 1848–1940*, ed. Ole Feldbæk (Copenhagen: C.A. Reitzel, 1992), 235.

[26] Chapter 5: 'Far Hjemmet,' (p. 16), of the unpublished Gade biography written by his eldest son, Felix Gade. The manuscript of this book is now held in DkB: Ny kgl. Saml. 1716, 4°, Gades efterladte papirer. 'I Begyndelsen var Høedt med sit kloge Hoved og som den eneste Akademier den ledende og den, der sagde det for 'Klumpen' afgørende Ord. Vennerne var fra Ungdommen paa en Maade vant til paa Forhaand at anerkende hans Overlegenhed. Edv. Helsted var en stille Mand, og Broderen havde en udviklet praktisk og mere magtege Sans for Tingene, medens Wiehe var taus, indtil noget tog hans kunstneriske Interesse helt, enten for eller imod, og han bruste op med Udtalelser og Anskuelser, der ofte var saa personlige og særegne, at de ganske gik for sig selv og hvad nye Baaer helt udenfor den Diskussion, man netop sad i.'

foreign literature and led lively discussions concerning contemporary philosophy.[27] In addition to his academic endeavors, Høedt was active in Copenhagen's theater life and was probably the one who introduced the young actor Michael Wiehe to the group in 1835.

Fritz Schram and Edvard Helsted were students with Gade at Wexschall's violin school.[28] Whereas Schram was recognized for his technical abilities, Edvard's style was characterized by great emotion and fervent expression. Carl Helsted, Edvard's younger brother, was also a member of the Davidsbund nucleus. An accomplished flutist and cellist, Carl probably entered the group with Edvard in 1834.[29] Other, more peripheral members of the Davidsbund included Peter Schram (1819–75) and Christian Ferslew (1817–83) – both notable singers; Vilhelm Holm (1820–86) and C.N. Lundgreen – students at the Royal Chapel's violin school; and Ferdinand Hoppe (1815–90) – a dancer at the Royal Theater. The actors Nicolai Peter Nielsen (1795–1860) and his wife Anna Nielsen (1803–56) were also associated with the Davidsbund as was Hans Christian Andersen (1805–75).[30]

The artistic interests of the Copenhagen Davidsbund were all-encompassing. Filled with an ideal ambition, they believed that the full development of talent required not only a musically-trained ear, but also a well-trained eye, an educated mind, a controlled imagination, and pure emotions.[31] The group's activities were numerous. They visited art galleries and museums, took long walks through the countryside, critiqued each others music and poetry, and spent many hours reading and discussing literary masterpieces and modern philosophy. Musically, preference was given to the compositions of Beethoven, Schubert, Mendelssohn, and Schumann, and to works by past masters mentioned in the *Neue Zeitschrift für*

---

[27] Robert Neiiendam, *Michael Wiehe og Frederik Høedt*, (Copenhagen: B. Pios, 1920), 12.

[28] According to Carl Thrane, *Fra Hofviolonernes Tid: Skildringer af Det kongelige Kapels Historie 1648–1848* (Copenhagen, Schønbergske Forlag, 1908), 325–27, Schram entered the school in 1830, Edvard Helsted in 1831.

[29] According to Frits Bendix, *Af en Kapelmusikers Erindringer: Miniaturportrætter fra Paullis Tid*, (Copenhagen: H. Hagerups Forlag, 1913), 63, the 'Davidsbund' meetings were often held in the Helsted brothers' attic apartment on Vingaardsstræde.

[30] In chapter 5 (Far Hjemmet) of the unpublished biography of Gade, Felix Gade describes the musical evenings his father shared throughout his life with a number of the original 'Davidsbund' members (p. 16): 'The gatherings often took place late at night, when the performance at the Theater was finished. Most of his closest friends were involved with the Theater. They included Høedt, Carl and Edvard Helsted – both of whom served in the Chapel, Michael Wiehe and a few others, perhaps Phisther, Peter Schram, Chapel master Paulli, or the singer Ferslev, etc. – It was mostly musical and on the whole artistic questions which were considered; but philosophical and similar topics popped up as well.'

[31] Dagmar Gade, 16–17. 'Opfyldte af en ideal Stræben, nærede de den Overbevisning, at ikke blot et musikalsk dannet Øre, men ogsaa et dannet Øje, skolet Tænkning, tøjlet Fantasi og lutret Følelse var nødvendige Betingelser for Talentets fulde Udvikling.'

Musik: (e.g. Palestrina, Allegri, Bach, Handel, Mozart, and Gluck). Attention was also given to compositions written by several of the Davidsbund members, most notably works by Gade and the Helsted brothers. A string quartet was formed around 1835 with Gade and Fritz Schram playing first and second violin, and Edvard and Carl Helsted playing viola and cello. When works for voice and piano were performed, generally Carl Helsted or Peter Schram sang while Gade served as the accompanist.[32]

Schumann's *Neue Zeitschrift für Musik* was read religiously and functioned as a springboard for the group's numerous discussions concerning criticism and aesthetics.[33] Rebelling against the conservative tastes of an older generation, the Copenhagen Davidsbund took as their motto Schumann's 1834 declaration in *Neue Zeitschrift für Musik*: 'Our aim...is simply this...to oppose the recent past as an inartistic period...and to prepare for and facilitate the advent of a fresh, poetic future.'[34] This search for a new 'poetic future' is perhaps best described as a search for 'autonomous music.' As Carl Dahlhaus stated in his *Foundations of Music History*:

> A musical creation is autonomous (1) if it manages to raise and enforce a claim to be heard in its own right, thus giving form precedence over function, and (2) if it constitutes a work of art in the modern sense, i.e. a work freely conceived and executed with no influence on the part of the patron or purchaser as regards its content or external form.[35]

---

[32] The acquisition of music was not easy for the group. None of the members could afford to buy new scores and the Royal Theater refused to supply music for private use. The group often turned to teachers and local lending libraries in search of new compositions. When an interesting work was found either Gade or one of the Helsted brothers transcribed the piece so that it could be studied by the group. Evidence of this practice still exists – for example, Gade's transcriptions of cadenzas to Mozart's Sinfonia concertante in E-flat major for Violin and Viola, (K. 364) and Beethoven's Piano Concerto in C minor (DkB: Gade Saml. C II 6); and his transcriptions of Handel's *Israel in Egypt*; a Mozart trio; *The Magic Flute*; an Onslow quintet; Haydn's quartet Op. 1 nr. 4; and Beethoven's String Quartet, Op. 74 and Fugue, Op. 135 (Dkb: Ny kgl. Saml. 1716, 4°, Gades efterladte papirer). The Helsted brothers' transcription of Spohr's Octet is preserved in a private collection.

[33] Felix Gade, Chap. 3: 'Neuer Aufschwung,' 3, reports: 'In his youth he [Gade] and his friends read a lot together, he also learned a lot from what he read; naturally most of these [books] were works dealing with aesthetics; a great deal of Golden age literature appeared just then. And he read books about the arts, both music and painting, for which he maintained a strong interest until his final days. In addition, he became acquainted with the philosophical treatment of various problems.'

[34] Schumann, *Neue Zeitschrift für Musik* 2 (2 January 1835): 3. 'Unsere Gesinnung ... ist einfach, und diese: ...die letze Vergangenheit als eine unkünstlerische zu bekämpfen,... [und] eine junge dichterische Zukunft vorzubereiten, beschleunigen zu helfen.'

[35] Carl Dahlhaus, *Foundations of Music History*, trans. J.B. Robinson (Cambridge: Cambridge University Press, 1983), 109.

Dahlhaus' idea of autonomy is a twentieth-century one, but similar ideas were expressed as early as the late-eighteenth century by Schiller, Schelling, A.W. Schlegel and Goethe.[36] Schumann believed that in experiencing poetic music, one responded subjectively, intuitively, as an individual. Music was not part of an 'enlightened' program geared towards the socialization and modification of behavior, but rather a liberating activity capable of shaking one free from the over-rationalized Enlightenment of an older generation. For Schumann and the Copenhagen Davidsbund, music served as a kind of de-centering experience that enabled the artist to transcend, or at least escape, mundane society.

The effects of this poetic approach to music on Gade's creative outlook is perhaps best reflected in a letter he wrote to Edvard Helsted in 1836. Here Gade describes a state of transcendence brought on by creative inspiration:

To [my] friend Helsted!
            Motto: 'I am lonely but not alone,'...
Dear friend, I miss you terribly; I also miss our leisurely evening strolls. It is very boring here now that Carl has left for Kjøge, and I am thus completely alone in this big city, no good music, wretched heat, no musical friends to talk to – and you well know that essentially nothing interests me outside of this one [thing]. Because of this absence of reciprocal communication, I have attempted to write down some thoughts that I confide to you in this letter. If you write to me, then write me what you think about the following – or, if such is the case, your criticisms.

Thoughts when my friends were off and traveling, – as always my consolation in this my loneliness is to receive now and then soft kisses from my darling in adoration and affection. She is the never-perishing eternal youth which is not seen by earthly eyes, but which floats in front of our imagination in a heavenly blue robe bearing all virtues – she, who leads us into the higher world and also draws the curtain aside and allows us to see a reflection of the glimmer of God's splendor – the harmonies of angels –

Suddenly the spectator loses consciousness and falls to earth again. – But the kind-hearted one does not allow him to remain in nothingness. She wakes him and allows him to see splendor in a mirror. – Art is the refreshing reflection. – The longer he looks, the more he is mastered by an indescribable emotion; he is excited by her – the Ideal, the highest measure of everything beautiful, good and virtuous. His spirit and thoughts broaden; he wants to throw himself in immeasurable rapture before the throne of the Creator. – He was on the highest step of Heaven's ladder that man can set foot upon, but now he climbs down again with serenity, constantly preserving the memory of the beautiful moment he attained. When temptations and heavy burdens try to shake him he recalls his Ideal, [and] they fly

---

[36] Sanna Pederson, 'Enlightened and Romantic German Music Criticism, 1800-1850,' (Ph.D. Dissertation, University of Pennsylvania, 1995), 16–24.

far, far away – just like the sun when, in all its majesty and clarity, it casts the fog away to all sides.

When she releases his burden with a fleeting kiss he is overwhelmed by an inexplicable longing to pour out his heart in a hymn of thanksgiving, and he himself becomes the creator of a mortal work. It springs out of his inner heart like a spark of the heavenly art which has inspired him.

You should consider the whole an incomplete sketch. Many of the expressions come from an unpracticed pen and are consequently not the best; but I nonetheless believe I will be able to make something out of it. In my thoughts, at least, it is clear to me what I want to say, but perhaps I am not very successful in expressing it. Read it and think it over.... If (when you are walking one evening) the wind should happen to blow from Zealand and cast a leaf from the trees upon your nose, do not be afraid; but put your imagination to good use and take it as a greeting from your friend, – N.W. Gade[37]

Gade's letter demonstrates the sentimental disposition obviously shared by members of the Copenhagen Davidsbund. Swept up in romantic theories concerning genius and divine inspiration, this group of young artists no doubt saw themselves as the embodiment of Hoffmann's Kreisler, Goethe's Werther, and Andersen's Christian.[38] On the whole, the Copenhagen Davidsbund brought together the most promising Danish artists of a new generation. Driven by dreams of success and fame, these young men never faltered in their quest for artistic excellence. Gade's ambition was especially keen. Intent on success by his twenty-fifth birthday, he placed a poster over his bed reading 'Year 25' to remind him of his formidable goal.[39] Gade reached his goal with a year to spare, but his road to fame was arduous. Like most of his friends in the Copenhagen Davidsbund, Gade searched outside the confines of his native land for musical guidance and inspiration. Consequently, Gade's formative years were defined by opposing musical philosophies: Berggreen's prosaic approach to music and Schumann's poetic outlook. The particular problems that resulted from this opposition and the ways Gade dealt with them influenced the development of his personal style and therefore serve as the focus of the following chapters.

---

[37] Dagmar Gade, 20–23. See appendix three for original Danish text.
[38] Christian was a young fiddler in H.C. Andersen's novel *Kun en Spillemand* (Only a Fiddler), whose genius and natural talent thrived despite a tragic life of poverty and misfortune.
[39] Dagmar Gade, 17–18.

Chapter Two

Emergence as a Serious Composer

In August of 1838 Niels W. Gade relinquished his position as a violinist in the Royal Chapel and began a concert tour of Norway and Sweden. Tired of his work as an orchestral player, Gade wanted to test his abilities as a concert soloist. His plan was to travel through Scandinavia, earning money along the way from concert revenues, and eventually settle in Cassel, Germany, where he hoped to study with Louis Spohr. Gade's sudden departure from Copenhagen worried his advisors at the Royal Chapel – students who resigned from the orchestra were rarely readmitted. Berggreen was also disappointed by Gade's decision. He had sensed his student's growing dissatisfaction with Copenhagen's music scene but was apparently unaware that Gade planned to study abroad. In a letter dated 30 August, several weeks after Gade's departure, Berggreen reflected on Gade's reasons for leaving and expressed, perhaps for the first time, the strong attachment he felt to his student. Berggreen saw in Gade a 'true disciple,' and he encouraged him to broaden his knowledge of folk music while traveling abroad:

My dear friend and disciple!
    I am taking advantage of your father's offer and sending this greeting to tell you how much it gladdened me to learn, through your letter to your parents, that you are doing so well. I think you must feel like a bird that has slipped out of its cage and now flies around free in God's nature. By this cage, however, I do not mean your home…but the prisoner's cage, wherein the conditions you hated held you so tightly. Even though the young are loved at home, they always want to go out into the world to gather a supply of experiences, ideas, thoughts, and pictures that will keep their minds busy in later years. I truly do not envy you your happiness, but should I completely give up the hope of seeing something more of the world than I have already seen? It would certainly thrill me and add a large part to my life's happiness.
    My melody collection for the *Historical Poems of the Fatherland* is almost finished. Since you do not want me to publish your composition to 'Absalon,' I have composed a melody for that poem. I played your melodies for your father the other day, and the two of us took great enjoyment in them and you. I miss you a lot. It seems to me as though you are flesh of my flesh and blood of my blood. At least you must allow me to look upon you as my musical son. Vanity does not cause me to see you in this relationship to me. Instead my feelings for you have grown, during the long time we have known each other, into an affection that is conscious of its own purity. With the eyes of a father, a brother, a friend, I want to follow you on your way. Therefore, do not let me wait in vain for news from you, my one and only disciple! But let me hear from you often! Truly, I now

have no one with whom I can discuss music in such a way as with you! We understood each other!

Don't forget the battle songs! And if you should manage to buy me some collections of Swedish songs (Romances), you would be doing me a great favor. In Stockholm some by Lindblad and Geier (poets) have come out, among which is included 'Soslargevisen' by Atterbom (as far as I know after a folk song).

I went to your house on the day you left at a little after three. I was hoping to see you off, but you had already gone! I stayed and talked with your mother for a while. Your father and mother miss you, but they are willing to dispense with the happiness of having you with them, since your happiness requires this sacrifice.... Live well, my dear Gade! Happy traveling! The good shall not want! Do not forget me!

Your friend,
A.P. Berggreen[1]

Gade responded several weeks later. He began his letter by addressing his teacher's outpouring of affection. Gade acknowledged his indebtedness to Berggreen and thanked him for his many years of support and guidance. He did not, however, respond to his teacher's comments concerning folk songs. Instead, Gade made a subtle, but definitive, break with his teacher's musical ideology. Unconcerned with the edifying purposes of folk music, Gade defined a new philosophical outlook; the wonders of nature had opened his eyes, and the power of literature had infused his soul with new inspiration:

Gothenborg, 24 September 1838

My dear Teacher and Friend!

You have given me the name 'Friend'! I am proud of this name, which your goodness has ascribed me and which makes me eternally happy. But how, and with what feeling, must I then call you my friend, to whom I am bound not only with affection, but also with such a strong bond of gratitude. – Yes to you, dear friend, I owe a great deal – you have looked deep inside me, your penetrating gaze has discovered the chains that fastened my feet and prevented, or would have prevented, regular steps. You broke them, and free, free breathes the bird again under the heaven's blue. I feel now, for the first time, my own self. Don't misunderstand me, however, and don't believe me to be a conceited fool who in following the sun's brightness flies into the flames – awakened as when a green-house plant from the artificial sunlight of the North is placed under the South's azure. My entire inner life is working, expanding, and preparing for a spiritual

---

[1] The original letter, dated 30 August 1838, is in DkB: Ny kgl. Saml. 1716, 4°. See appendix three for Danish text. Berggreen expressed a similar sentiment in a letter to one of his colleagues: 'Gade is really my true disciple. With him I can tell that my principles have been worthwhile. But how often does one also expect to find so much pleasure, seriousness, perseverance, and talent combined?' (c.f. Kjerulf, 31).

rebirth; my previous life lies formless [and] lifeless in the background like a chaos, from which the Creator calls forth the hard and the soft, the heavy and light to unite.

Many great, glorious conditions of nature that my corporeal eyes have had the pleasure to view have spiritually awakened new emotions and thoughts and given my intellectual activities inspiration and nourishment for a long time. However, I miss you friend. [I miss] a colleague in my proximity with whom I can rework this material, with whom I can exchange thoughts and opinions, a brother, a partner, who according to me is – 'flesh of my flesh, blood of my blood,' – you.

In this my need, missing my friends, I pleaded to the spirits for help and relief – and I was heard! A spirit, as great and powerful as any, let me read his joy and pain. He told me the story of Prince Hamlet's melancholy, of Romeo's love and Othello's jealousy. Shakespeare is his name, the great spirit with the large, all-encompassing heart, whose warmth and enthusiasm charmed me and likewise refreshed and ripened a plan, which has already haunted my heart for a long time. – I will tell you this and with pleasure will hear your opinion of it.

The fairytale about Agnete and the Merman has always seemed to me a very musical subject. Although I have never before actually made plans about how to work it out further as a composition, it has nonetheless constantly been an idea to me. ('Watch out for the pretty Melusine,[2] Herr Gade! a dangerous beauty and an equally dangerous rival.' 'I know that, I know that quite well, my sir, and in no way [do I] make a comparison between the maiden Agnete and the beautiful Melusine; but should a painter lay his hands in his lap for the sake of a less beautiful neighbor and dare not paint a portrait of a woman? No! I know for certain that there is room for us all, if not on the main street, then on a dirty little side street.')[3]

Now I have begun the work and given it the form of an overture. I have intended Agnete's yearning at the sea over an object unknown to her as the primary moment in this piece. The Merman's lamentation of love and her own conscious voice (in that she knows that to love the Merman will cause both joy and pain) appear as two opposing principles. This fight between good and evil makes up the mid-point until, towards the end, she surrenders herself unconditionally into the Merman's embrace. I am almost halfway finished with composing the music, and I am relatively pleased with it. I am working hard and it is coming along nicely.

I still want to write more, but I see the paper disappearing, bit by bit, under my hand. So, I now must begin thinking about the many greetings that lie in my heart. My dear parents, then next you and your family, then next – well, you know well enough yourself to whom you should offer my heartfelt greetings and warmest wishes for their continued well being.

---

[2] Undoubtedly a reference to Mendelssohn's *Ouvertüre zum Märchen von der schöne Melusine*, Op. 32 (1833).

[3] Here Gade has made a clever pun on his name. 'Gade' in Danish is the word for street.

Wednesday or Thursday I will travel to Stockholm. I'm waiting to receive a
little something from your hand soon. How is your opera coming along? I don't
know how I should sign off, Yours sincerely, or – I will just say

Yours,

Niels W. Gade[4]

This exchange of letters represents a significant turning point in Gade's musical
career. Free of the 'imprisoning cage' of his native Copenhagen, Gade redefined
his role as a musician. He abandoned his plans of becoming a concert soloist and
began to pursue a career in composition. Having finally discovered his 'true self,'
Gade found the courage to begin a compositional project that had 'haunted' him
for a long time – an overture based on the Danish fairy tale, 'Agnete and the
Merman.'

The story of Agnete and the Merman exists in many versions. In its earliest
ballad form (ca. eighteenth century) Agnete is portrayed as a selfish, rebellious girl
who deserts her family to live with the Merman and bear his children, only to
callously abandon him as well at the end of the story. Contrary to this egocentric
characterization, the Agnete of most nineteenth-century versions displays kind,
loving feelings of familial loyalty. She is torn between her loyalty to God (being
a faithful wife) and her love for the Merman. Thus the predominating theme of
most nineteenth-century versions is a tragic split between the Christian and the
human.[5]

Gade's choice of subject for his overture clearly reveals the influence of
Mendelssohn's *Die schöne Melusine*: 'Watch out for the pretty Melusine, Herr
Gade! A dangerous beauty and an equally dangerous rival.' Although *Die schöne
Melusine* was not premiered in Copenhagen until 1846, no great leap of faith is
needed to imagine that Gade was familiar with the piece; the overture received
favorable notices in various music journals, including one written by Robert
Schumann and published in the *Neue Zeitschrift für Music* in 1836. Gade's
description of his *Agnete and the Merman* program reveals that he was familiar
with Schumann's review and was likely influenced by it.

Schumann began his review with a discussion of Mendelssohn's program,
tracing the tale of the ill-fated water nymph and the mortal knight she loves back
to its origins in a story by Ludwig Tieck:

---

[4] C. Skou: A.P. Berggreen, (Copenhagen, 1895), 55-58. See appendix three for Danish text.
[5] This split between the Christian and human also plays a role in E.T.A. Hoffmann's *Undine*.
For further discussions of 'Agnete and the Merman' see: Thomas Bredsdorff, 'Nogen skrev et
sagn om 'Agnete og Havmanden,' hvem, hvornår og hvorfor?' *Fund og Forskning* 30 (1991):
67–80; Peter Meisling, *Agnetes Latter*, (Copenhagen, 1988) and 'De sympatiske Havmænd – En
lille replik til Thomas Bredsdorff,' *Fund og Forskning* 30 (1991): 81– 86; Iørn Piø, *Nye veje til
Folkevisen II: DgFT 38, Agnete og havmanden*, Stockholm, 1970.

With characteristic poetic grasp, Mendelssohn sketches here only the characters of the man and woman, the proud, knightly Lusignan and the alluring, devoted Melusine; but it is as if the swells of water joined in their embraces, overwhelmed them and divided them.... This it seems to me, distinguishes the overture from [Mendelssohn's] earlier ones – that such events, much as in fairy-tale, are recounted at a certain remove: the narrator keeps his distance.[6]

Schumann continued by associating the characters of the drama with specific passages in Mendelssohn's overture: Melusine is portrayed by the gentle, pliant theme in A-flat major, while the theme in F minor represents the knight, Lusignan. In addition, the overture begins and ends with a striking wave figure in the clarinets that 'has the effect of transporting one from the battleground of tense human passion to the sublime, all-encompassing universe of water.'[7]

In Gade's description of his overture, *Agnete and the Merman*, he too appears to be associating the various thematic elements of his composition with characters from the fairy tale. Gade develops a program that focuses on characterization and plot; and he uses this program as a structural guideline for his overture, dividing it into three separate sections: 'Agnete's yearning by the sea after an unknown object,' 'Agnete's moral struggle with good and evil,' and 'Agnete's unconditional surrender to the Merman's embrace.'

Gade never completed *Agnete and the Merman*, but his earliest sketches for the work, which only recently came to light, reveal his early struggles. In the Royal Library's Gade Collection is preserved a set of autograph sketches labeled *Agnete and the Merman* and dated 'September 1838 – Gothenborg.'[8] Bearing the incorrect date of 1858 in the handwritten catalogue of Gade's manuscripts (a.k.a. 'Abelones Liste'), these sketches have been overlooked by previous scholars. The sketches comprise six pages and appear as though they were worked on at various times. Two different shades of ink have been used (first brown and then black), and the manuscript paper is of different sizes (22 cm x 35 cm and 22.7 cm x 34.5 cm). Composed the same month as Gade's letter to Berggreen, these sketches probably represent Gade's earliest setting of *Agnete and the Merman*.

Gade's description of 'Agnete's yearning by the sea after an unknown object' appears to have been the inspiration for the opening measures of the 1838 sketches (ex. 2:1). Note the depiction of the waves in the lower strings (cello) and the use of an impassioned A-minor clarinet solo for the portrayal of Agnete's yearning. After this opening section Gade recorded two contrasting themes – the opposing principles mentioned in his letter to Berggreen. Perhaps Gade envisioned these themes as representations of the Merman's lamentation of love (ex. 2:2), and the

---

[6] R. Schumann, *Gesammelte Schriften*, 1:143.
[7] Ibid.
[8] DkB: Gade Sml. C II, 6. Both the date and title are written in Gade's hand.

voice of Agnete's conscience (ex. 2:3). While the Merman is characterized by a trombone, Agnete is again represented by the clarinet.

The overture's midpoint represents Agnete's moral struggle between good and evil (ex. 2:4). Finally, Gade describes the closing of the overture as Agnete's unconditional surrender to the Merman's embrace (ex. 2:5). Unfortunately the sketches abruptly end at this point, and it is unknown whether Gade completed the draft. He included only a few indications concerning harmony and orchestration, and his corrections reveal that he struggled with the overture's formal structure. Gade's use of two different ink colors indicates that he worked on the sketches more than once, but he apparently grew frustrated with his progress and set the project aside shortly after his letter to Berggreen.

Gade traveled to Stockholm in early October, and this change of scenery appears to have facilitated interest in a new compositional project, an overture entitled *Jugendträume*. We can only speculate about the source of inspiration for *Jugendträume* – Gade makes no mention of it in letters home, and no program for the work now exists. I propose *Jugendträume* was inspired by a poem with the same title written by the Swedish/German poet, Ernst Moritz Arndt (1769–1860). Arndt was a popular figure in the nineteenth century, and his works were read widely by Gade's generation. Arndt spent a large portion of his early career in Stockholm; and his poetry would have been readily available in the city during Gade's visit.[9] Reading the opening stanza to 'Jugendträume,' we can see why it might have appealed to the struggling composer:

Was du geträumt in grüner Jugend,
Das mache wahr durch Männertugend –
Die frühsten Träume täuschen nicht.
Doch wisse, Träume sind nicht Thaten:
Ohne Arbeit wird dir nichts geraten.
Die Tugend trägt ein ernst Gesicht.[10]

(What you dreamed in your green youth
Can be realized through manly virtue –
The earliest dreams do not deceive,
But be aware, dreams are not deeds:
Without work nothing succeeds.
The virtuous wear a serious expression.)

---

[9] Henry Garland, *The Oxford Companion to German Literature*, second ed., (Oxford and New York: Oxford University Press, 1989), 37–38.

[10] For the complete poem see Günther Deicke, ed. *Deutsches Gedichtbuch*, (Berlin, 1959) or Georg Wirnsberg, ed. *Vom Reichtum der deutschen Seele*, (Leipzig, 1928).

Example 2:1. Opening measures of Gade's *Agnete and the Merman* Overture.
(DkB: Gade Saml., C II 6)

Example 2:2. The primary theme (the Merman's lamentation of love) in *Agnete and the Merman*. (DkB: Gade Saml., C II 6)

Example 2:3. The secondary theme (the voice of Agnete's conscience) in *Agnete and the Merman*. (DkB: Gade Saml., C II 6)

Example 2:4. Development section (Agnete's struggle between good and evil) of *Agnete and the Merman*. (DkB: Gade Saml., C II 6)

Example 2:5. Concluding measures (Agnete's surrender) of Gade's *Agnete and the Merman* Overture. (DkB: Gade Saml., C II 6)

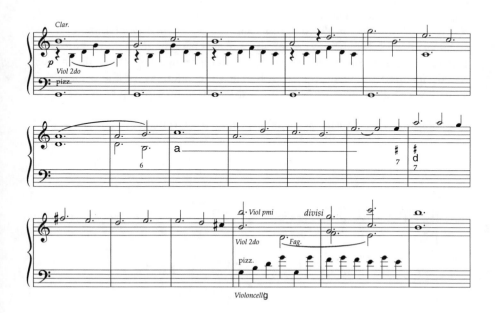

Gade never completed *Jugendträume*, but two drafts of the work still exist: a complete score in piano format and an incomplete orchestral score. The piano score carries the title *Jugendträume*. The first page is dated '16/10 – 38. Stockholm,' and the closing date on page nine reads: 'Fin den 1ste December 1838. Stockholm.' The orchestral score is undated and labeled simply 'Ouverture.'[11] The completed draft in piano format reveals something of a free sonata form with two themes predominating and changing form throughout (exx. 6 and 7). It is tempting to view these themes as representations of the 'dream' and 'deed' featured in Arndt's poem. Perhaps the interplay of these themes is somehow representative of Gade's own struggles as an aspiring composer.

Example 2:6. Primary theme of Gade's *Jugendträume* Overture.
          (DkB: Gade Saml., C II 6, Supplement 17)

---

[11] DkB: Gade Saml., C II, 6, Supplement #17.

Example 2:7. Secondary theme of Gade's *Jugendträume* Overture.
(DkB: Gade Saml., C II 6, Supplement 17)

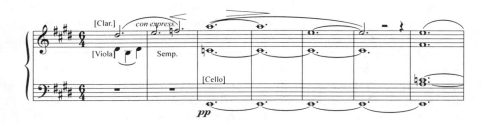

Gade's Scandinavian tour was successful on a personal level – he separated himself from unwanted influences in Copenhagen and began to develop independently as a composer. On a financial level, however, it was a disaster. Concerts were not as easy to arrange as Gade had hoped they would be, and the revenues scarcely covered his room and board. By mid December, Gade had reached the end of his rope. Destitute and alone in a foreign land, he wrote to his father and asked for money to cover his travel fare home. When Gade returned to Copenhagen in late December, he feared his parents would chastise him for the financial burden he had placed on them. But as he later recalled, his family's reaction was anything but judgmental: 'And so, both Father and Mother were so overjoyed at seeing me again, that they couldn't be the least bit angry with me – the dear, good parents.'[12]

---

[12] Dagmar Gade, 24–25. 'Og saa var dog baade Fader og Moder kun saa himelglade over at se mig igjen, at de kun slet ikke kunde være vrede paa mig, de kjære, gode Forældre.'

Gade attempted to resume his musical activities when he returned to Copenhagen, but the Royal Chapel barred his readmittance to the orchestra for several months. Berggreen, however, welcomed his student with open arms. In 1839 Gade published several part songs under Berggreen's tutelage and began to take a stronger interest in his teacher's preoccupation with folk music. In 1840 he contributed to Berggreen's *Melodier til de af 'Selskabet for Trykkefrihedens rette Brug' udgivne fædrelandshistoriske Digte* (Melodies to National-Historic Poems Published by the Society for the Proper Use of Freedom of Press),[13] and in 1842 he assisted Berggreen with the multi-volume folk-song anthology *Folke-Sange og Melodier* (Folk songs and Melodies). Gade harmonized the Swiss folk song 'Kuhreigen' for volume one of this collection, and for volume four he composed arrangements of 'Tordenskiolds Vise' and 'Regnar Lodbroks Dødsang.' This last arrangement, however, was not used – Berggreen considered it 'too modern' and consequently published his own arrangement instead.[14]

Berggreen was indisputably the primary influence behind Gade's new interest in folk music, but other prominent members of Copenhagen's musical community, namely the ballet master August Bournonville (1805–79) and the concertmaster/ opera director of the Royal Theater Johannes Frederik Frøhlich (1806–60), gave the young composer encouragement as well. Dedicated to creating a Danish theater-repertoire, Bournonville and Frøhlich produced a number of national-historic ballets during the first half of the nineteenth century.[15] Bournonville had a reputation for encouraging up-and-coming Danish artists, and he took an interest in Gade after hearing about his experiences abroad. In 1839 he commissioned Gade to write the melodramas for a production of Oehlenschläger's dramatic adventure *Aladdin*,[16] and in 1840 he asked him to collaborate with Frøhlich on music for the pantomime prelude *Fædrelandets Muser*.[17] Gade's compositions were not used in the public performance of *Fædrelandets Muser*, but early manuscripts show that he submitted music for several scenes.[18] His contribution for the seventh scene was especially interesting. Here he used a number of folk-

---

[13] Gade contributed five arrangements to the collection. The dates on the manuscripts of these pieces (DkB: Gade Collection C II, 6) show that they were composed shortly before Gade's departure in 1838.

[14] Niels Martin Jensen, 'Niels W. Gade,' 218.

[15] One of these, *Valdemar*, used folksong melodies as thematic material. According to Jensen, 'Niels W. Gade,' 222, the opening scene of this ballet uses the folk melody 'Den Konning han lader en havfru gribe' as a subject for thematic development and variation.

[16] The rest of the music for *Aladdin* was taken from Kuhlau's *Trillingbrødrene fra Damask* and arranged by the concertmaster, Peter Funck.

[17] *Fædrelandets Muser* is an allegorical work in which nine musicians gather in a number of *tableaux vivants*.

[18] Frøhlich's autograph score for *Fædrelandets Muser* is found in DkB: Musik afdeling, CII, 107 Tv. fol.

song melodies as thematic material. These included: 'Jeg lagde mit hoved til Elvehøj,' 'Det var ridder Hr. Aage,' 'Dronning Dagmar' (Oehlenschläger), and the patriotic tune 'Danmark, dejligst vang og vænge' (P.E. Rasmussen).[19] Like Berggreen, Bournonville, and Frøhlich greatly influenced Gade's evolution as a composer. In addition to giving him the opportunity to concentrate on orchestral writing, they encouraged his interest in folk music and helped him learn how to integrate successfully folk melodies into large-scale orchestral works – a technique that would later become a major component in Gade's international success.

But Gade's new interest in folk music did not diminish his pursuit of the poetic. His participation in the Copenhagen Davidsbund never faltered, and his travels only strengthened his interest in Schumann's critical works and music. Gade became fascinated with Schumann's character pieces during his time abroad, and in 1839 he began to experiment in the genre. In an unpublished work entitled *Kleine Claviergeschichte* (1839), Gade used a narrative keyboard style similar to the one found in Schumann's *Carnival*.[20] Closer still to Schumann's piano music is Gade's *Dithyrambe* (1840). Dedicated to 'Capellmeister Johannes Kreisler,' this work is infused with an intellectualism reminiscent of Schumann's *Kreisleriana*. In addition, Gade followed the initiative of Schumann's *Carnival* and used the letters of his own name, G-A-D-E, as the composition's central motive.[21]

Gade was apparently the first to introduce the music of Schumann to the Copenhagen Davidsbund. While Carl Helsted was visiting Leipzig in 1840/41 Gade wrote to him:

> ...the only thing you mentioned in your letter that makes me envious of you is that you can go in and out of Schumann's home – nonetheless I am happy that you are able to recognize his compositions as being something quite good!!!!!! Furthermore, I am glad that it was me who first took notice of him and hacked through [his compositions] as well as I could. You can tell him that his unseen friend sends greetings.... Next time write more about R. Schumann.[22]

---

[19] Jensen, 'Niels W. Gade,' 220. For the original form of these folk melodies see *Udvalgte danske Viser fra Middelalderen* (Copenhagen: Abrahamson, Nyerup og Rahbek, 1812–14), vol. 5.

[20] Perhaps Gade's title choice reflects a connection with Schumann's recently published *Noveletten* (1839).

[21] Gade's *Claviergeschichte* and *Dithyrambe* were never published. The original manuscripts of these works are in DkB: Gade Saml., CII, 6.

[22] William Behrend, 'Omkring Niels W. Gade,' *Aarbog for Musik* (1922/23): 64. '...Det eneste jeg misunder dig af Alt hvad du har fortalt i dine Breve er at du saaledes kan gaae ind og ud hos Schumann – det glæder mig dog at du maatte erkjende hans Compositioner for noget ganske godt !!!!!! endvidere glæder det mig at det var mig der først blev opmærksom paa ham, og hakkede dem igjennem saa godt jeg kunde. Du kan hilse ham fra hans usynlige Ven. ... Skriv næste Gang noget mere om R. Schumann.'

Further evidence of Gade's devotion appears in a letter written by Clara Schumann in 1842, when she visited Copenhagen as part of an extended concert tour. During her stay she met privately with Gade and then wrote to her husband:

> Gade visited me today and went into raptures over you. He knew everything by you and played everything (to the best of his ability) himself. ... I really like him; I have asked him to come again tomorrow so that I can play some things by you – today he heard the Nachtstücke.[23]

Two years passed before Gade had the opportunity to meet his idol in person. Still, his 'rapture' over Schumann's compositions and philosophical ideas never waned. Gade continually sought out Schumann's opinions in the *Neue Zeitschrift für Musik* during the late 1830s and early 1840s, and he took them to heart when mapping out his own compositional plans. Although Berggreen was a constant presence in Gade's life during his formative years, he did not overshadow Schumann's influence. In fact, Gade's early career as a composer is perhaps best described as a struggle between two distinct musical ideologies: prosaic (folk) music as defined by Berggreen and Bournonville and poetic music as defined by Schumann and his *Neue Zeitschrift für Musik*. Perhaps in an effort to keep these two ideologies separate, Gade began keeping what is best described as a composition diary in July 1839. Spanning a period of roughly two and a half years, this diary contains the programmatic origins for seven of Gade's early 'poetic' compositions: the incomplete B-flat-major Piano Trio and F-minor String Quartet, the Piano Sonata in E minor (Op. 28), a five-movement symphony entitled *Agnete and the Merman*, the famous *Echoes of Ossian* Overture (Op. 1), the *St. Hans' Evening Play* Overture, and the Symphony No. 1 in C minor (Op. 5). Tracing the development of these compositions from their programmatic origins to their final form, the second part of this book presents the first in-depth examination of these works, offering new insights into Gade's creative interests and compositional methods.

---

[23] Berthold Litzmann, *Clara Schumann. Ein Künstlerleben. Nach Tagebüchern und Briefen* (Leipzig: Breitkopf und Härtel, 1905), vol. 2, 48. 'Gade besuchte mich heute und schwärmte von Dir. Er kennt alles von Dir, spielt alles (nach Kräften) selbst.... Er gefällt mir ganz gut; ich hab ihn morgen wieder zu mir bestellt, um ihm von Dir vorzuspielen – heute hörte er die Nachtstücke.'

Part Two

In Search of the Poetic (1839–42)

Chapter Three

Gade's Composition Diary

'Formel hält uns nicht gebunden. Unsre Kunst heißt Poesie.'[1]

More than just a motto for the *Echoes of Ossian* Overture, these words served as Gade's artistic manifesto. Intent on creating 'Poesie,' Gade looked beyond the realms of music for inspiration. Literature, and later the theater, served as the impetus for his creative output during his early years, and the result was a unique compositional style influenced equally by Danish and German traditions.

For the whole of his career, Gade looked to literature as an artistic stimulus. Reading was a crucial stage in his creative process: it aroused his inner emotions, kindled his imagination and provided the creative foundation for numerous compositions. As the composer himself once wrote:

> It is not so much what you read ... but how you read that matters. ... First of all, what I read must be written by an author who himself is a complete person, someone who has something to express and who, in addition, is an artist. In short, [one who] understands how to express himself clearly. Because it doesn't matter if he has profound and beautiful thoughts if he cannot express them in a way that enables me to understand easily what he wants to say.
>
> In truth, artistic production is nothing more than a desire to express one's own emotions and frame of mind to others. This can be done with various materials: colors, words, tones. The clearer one is able to express with these materials the inner-most state of his soul, the greater an artist he is.[2]

---

[1] This motto is taken from a popular poem by Uhland entitled 'Freie Kunst.' For an excellent discussion of the importance of this poem in relation to the aesthetics behind Gade's creation of his *Echoes of Ossian* Overture, see Oechsle, 135–36.

[2] Johannes Gade, *Omkring Niels W. Gade, Breve fra fader og søn*, Hasselbachs Kultur-bibliotek nr. 265, (Copenhagen: Steen Hasselbachs, 1967). 'Det er nemlig ikke saa meget hvad Du læser – naturligvis hverken Thevandsromaner eller filosofiske Skrifter underforstaaet – som hvorledes Du læser at det kommer an paa. Du siger selv, at Du tidligere har læst blot til Tidsfordriv. Naa, det kan man ogsaa en Gang imellem efter strængt aandeligt eller legemligt Arbejde; og det gjør jeg ogsaa undertiden faae Tankerne bort fra et Arbejde, som interesserer mig, da man jo ikke har godt af bestandig at fixere Tankerne paa et Punkt, hvorved let den aandelige Friskhed og Qvikhed kan afmattes. – Men Læsningen, hvorved man vil erhverve sig et aandeligt Udbytte, forfriske sin Tanke og ligesom berige sit eget Jeg, er af en heel anden Art. – Først maa det jeg læser være af en Forfatter, som selv er et heelt menneske, som har Noget at udtale – og som tillige er Kunstner – det vil sige: forstaaer at tale tydeligt – thi det kan ikke nytte noget, at han har dybsindige og skjønne Tanker, naar han ikke kan udtale disse saaledes, at jeg med nogenlunde Lethed kan forstaae, hvad han vil meddele mig. Al kunstnerisk Produktion er jo egentlig kun en Trang til at meddele andre sine Følelser og Stemninger; dette kan skee ved

Expressing 'the innermost state of his soul' was Gade's primary objective during his early years in Copenhagen. With Schumann as his guide, he devoured tomes of contemporary literature and criticism, looking for that spark of inspiration that might lead to the poetic. There was no doubt in Gade's mind as to his duty as a composer – he self-consciously transposed the extramusical into the musical, turning the subjective experience of art and emotion into cognitive form.

Looking at the entries in Gade's composition diary, we can tell that, as a reader, he sensed the experience of the act of writing. Moreover, the process of subjective reaction to the world of art was at the center of his creative process. Reading contemporary literature held a singular importance in the rapid development of his compositional style, and the entries in his composition diary trace the evolution of his skills as an interpreter and connoisseur. Written between July 1839 and September 1841, Gade's diary contains the programmatic origins for seven of his early compositions: the incomplete B-flat-major Piano Trio and F-major String Quartet, the Piano Sonata in E minor (Op. 28), a five-movement symphony titled *Agnete and the Merman*, the overtures *Echoes of Ossian* (Op. 1) and *St. Hans' Evening Play*, and the Symphony No. 1 in C minor (Op. 5). In the case of each of these pieces, Gade recorded a literary program based on excerpts of poetry and/or prose. No commentary was added explaining his reactions to the texts. Instead, the act of composing itself served as a means of interpreting the literary excerpts. Gade let musical sketches, and later complete compositions, stand as his personal commentaries to the texts preserved in his diary. Perhaps this is what makes his diary, and the compositions it engendered, so unique. For Gade's early works are not simply a set of compositional studies focused on the craft of musical creation; rather they are a series of creative reactions to the subjective experience initiated by another art form. Similar in spirit to Schumann's literary reactions to contemporary music as presented in the *Neue Zeitschrift für Musik*, Gade's early compositions represent musical reactions to the literature of his age.

Turning to the diary entries themselves, we see that Gade usually included only the most basic outlines for his pieces (figures 2–5). No music notation was added, and comments concerning instrumentation and key signatures were rare. In the case of programs for multi-movement compositions, Gade always divided the programs according to the various movements and noted which excerpts were to serve as inspiration for each part. The literary excerpts in each program served as a set of blueprints for a specific musical composition. After completing these

---

forskjellige Midler: Farver, Ord, Toner. – Jo tydeliger han ved disse Medier kan udtrykke sit inderste Væsens Stemning, jo større Kunstner er han.'

'blueprints,' Gade usually began on the musical sketches right away, taking great care to preserve and date each stage of the process. Consequently, we can compare the original literary programs for each piece with the musical sketches and drafts that followed. This process enables us to trace Gade's experiments in what might best be called 'interpretive composition;' in so doing, we can document the composer's earliest attempts to capture in music the aesthetic essence he termed 'Poesie.'

The programs for the first three works mentioned in Gade's diary – the Piano Trio, Piano Sonata, and String Quartet – are three separate attempts to capture in music the same poetic idea. The programs for these pieces reveal that all three were concerned with the same extra-musical topic of 'departure and return.' This idea was by no means new to music during Gade's formative years; it had already been treated by a number of German composers – e.g. J.S. Bach in his Capriccio for his departing brother, BWV 992; Ludwig van Beethoven in his Piano Sonata, 'Das Lebewohl, Abwesenheit und Wiedersehen,' Op. 81a; and Carl Maria von Weber in his *Concertstück* for Piano and Orchestra Op. 79. Gade likely knew these works; they would have been available to him at Copenhagen's various lending libraries. Thus it is tempting to imagine that he chose this topic for his first experiments with musical 'Poesie' precisely because it had already been successfully tested in the past.

The dates in Gade's composition diary show that he recorded the programs for the trio, piano sonata, and string quartet within a few months of each other. The program for his trio was recorded first, in July 1839. Gade's sketches show that he worked on this piece throughout the summer, making his final attempts on 2 September. Apparently dissatisfied with his progress at this point, Gade put the piece aside and designed similar programs for the piano sonata and string quartet. These were entered in his diary in September. Gade worked on the piano sonata for roughly six weeks, 20 November through 3 January, but did not finish it. In June he wrote the first musical sketches for the string quartet, but this work too was eventually abandoned. In the past, the unfinished state of these pieces has caused scholars to overlook them when discussing Gade's early career. This is unfortunate, for although these works were left incomplete by the composer in the 1840s, they nonetheless played a crucial role in his compositional process. Gade's continued attempt early in his career to capture a specific poetic concept in various genres reveals his determination as an aspiring composer and his commitment to the idea of 'Poesie.' In addition, his multiple sketches and drafts for these works clearly display the frustrations and struggles he faced when trying to alleviate the tension between form and content that inevitably arose in his early works.

For the fourth program in his composition diary, Gade abandoned the idea of using excerpts of poetry and turned instead to narrative works. In his program for a five-movement symphony called *Agnete and the Merman*, he quoted excerpts from two Danish texts inspired by native folk poetry: Jens Baggesen's *Agnete from Holmegaard* and Hans Christian Andersen's *Agnete and the Merman*. Like his earlier programs, Gade's program for the symphony was constructed along the lines of a narrative plot. No musical realization of this program exists, and we can only assume that in sketching out this piece Gade ran into some of the same structural pitfalls involving form and content that he had struggled with when working on the chamber pieces.

After recording the programmatic outline for *Agnete and the Merman* in October 1839, Gade appears to have taken a brief hiatus from his pursuit of the poetic, concentrating instead on setting folk texts for Berggreen and writing theater music for Bournonville. When Gade returned to his pursuit of the poetic in November 1840, his taste in sources and approach in interpreting them had changed in a subtle, but significant, way. Looking at the programs and musical sketches for the first four compositions mentioned in Gade's diary, one gets the sense that he was trying to re-create musically the intimate relationship a reader might have to a book or poem, using plot and tone as a means of expression. After his brief hiatus, however, Gade's approach to texts appears to have changed. Drawing on folklore, dramatic works, and ballad texts, Gade altered his approach to literary sources, using characterization and mood in an effort to recreate the sort of multi-sensory experience most commonly associated with the stage.

Gade's first project in this new mode of writing is represented by the fifth entry in his composition diary, the program for a concert overture called *Echoes of Ossian*. *Echoes of Ossian* was Gade's first great success, and he symbolically labeled it his Opus 1 upon publication. In preparing the program for this piece, Gade used excerpts from Steen Steensen Blicher's translation of the *Poems of Ossian*, and like the literary source itself, Gade's program is characterized by striking landscape descriptions and emotive characters. Gade completed the overture within two months of writing his program for the piece, and upon hearing the music one quickly realizes that he drew on his experience and love of the theater, not just his love of literature, when composing the work. Instead of attempting to capture a plot in music, his mistake in previous compositional projects, Gade focused on the expression of characterization and mood, much as an actor or playwright might do when preparing a work for the stage.

The thematic material in *Echoes of Ossian* shows an indebtedness to Danish folk music. Consequently, many twentieth-century scholars have looked to this work as the first of Gade's 'nationalistic' compositions. But this assumption is misguided. Blicher's translation of the *Poems of Ossian* never served as part of Denmark's folk heritage, and a study of Danish literature shows no link between

Ossian and Danish nationalism.[3] Gade did not choose Ossian for nationalistic reasons – such a connection never would have been understood in early to mid-nineteenth-century Denmark. Instead, he chose the *Poems of Ossian* for its striking descriptions and perceived literary worth. Quite simply, it was a source of poetic inspiration.

The same appears to be true for the literary work behind the next composition mentioned in Gade's diary, Adam Oehlenschläger's *St. Hans' Evening Play*. As he did in the *Echoes of Ossian*, Gade turned to his source's primary characters and scenic changes for inspiration, and in so doing created an orchestral work similar in nature to Felix Mendelssohn's *A Midsummer Night's Dream* Overture.

The final piece given a literary program in Gade's composition diary is his Symphony No. 1 in C minor. On the whole, this work reflects a tension between Danish and German elements. Gade based his program on Danish ballad texts, yet the music itself verifies the influence of German romantic models, i.e. Beethoven, Mendelssohn, and Schubert. Gade's Danish colleagues were clearly aware of the symphony's Germanic leanings; and when Gade first attempted, in 1842, to have it premiered in Copenhagen, it was rejected by the Music Society – 'too German' being the reason for refusal. The final chapter of this book traces the unique reception history of this composition, showing that it was the music's reception, not the original circumstances of its creation, that lead to Gade's present status as a nationalist composer.

Unfortunately, Gade's composition diary is the only surviving source of its kind – other composers no doubt followed a similar practice of literary inspiration, but none appear to have preserved the process with such care and in such detail. Even Gade himself appears to have abandoned the practice of keeping a composition diary after his initial success, though we know he continued to look to literature as a primary source of inspiration. Indeed, the composer's son, Axel, once reported in a description of his father's later career:

> Father repeated his favorite authors – again and again the same. ... Occasionally the door opened and father would stick his head in and say: 'Now this is exceptional – you must hear this.' Then he would read in his clear, expressive voice one thing or another; for example a poem by Oehlenschläger, his favorite Danish poet, [or] one of Falstaff's monologues, ... Father's laughter was contagious and his light-blue eyes were beaming with roguishness! Still gloating over the 'priceless Shakespeare,' he would retire again to his dear studio

---

[3] See my article, '*Efterklange af Ossian*: The Reception of James MacPherson's *Poems of Ossian* in Denmark's Literature, Art and Music,' *Scandinavian Studies* 70 (1998): 359–96.

and beloved books, in whose company he frequently would remain until late in the evening. ... Here he often got ideas for new compositions.[4]

Committed to the development of a personal, poetic style, Gade created the programs in his composition diary in order to facilitate his absorption of the poetic as he found it in contemporary German literature and Danish folk culture. Discovering 'Poesie' and making his mark in the world of composition were his primary goals. And by crossing the Danish/German cultural divide and drawing on his love of literature and the theater, he soon created a unique compositional style recognized both at home and abroad.

---

[4] Behrend, *Minder om Niels W. Gade. Kendte og Kvinders Erindringer* (Copenhagen, 1930), 41–2. 'Fader repeterede sine Yndlingsforfattere, – om og om igen de samme.... Af og til gik Døren op, og Fader stak Hovedet ind: 'Nej, det er mageløst, – det maa I høre.' Saa læste han med sin klare, udtryksfulde Stemme et eller andet op, f. Eks. et Digt af Oehlenschläger, hvem han elskede højest af danske Digtere, [eller] en af Falstaffs Monologer, ... Hvor smittende var ikke Faders Latter, og hvor kunde de mærkelig lyse, blaa Øjne ikke straale af Skælmeri! Endnu gottende sig over den 'kostelige Shakespeare' trak han sig igen tilbage til sin kære Stue og de kære Bøger, i hvis Selskab han kunde blive til sent ud paa Aftenen.... Her fik han sikkert ogsaa tidt Ideer til nye Kompositioner,...' Further evidence supporting Gade's use of literature as inspiration is found in a statement made by Ingeborg Simesen, also published in Behrends: 'When his books were organized after his death I found, in an edition of Dante, sections of text underlined in pencil in preparation for possible musical treatment.' (Da hans Bøger blev ornet efter hans Død, fandt jeg i en Udgave af Dante med hans Blyantsindstregninger med Henblik paa mulig musikalsk Behandling.)

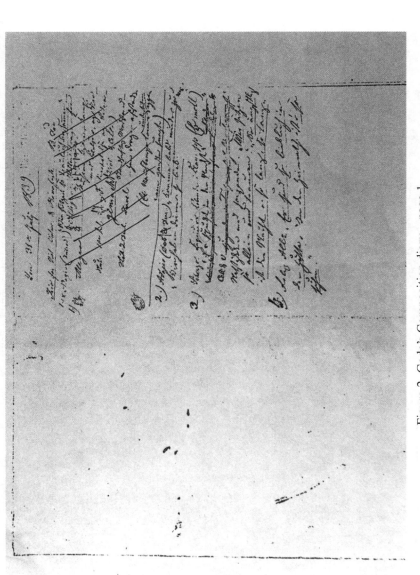

Figure 2 Gade's Composition diary – page 1.
(Olm DkB. Photocopies of the original supplied by Niels Martin Jensen)

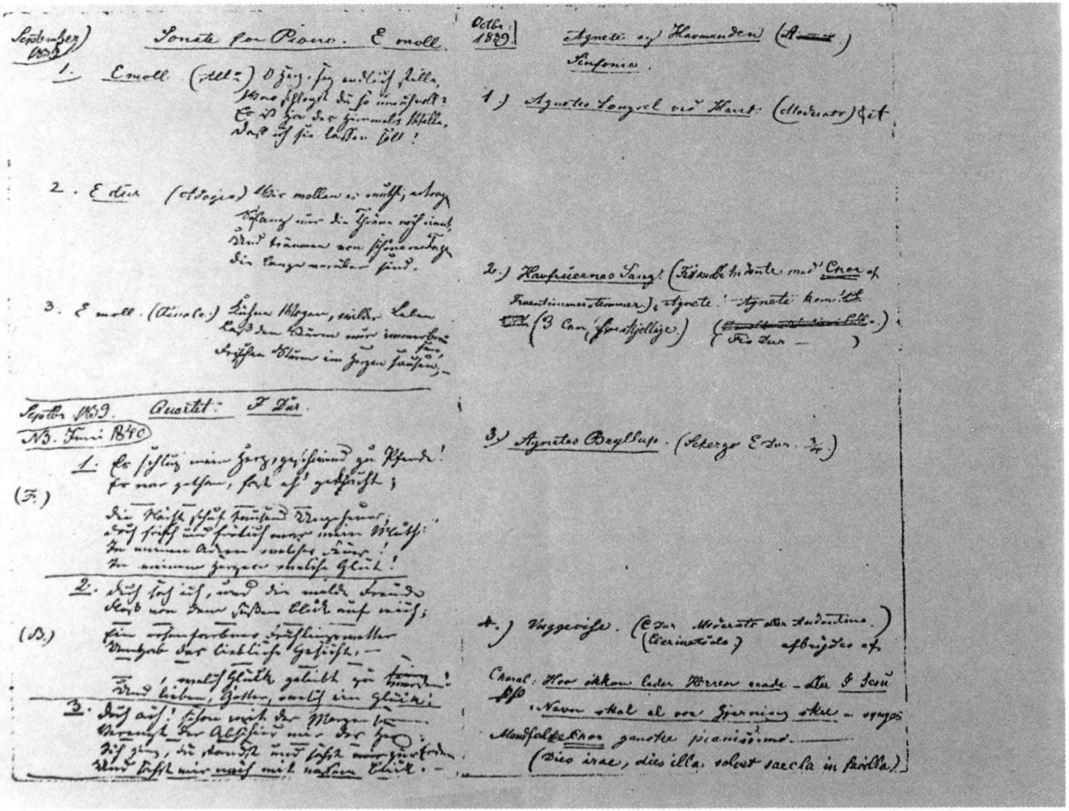

Sonate for Piano. E moll

1. Emoll

2. E dur

3. E moll

Quartet: F Dur

Agnete og Havmanden

Sinfonia.

(Dies irae, dies illa, solvet saecla in favilla.)

Figure 3 Gade's Composition diary – pages 2 and 3.
(Olim DkB. Photocopies of the original supplied by Niels Martin Jensen)

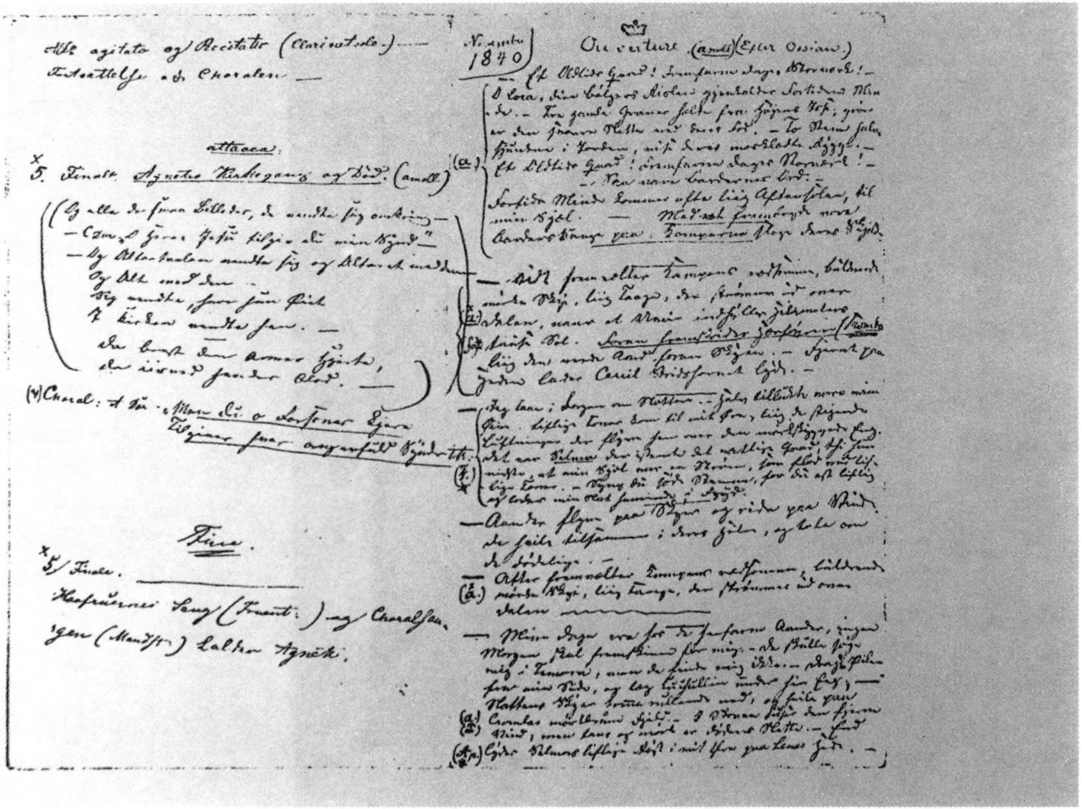

Figure 4 Gade's Composition dairy – pages 4 and 5.
(Olim DkB. Photocopies of the original supplied by Niels Martin Jensen)

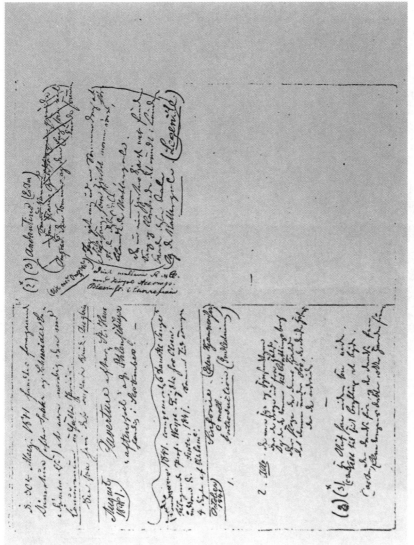

Figure 5 Gade's Composition diary – pages 6 and 7.
(Olim DkB. Photocopies of the original supplied by Niels Martin Jensen)

Chapter Four

The Chamber Works
(1839–40)

Chamber music for strings played a marginal role in Denmark's musical culture during Gade's formative years. Nonetheless, to fully understand the significance of Gade's early attempts in the genre, we must first acquaint ourselves with the history of chamber music in Denmark in the early nineteenth century.

Claus Schall (1757–1835), concertmaster of the Royal Chapel orchestra from 1792 and director of that organization's violin school from 1816 until 1834, was influential in sparking Denmark's first interest in chamber music for strings. Shortly after the turn of the century, Schall built what he called the Musikhus (Music House) behind his summer residence in Lyngby – a small town on the outskirts of Copenhagen. Designed especially for the performance of string quartets, the Musikhus became a popular meeting place for many of Copenhagen's finest string players. In the late 1830s, Gade and the Helsted brothers frequently performed there during the summer months.[1]

Other venues for the performance of chamber music included the homes of wealthy dilettantes such as Carl and Ernst Weis, Johann Friedrich Zinn, and Christian Waagepetersen. Waagepetersen, especially, spared no expense when sponsoring musical soirees. A painting by Wilhelm Marstrand entitled 'Musical Soiree at the Waagepetersen Home' (1834) presents a rare glimpse of how these evenings functioned (fig. 6).

Seated in the back room are members of Copenhagen's bourgeoisie – their chief function was to serve as an attentive audience. In the foreground are the artists and connoisseurs.

---

[1] Among these performers were George Gerson, Johannes Frøhlich and Frederik Thorkildsen Wexschall. Another player often in attendance was a student named Holger Simon Paulli. He described the meetings at Schall's Musikhus in a biographical essay published in Knud Hendricksen, *Fra Billedmagerens Kalejdoskop* (Copenhagen, 1954), 76: 'During the summer I spent many months with Schall at his estate in Lyngby. As a rule his students walked to Lyngby once a week and spent the day playing quartets.' (I Sommermaanederne, som Schall tilbragte paa sit Landsted i Lyngby, var jeg ofte flere Maaneder derude, medens Eleverne i Reglen 1 Gang om Ugen spaserede til Lyngby, hvor de tilbragte Dagen og spillede Qvartetter.) We know from letters between Gade and other members of the Copenhagen Davidsbund that Gade, Fritz Schram, and Edvard Helsted were among the students who participated in the quartet playings at Schall's Musikhus in the summer of 1834.

Figure 6 'Musical Soiree at the Waagepetersen Home' (1834) by Wilhelm Marstrand. (Det Nationalhistoriske Museum at Frederiksborg.)

Although the identity of each figure is no longer known, many of Copenhagen's most notable musicians are recognizable: for example, Claus Schall and Frederik Wexschall are seated in the left foreground. Above them stand the flautist Niels Petersen (darkened profile) and Ludvig Zinck (facing forward). To the right of the four string players (still unidentified) stands the cellist, Frederik Funk. C.E.F. Weyse is seated at the piano; surrounding him are I.F. Bredal, Hans Matthison-Hansen, and J.P.E. Hartmann. The large portrait on the back wall is the late Frederik Kuhlau (who had died two years earlier). Unfortunately the piano quintet about to be performed is unidentifiable. But if we are to assume that it is by a Dane, then it is probably that of P.C. Krossing, the only Danish composer known to have been composing piano quintets at that time.[2]

The number of private musical soirees grew steadily during the 1830s. In fact, by the end of the decade many string players from the Royal Chapel were supplementing their salaries by moonlighting as chamber players.[3] As Paulli explains, Copenhagen's eventual acceptance of chamber music as a serious art form was greatly due to the efforts of Frederik Wexschall and the brothers Ernst and Carl Weis:

The first public quartet soirees took place, if I remember correctly, in 1837–38. The Weis brothers, Ernst and Carl, were very gifted music dilettantes. During a stay in Braunsweig, Carl Weis became acquainted with the first epoch-making quartet players, the Müller brothers.[4] He had attended their rehearsals of classical works, and when he came home he recommended to Wexschall that the four of us – Wexschall 1st violin, Carl Weis 2nd violin, myself viola, and Ernst Weis cello – should rehearse quartets à la Müller [i.e. quartets in the classical style].

---

[2] Nils Schiørring, *Musikkens Historie i Danmark*, vol. 2: 1750–1870 (Copenhagen: Politikens Forlag, 1978), 175.

[3] According to H.S. Paulli: 'The capital was full of music-playing dilettantes. In their homes quartets were constantly being played, and I was summoned there many evenings after the theater…to play in quartets, often until the early hours of morning.' (Hovedstaden var riig paa musikdyrkende Dilettanter, i hvis Hjem der stadig spilledes Qvartetter, og hvortil jeg blev søgt, kunde jeg de fleste Aftener gaa fra Teatret…og deltage i Qvartetter ofte til langt ud paa Morgenstunden.) Cf. Knud Hendricksen's *Fra Billedmagerens Kalejdoskop* (Copenhagen, 1954), 76. In the 1830s the first professional chamber music society, Arken, was founded by Wexschall, Frøhlich and and Paulli (see Hendricksen, 77 and Ravn, 191). Arken's meetings took place one to two times a month in Knirsch Hotel (now the Hotel Angleterre). Preceded by a meal, the meetings often involved the performance of various chamber works – most commonly works for either voice, piano, or strings. The membership was limited to 29 people, but additional invitations were often extended to selected guests and visiting foreign musicians.

[4] These four brothers, Karl (1797–1873), Georg (1808–55), Gustav (1799–1855), and Theodor (1802–75), made their public début as a professional string quartet in Hamburg in 1831. During the following years they embarked on a number of tours which took them to Germany, France, Denmark, the Netherlands and Russia. Their principal repertory comprised works by Haydn, Mozart, and Beethoven. The quartet was dissolved in 1855.

Although this genre did not particularly appeal to Wexschall – a bravour player like few others – it was not long before he saw fit to regulate his playing according to Weis' recommendations....[5] After a half year of concentrated rehearsals we had come so far, that we dared to present ourselves as quartet players. According to my memory we were invited to play at three soirees. These [performances], which took place in the Harmony Club's meeting hall on Vingaardsstræde, were very popular and greatly appreciated.[6]

In addition to performing string quartets, a few Danish musicians also tried their hand at composing in the genre. Not surprisingly, the first composer to take such an initiative was Claus Schall. Schall's composers of choice were Gluck, Haydn, and Mozart,[7] but his string quartets show a predilection for the *quatuor brillant* style. Popularized in France, this style of quartet writing was transplanted to Germany in the early nineteenth century and adopted by composers such as Andreas Romberg, Rodolpho Kreutzer, and Louis Spohr.[8]

---

[5] This essentially meant that he should restrain his virtuosic playing, which could easily eclipse the other parts. Not surprisingly, Wexschall was one of Copenhagen's strongest *quatuor brillant* advocates.

[6] Hendricksen, 77–78. 'Den første offentlige Qvartet-Soirée fandt efter mit Vidende Sted i 1837–38. Brødrene Ernst og Carl Weis vare høit begavede Musik-Dilettanter. Carl Weis havde under et Ophold i Braunsweig gjort Bekjendskab med de første epokegjørende Qvartet-Spillere, Brødrene Müller; han havde overværet deres Indstudering af de klassiske Værker, og da han kom herhjem, forslog han Wexschall, at vi fire, Wexschall 1ste Violin, Carl Weis 2den Violin, jeg Bratsch, og Ernst Weis Violoncel, skulde indstudere Qvartetter à la Müller. Skjønt denne Genre egentlig ikke laa for Wexschall, der var Bravourspiller som faa, varede det dog ikke længe, føren han med Interesse saa at sige underordnede sit Spil efter Weis' Angivelse, thi det gjalt væsentligst om at slaa af paa hans enorme Technik, som let kunde faa Overhaand. Efter ½ Aars flittig Indøvelse, var vi kommen saavidt, at vi turde fremtræde som Qvartetspillere. Der blev indbudt, saavidt jeg erinder, til 3 Soiréer og disse, der blev meget søgte og paaskjønnede, fandt Sted i Harmonien's Lokaler i Viingaardsstræde.' A letter from Wexschall to Paulli in DkB testifies to these rehearsals. For a full transcription of this letter see Nils Schiørring, 'H.S. Paulli og Dansk Musikliv i det 19. Århundrede,' *Fund og Forskning* 4 (1957): 100.

[7] Mozart, especially, was a favorite of Schall. In the late 1780s Schall made a study tour of various European cities. While in Prague he had the good fortune to meet privately with Mozart.

[8] In a chapter of his *Violinschule* entitled 'Vom Vortrage des Quartets,' Spohr drew a clear distinction between the *quatuor brillant* and the 'regular' quartet (i.e. the motivically elaborated quartet developed by Haydn and Mozart). Schall's interest in the *quatuor brillant* was probably piqued by the amateur musician George Gerson (1790–1825). Born in Copenhagen, Gerson studied violin with C. Tiemroth and then moved to Hamburg in 1805 to study business. He composed a number of chamber works while in Germany – among these the string quartets nos. 2–4. Although lacking in musical invention, these works show an assured handling of form and texture and the strong influence of Gerson's mentor, Andreas Romberg. Few of Gersen's works were ever published, but his collected works are preserved in five autograph volumes in the Music Collection of DkB.

Two additional composers of chamber music for strings were Johannes Frederik Frøhlich (1806–60) and J.P.E. Hartmann (1805–1900). A noted violinist and student of Schall since 1821, Frøhlich made his debut as a composer in 1823 with the String Quartet in D minor, Op. 1. No doubt influenced by Schall, Frøhlich composed this work in the *quatuor brillant* style.[9] Frøhlich composed four string quartets. Whereas his String Quartet in A major, Op. 2 (1823) still adheres to the *quatuor brillant* style, the String Quartet, Op. 17 (1827, also in A major) reveals a strong allegiance to the classical styles of Mozart and early Beethoven. Unfortunately the B-minor String Quartet, Op. 15 (1826) is now lost.[10]

J.P.E. Hartmann made his debut as a chamber music composer in 1823 with his Piano Quartet, Op. 12. Clearly indebted to the chamber works of Mozart, Hartmann's piano quartet testifies to the growing popularity of the Viennese classical style in the 1820s. Frøhlich and Hartmann paved the way for the arrival of the classical style in Denmark, but it was Frederik Kuhlau who served as Denmark's foremost representative of the period. The majority of Kuhlau's chamber works were written for flute,[11] but he occasionally composed for strings as can be seen by his three Piano Quartets (C minor, A major, and G minor, Opp. 32, 50 and 108), four Violin Sonatas (F minor, Op. 33; and F major, A minor, and C minor, Op. 79) and single String Quartet (A minor, Op. 122). This latter work is especially important. Written in 1831 and commissioned by Waagepetersen, it was originally intended to be the first of a set of six quartets.[12] But Kuhlau's untimely death in 1832 precluded the completion of the commission and thus brought to a close the Viennese-inspired classical period in Danish chamber music for strings.

Kuhlau's death dealt a heavy blow to Danish chamber music. Although the late 1830s witnessed a rise in public performances of string quartets, the production of such pieces was all but abandoned by Denmark's most notable

---

[9] For a description of this quartet see Kai Aage Bruun, *Dansk Musiks Historie fra Holberg-tiden til Carl Nielsen* (Copenhagen: J. Vintens Forlagsboghandel, 1969), vol. 1, 286–7.

[10] An autograph chronological list of Frøhlich's compositions can be found in DkB: Ny kgl. Saml. 3258 A, 4°. Sent to August Bournonville in 1866 by Frøhlich's niece, Rikke Kittler, this list reveals that approximately one third of the composer's works are now lost.

[11] Kuhlau was not a flutist himself – he wrote for this instrument in order to satisfy the great demand for flute music in early nineteenth-century Denmark.

[12] In a letter to J. H. A. Farrenc dated 18 July 1831 Kuhlau wrote: 'Dann muss ich aber eine Composition grösserer Art schreiben, worüber mir wohl der ganze nächste Winter vergehen wird, nämlich: ein hiesiger reicher Kaufmann und grosser Musikfreund [Christian Waagepetersen], hat mich aufgefordert für ihm 6 Quartetten für 4 Bogeninstrumentente zu componiren. Er honorirt mir diese Arbeit sehr generös, und will die Herausgabe selbst besorgen. Da ich nun schon lange wünschte mich auch in dieser Gattung von Composition zu versuchen, so habe ich diesen Auftrag mit Vergnügen angenommen.' Quoted from Gorm Busk, *Kuhlau Breve* (Copenhagen: Engstrøm & Sødring, 1990), 176.

composers. Only a few students in Wexschall's violin school – i.e. Gade, and the Helsted brothers – appeared to show an interest in the genre.

Looking at Gade's early chamber works for strings, we quickly recognize the emergence of what might be best described as a romantic manner. In his first piece, a single *Allegro* movement in A minor composed in 1836,[13] we encounter an experimental style likely influenced by Wexschall's virtuosic taste – the dominating first violin part shows the influence of the above-mentioned *quatuor brillant* style. Yet even at this early stage one can recognize several enterprising traits: intemperate dynamic changes, a bold attempt toward harmonic ingenuity, and the first violin's *ad libitum* solo at the opening and closing of the movement.[14]

Gade's next attempt at chamber music is a single *Andante and Allegro molto* movement for string quintet (1837). Composed only one year after the *Allegro* in A minor, this work clearly reveals the rapid development of his romantic style. The piece is quite long, 493 measures, and the introductory *Andante* has considerable weight. The *Allegro* section is rather free in form and alternates between *allegro molto* and *meno allegro*. A *presto* coda brings the movement to a close. This extended movement reveals Gade's experimentation with dramatic musical expression and unconventional formal structure.[15]

But Gade's true progress in chamber music came in 1839 and 1840, when he began work on his B-flat-major Piano Trio and F-major String Quartet. Here we finally see a serious approach toward large, multi-movement chamber works for strings in the romantic style. Left incomplete by the composer, these works have received little attention in the scholarly literature – an unfortunate oversight.[16] Though never published during Gade's lifetime, the piano trio and string quartet symbolize a crucial stage in the history of chamber music in Denmark and, perhaps

---

[13] This work was never published. The autograph score is found in DkB: Gade Samling, C II 6, supplement #22, 4°.

[14] This solo may have been a response to Mendelssohn's violin solo *ad libitum* in the second movement (mm. 91–92) of his String Quartet in A minor, Op. 13. For a discussion of Gade's *Allegro* see Juddi Winkel, 'N.W. Gades og J.P.E. Hartmanns strygekvartetter set på baggrund af den romantiske strygekvartet iøvrigt, specielt hos Mendelssohn og Schumann,' Masters Thesis, Copenhagen University, 1975, 51–53.

[15] It is tempting to view Gade's employment of two cellos (instead of the traditional doubling of the viola) as a response to Schubert's monumental quintet (composed in 1828), but this is unlikely. Schubert's quintet was practically unknown before 1850 and was not published until 1853.

[16] Apart from occasional citations, the only discussions occur in Povl Ingerslev-Jensen, 'Et Ukendt Værk af Niels W. Gade,' *Dansk Musik Tidene* (1942): 138–42 and Winkel. Neither Asger Lund Christiansen, 'Gades Strygekvartetter,' *Musik* 1 (1967): 7–9 nor Friedhelm Krummacher, 'Gattung und Werk – Zu Streichquartetten von Gade und Berwald,' *Kieler Schriften zur Musikwissenschaft* 26 (Kassel 1982): 154–75, mention Gade's F-major String Quartet.

more relevant to this study, reveal the first definitive step in Gade's advancement towards creative maturity.

Gade created the program for his Piano Trio in B-flat major on 31 July 1839 and recorded it in his composition diary. Comprised of a series of mottos and musical indications, this program contains outlines for four separate movements: *Allegro* (preceded by an Adagio introduction), *Adagio*, *Scherzo* and *Finale*. A look at Gade's program reveals that he based his trio on the idea of a hero's departure and eventual homecoming. The poetic mottos used in the program obviously came from a variety of Danish and German sources, and it appears that in his devising of the program, Gade was attempting to formulate some kind of stylized plot (table 1).

Only two musical sources still exist for the trio: a manuscript score containing sketches for movements one, two and three, and a set of string parts for the first movement.[17] We know from dates in Gade's score that he began writing the first movement on 23 August 1839, completing it ten days later (2 September). Written in sonata form, this movement begins with a slow introduction that clearly imitates the melancholy expressed in the program's opening motto: 'Wir sitzen so traulich beysammen' (We sit together so sorrowfully). Gade was likely thinking of Wilhelm Müller's celebrated 'Thränenregen' when he composed his program;[18] and a sense of restlessness characterizes the opening measures, where descending arpeggios mask the downbeat. But this restlessness is soon resolved by the entrance of a stirring, melodic theme in measure 4 (ex. 4:1). Measures 12–20 bring back the arpeggio motive. Played in unison by the violin and piano in measures 12–14 and by the cello in measures 16–17, this motive alternates with melodic figures derived from the introductory theme (ex. 4:2). A transition section (m. 21ff) leads to the opening of an *Allegro con fuoco* section. Here the duality of the hero/sweetheart relationship in the trio's literary program is emphasized by an exchange of sweeping melodic lines in the violin and cello. This imitative counterpoint was to have been supported by a slow, ascending bass-line in the piano (ex. 4:3).

---

[17] Both the score and the set of parts are found in DkB: Gade Saml. C II 6, supplement #32, 4°.

[18] Müller's text reads: 'Wir saßen so traulich zusammen.' Gade probably knew this poem from Franz Schubert's setting of it in the cycle, *Die schöne Müllerin*.

Table 1
Program for the Piano Trio in B-flat major

The 31ˢᵗ July 1839 –
          Trio for Violin, Viola and Piano. B-flat major

1)x Adagio (Introd.) 'Wir sitzen so traulich beysammen.'[19]
          Allegro: 4/4 3/4
1)//[20]   Allegro......................The hero departs from his sweetheart –
                                          Struggle with emotions and unrest –
        cadence 1ˢᵗ part A and F: Persuasion and pleading (Violin and Cello)

                  Finished   Steadfast resistance –

        cadence: 2ⁿᵈ part, Farewell   – He departs.
                                    (In the meantime, a march tempo sounds
        //   Again, but very weakly)

             ----

2)   Adagio (D-flat Maj.) 'Komm bald wieder zu uns.'
                           'Wir haben deins so lieb.'

2 3)   Scherzo. Capriccios running in piano. *pp.* (B-flat minor)
                'Es spukt in der Nacht,'
           ///
           Cello and Violin ////////////////////////////
           Evening piece with sforzando: 'Wir sitzen
           so allein und trauern.' 'So ängstlich
           Ist die Nacht und so lang, so lang.'

3 4)   Calm Allegro: 'Es sind so lieblich in der Hütte'
                       'In der Heimat ist's so schön.'

---

[19] First line of Wilhelm Müller's 'Thränenregen' from *Die schöne Müllerin.*
[20] // indicates illegible, crossed-out text.

Example 4:1. Piano Trio in B-flat major, first movement, measures 1–11.

Example 4:2. Piano Trio in B-flat major, first movement, measures 12–20.

Example 4:3. Piano Trio in B-flat major, first movement, measures 21–44.

(Example 4:3 cont.)

Example 4:4. Piano Trio in B-flat major, first movement, measures 45–58.

(Example 4:4 cont.)

A trumpet-like fanfare announces the beginning of the *Allegro con fuoco* in measure 45. As indicated in Gade's program, this fanfare serves as a leitmotif for the hero. Measures 45–58 function as a bridge to the primary theme. Here the program's second motto, 'The hero departs from his sweetheart,' is musically expressed through a long, emphatic cadential section (ex. 4:4). The program's third motto, 'struggle with emotions and unrest,' is represented by the primary theme. Two distinct melodic ideas are separated by a reappearance of the hero's leitmotif (ex. 4:5a–c). A quiet march theme begins in the piano in measure 105 and is soon joined by impassioned melodic passages in the violin and cello. Returning to Gade's original program, we see that this transition section undoubtedly illustrates the fourth and fifth mottos, 'Persuasion and pleading' and 'Steadfast resistance' (ex. 4:6). As indicated in Gade's program, this section ends in the key of F major. A lyrical secondary theme begins in measure 137 (ex. 4:7). Played first by the piano and then by the strings, the resolved character of this simple and balanced melody stands in stark contrast to the fervent qualities displayed in the preceding sections and thus perfectly represents the hero's departure.

Gade's development begins with some variations on the hero motif. As indicated in the program, 'a march tempo sounds again, but very weakly.' Various thematic elements from the exposition are elaborated and intertwined. The return of the primary theme in its original form marks the beginning of the recapitulation. The coda closes with a final statement of the secondary theme and 'the hero departs.'

We know from the surviving set of parts that the first movement of the Piano Trio was completed and performed in the late 1830s. Whereas the score is obviously a working manuscript – the piano part contains occasional lacunae, and movements two and three are incomplete – the set of parts for the first movement are cleanly written and contain several fingering indications. These parts were more than likely prepared for a performance with friends from the Copenhagen Davidsbund (perhaps Carl and Edvard Helsted).

Example 4:5. Piano Trio in B-flat major, first movement.

a) primary theme (first melodic idea), measures 58–71.

b) reappearance of hero's leitmotive, measures 72–75.

c) primary theme (second melodic idea), measures 76–85.

Example 4:6. Piano Trio in B-flat major, first movement, measures 105–37.

(Example 4:6 cont.)

(Example 4:6 cont.)

Example 4:7. Piano Trio in B-flat major, first movement, measures 137–45.

Only skeletal musical sketches exist for the second and third movements. The second movement, an *Adagio* in D-flat major, appears to conform to Gade's original program. Written primarily in imitative counterpoint, this movement follows an A B A^i outline and is dominated by a theme reminiscent of the hero's leitmotif from the first movement (ex. 4:8). The third movement is less complete; only the opening scherzo section is represented. Written in the key of B-flat minor, this section reveals little more than the 'running capriccios' mentioned in Gade's program (fig. 7). There is no trace of the proposed fourth movement, and it is reasonable to assume that it was never begun. The dates in Gade's sketches show that he worked on the trio throughout the summer, making his final attempts on 2 September. Apparently dissatisfied with his progress at this point, he put the project aside and designed similar programs for a piano sonata and string quartet. These were entered in his diary in September. Gade worked on the piano sonata for roughly six weeks but did not finish it. In June 1840 he recorded the first musical sketches for a string quartet in F major.[21]

Example 4:8. Piano Trio in B-flat major, second movement, measures 1–6.

---

[21] DkB: Gade Saml. C II 6, Supplement # 23. Dates in the sketches show that Gade began work on the quartet 8 June 1840. The final page of the first movement is dated 13 July 1840.

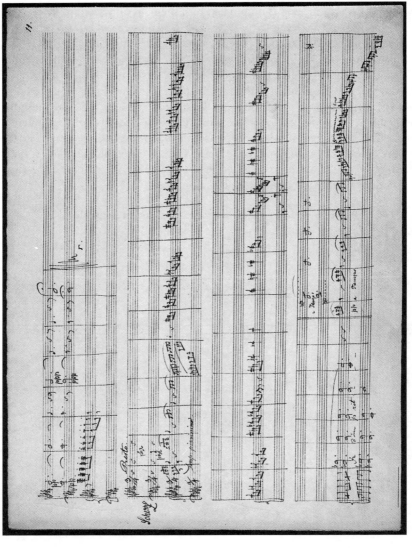

Figure 7 Piano Trio in B-flat major, first page of the third movement.
(DkB: Gade Saml., C II 6)

Like the piano trio, Gade's string quartet was probably written for his friends in the Copenhagen Davidsbund. We know from contemporary accounts that four members of the group – Gade, Fritz Schram, Edvard and Carl Helsted – formed a string quartet in 1835. The inspiration for the program was Goethe's poem 'Wilkommen und Abschied.' As shown in tables 2 and 3, Gade did not use the entire poem, but instead chose excerpts from each stanza and arranged them according to his own programmatic idea.

Written in sonata form, this movement appears to express the same spontaneous passion communicated in the first stanza of Gade's literary program. The length of this movement, 531 measures, is quite impressive; and although it occasionally suffers from a lack of proportion, it nonetheless contains moments of true ingenuity. One such example is the construction of the primary theme in measures 1–81 (ex. 4:9). Characterized by a driving melody in the first violin and dramatic dynamic changes, this typically romantic theme conjures up the sense of restless movement found in the first two lines of Gade's program:

Es schlug mein Herz, geschwind zu Pferde!
Es war gethan [sic.] fast eh' gedacht;

(My heart beat fast; quick, to the horse,
It was done almost before it was thought;)

While the primary theme departs from the tonic, the secondary theme clings to its key, the dominant C major (ex. 4:10). In measures 140–68, with a turn to the dominant minor and exploitation of the dark colors of the lower strings, we encounter what appears to be a clear depiction of the third line in Gade's program: 'Die Nacht schuf tausend Ungeheuer' (The night created a thousand monsters) (ex. 4:11). This is followed by a *risoluto* return of the primary theme in measure 210. Unquestionably, this return was conceived as a musical representation of the hero's undaunted resolve expressed in line four of the program: 'Doch frisch und fröhlich war mein Mut' (But fresh and merry was my courage) (ex. 4:12).

Table 2
Goethe's 'Wilkommen und Abschied'[22]

Es schlug mein Herz, geschwind zu Pferde!
Es war getan fast eh gedacht.
Der Abend wiegte schon die Erde,
Und an den Bergen hing die Nacht.
Schon stand im Nebelkleid die Eiche,
Ein aufgetürmter Riese, da,
Wo Finsternis aus dem Gesträuche
Mit Hundert schwarzen Augen sah.

Der Mond von einem Wolkenhügel
Sah kläglich aus dem Duft hervor,
Die Winde schwangen leise Flügel,
Umsausten schauerlich mein Ohr.
Die Nacht schuf tausend Ungeheuer,
Doch frisch und fröhlich war mein Mut:
In meinem Adern welches Feuer!
In meinem Herzen welche Glut!

Dich sah ich, und die milde Freude
Floss von dem süssen Blick auf mich;
Ganz war mein Herz an deiner Seite
Und jeder Atemzug für dich.
Ein rosenfarbnes Frühlingswetter
Umgab das liebliche Gesicht,
Und Zärtlichkeit für mich – ihr Götter!
Ich hoffe es, ich verdient es nicht!

Doch ach, schon mit der Morgensonne
Verengt der Abschied mir das Herz:
In deinem Küssen welche Wonne!
In deinem Auge welcher Schmerz!
Ich ging, du standst und sahst zur Erden,
Und sahst mir nach mit nassem Blick.
Und doch, welch Glück, geliebt zu werden!
Und Lieben, Götter, welch ein Glück!

---

[22] The underlined text indicates the lines appearing in Gade's program for the F-major String Quartet.

Table 3
Gade's program for the F-major String Quartet

Septbr. 1839   Quartet: F major
(NB. June 1840)

1.   Es schlug mein Herz, geschwind zu Pferde!
          Es war gethan [sic.] fast eh' gedacht;
(F.)   – – – –

          die Nacht schuf tausend Ungeheuer;
          doch frisch und frölich [sic.] war mein Muth [sic.]:
          In meinem Adern welches Feuer!
          In meinem Herzen welche Glut!

----

2.   dich sah ich, und die milde Freude
          floß von dem süßen Blick auf mich;

                  – – – –
(B.)   Ein rosenfarbnes Frühlingswetter
          Umgab das liebliche Gesicht,--

                  – – – –

          – , welch Glück, geliebt zu séín werden!
          Und Lieben, Götter, welch ein Glück!

----

3.   doch ach! schon mit der Morgensonne
          Verengt der Abschied mir das Herz:

                  – – – –

          Ich ging, du standst und sahst mít zur Erden,
          Und sahst mir nach mit naßem Blick –

Example 4:9. String Quartet in F major, first movement, measures 1–9.

Example 4:10. String Quartet in F major, first movement, measures 82–89.

Example 4:11. String Quartet in F major, first movement, measures 140–47.

Example 4:12. String Quartet in F major, first movement, measures 209–16.

Example 4:13. String Quartet in F major, first movement, measures 241–60.

Fluctuating between the keys of A-flat major and F minor, the first thirty-two measures of the development section show little sign of thematic development. However, new motivic material appears in measure 241 (ex. 4:13).[23] Labeled 'Agitato,' this material was clearly inspired by the closing lines of the movement's program:

> In meinem Adern welches Feuer!
> In meinem Herzen welche Glut!
>
> (In my blood, what fire!
> In my heart, what ardour!)

A return of the secondary theme in measure 366 marks the beginning of the recapitulation. This is followed by a condensed version of the primary theme (mm. 418–55) and a final statement of the secondary theme. A coda begins in measure 493. Marked *poco lento*, the first twelve measures present a melody in the viola which appears to be a hybrid of the primary and secondary themes. Finally, a return of the *agitato* motive first found in the development section brings the movement to a close.

The second movement, an *Adagio con expressione* in B-flat major dated 13 July 1840, presents a musical interpretation of the second part of Gade's program. Like the program itself, this movement divides into three distinct sections, A B A[i]. A single thematic idea serves as the movement's foundation[24] (ex. 4:14). Appearing first in the opening measures, this theme represents the 'milde Freude' (gentle bliss) described in Gade's program.

The movement's middle section occupies measures 33–60 and in many ways functions as a development section – the first measures of the central theme serve as motivic material. Returning to Gade's program we see that this section was apparently envisioned as a musical portrait:

> Ein rosenfarbnes Frühlingswetter
> Umgab das liebliche Gesicht.
>
> (Rose-colored, spring weather
> Surrounded the lovely face.)

---

[23] The descending arpeggio played by the first violin in measures 241–43 appears again later as the cyclical motive in Gade's Piano Sonata in E minor, Op. 28. For a complete discussion of this work see chapter five.

[24] Here true signs of Gade's adherence to an expressive romantic style can be seen in the irregular metrical construction of the antecedent and consequent phrases and the employment of numerous dynamic fluctuations as a means of emphasizing the music's expressive character.

Example 4:14. String Quartet in F major, second movement, measures 1–7.

As might be expected, this middle section goes through a number of harmonic changes. Beginning in the key of F minor, it modulates to D-flat major in measure 42 and then B-flat minor in measures 46–49. After a brief suspension of harmony in measures 49–53 (here the harmony appears to be floating between B-flat minor and E-flat minor) the tonic key of B-flat major returns (ex. 4:15).

The final section of the second movement begins in measure 61. Marked *tempo primo*, this section is no more than a condensed version of the opening thirty-two measures. Based on the final lines of Goethe's poem – 'welch Glück, geliebt zu werden!/ Und lieben, Götter, welch ein Glück!' (What joy, to be loved!/ And to love, Oh Gods, what a joy!) – this section, like the opening, is an attempt to represent musically the joy of love.

Whereas the first and second movements of the string quartet are complete, the final movement, a *Serenata scherzando* in F major, is finished only up to measure 86. As Richard Carpen observed in his recent edition of this work:

> From that point, and until measure 272, there are substantial sections in which only the first violin and/or cello are indicated, the majority being repetitions of earlier passages the composer intended to 'fill-in' later. In transitional passages and in sections deviating from what was written earlier, Gade again wrote for all four instruments.[25]

Though the movement is unfinished, we can surmise that Gade intended to use a five-part rondo structure composed of two alternating thematic ideas: ABABA.[26]

Section A presents a sanguine melody in the first violin accompanied by broken staccato chords in the viola and pizzicato quarter notes in the second violin and cello. In contrast, section B is characterized by an airy, carefree melody in the upper-register of the cello accompanied by staccato eighth-note figures in the violins and viola (ex. 4:16a and b). Whereas section A is always presented in F major, the tonic key, section B appears in D major the first time and F major the second time.

---

[25] Richard Carpen, 'Editor's Note,' *Gade's String Quartet in F Major* (Copenhagen: Dan Fog, 1995).

[26] Winkel, 56, correctly observes that on the last page of the score one finds the opening measures of the A theme marked *Sempre forte*. Due to the length of the surviving movement, we can assume that this returning A section is, in fact, the final coda. Winkel continues by noting that Gade uses the same motivic material to link the movement's five sections, and she states that the melody used in this transition is an allusion to the third melody line from Gade's song 'Kong Valdemars Jagt.' I disagree with this conclusion. Although the two melodies contain some similarities, they do not appear to be motivically related to one another.

Example 4:15. String Quartet in F major, second movement, measures 46–53.

Example 4:16. String Quartet in F major.

a) third movement, section A, measures 1–10.

b) third movement, section B, measures 45–54.

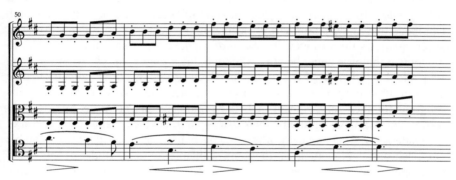

According to Gade's program, he originally envisioned the final movement as an expression of pain and sorrow:

Doch ach! schon mit der Morgensonne
Verengt der Abschied mir das Herz:
Ich ging, du standst und sahst zu Erden,
Und sahst mir nach mit naßem Blick.

(But alas! Already with the morning sun
The farewell made my heart constrict.
I went, you stood looking down at the ground
And gazed after me with wet eyes.)

But nothing in the animated character of the third movement in Gade's sketches reflects this program, and we are left with the question: Was the *Seranata scherzando* actually inspired by the third part of Gade's program? Probably not. I propose that Gade's program for a final movement was not intended for the string quartet's third movement, *Seranata scherzando*, but rather for a fourth movement that was never begun. Although this argument might seem forced at first, a look at other programs written by Gade around this time indicates that he often omitted programs for scherzo movements. Such was the case with his program for the Piano Sonata in E-flat minor and his program for the five-movement symphony entitled *Agnete and the Merman* (see chapters five and six).

Gade's early chamber works do not belong among his most notable compositions. Nonetheless, they are valuable to any study of his early development as a composer. The Trio in B-flat major and the F-major String Quartet serve as important examples of Gade's early struggles toward creative maturity. They represent the earliest examples of the composer's emerging romantic style, and as such they signify a crucial stage in Denmark's music history – the belated arrival of Romanticism in Danish chamber music for strings.

Chapter Five

The Piano Sonata in E Minor, Op. 28 (1839–54)

The Piano Sonata in E Minor, Op. 28 represents Gade's only attempt in the genre and one of only two cyclical works he published for piano in 1854.[1] As the dates in the title of this chapter suggest, the piano sonata underwent a long period of gestation before reaching its final form. Curiously, Gade's numerous revisions of the work coincided with articles about the genre published in the *Neue Zeitschrift für Musik*. As this chapter will show, it appears that Gade's initial interest in the piano sonata may have been fueled by Schumann's published thoughts and opinions about the genre.

In an article appearing in April 1839, Schumann bemoaned the mediocre quality of recently-composed piano sonatas and criticized young composers' treatment of the genre as 'a kind of specimen' or 'studies in form.' He reproached composers whom he felt treated the sonata too lightly (i.e. Ries, Berger, Onslow and C.M. von Weber) and declared that the genre, as a whole, was stagnating:

> The sonata is the same as it was ten years ago. A few nice appearances of this genre will surely come to light now and then. But in general, it seems this genre has passed through its life cycle. After all, this is the order of things, and we should not repeat the same thing for a century without showing concern for what is new.[2]

Schumann awaited the impending demise of the sonata, but he also held out hope for the future. To composers still interested in composing in the genre, he offered the following advice: 'If one should wish to write sonatas, or fantasies (what lies in a name), one should be sure not to forget about the music, and good genius will take care of all the rest.'[3]

These words appear to have served as a catalyst for Gade. In September 1839 he recorded in his composition diary the program for his Piano Sonata in E minor. Based on stanzas from three different poems, this program, like those for the B-flat-major Piano Trio and F-major String Quartet, was founded on the idea of a loved one's departure and return. The author(s) of the verses is still unknown, but it is likely the original poetry was written by Gade himself and/or friends in the

---

[1] The other work was the *Arabeske*, Op. 27. Like the piano sonata, this piece was begun in the late 1830s, eventually evolved into a cyclical work, and was revised and published in 1854.

[2] Schumann, 'Sonaten für das Klavier,' *Neue Zeitschrift für Musik* (26 April 1839): 134.

[3] Ibid.

Copenhagen Davidsbund. The only musical indications in Gade's program are the key and tempo designations assigned to each stanza (table 4).

Gade's piano sonata underwent numerous changes before reaching its final form. Four autograph sources still exist for the work: three sketch sets, which I have labeled chronologically A, B and C, and a final draft dating from 1854 (table 5).

Sketch set A was written between 20 November 1839 and 3 January 1840.[4] These sketches contain rough outlines for four movements: an *Allegro appassionato* in E minor, an *Allegretto grazioso, quasi Andantino* in E major, a *Scherzo* in B minor, and the *Finale* in E minor. Gade later revised set A in pencil.

Sketch set B is not dated, but corrections for the first movement and the inclusion of an alternate second movement indicate that it was written after sketch set A. Gade edited these sketches in black ink and pencil.[5]

Sketch set C also lacks a precise date. Written on the backside of a discarded cover page dated 23 January 1841, these sketches must have been written sometime after this date.[6] Sketch set C contains the finished version of the third movement and a fragment of the first movement's development section.

In addition to these three sketch sets, the autograph Stichvorlag sent to Breitkopf und Härtel for the publication of the first edition can be found in Leipzig.[7] Dated June 1854, this neatly written autograph presents the final stage of the sonata's long evolution. Thanks to the survival of Gade's various drafts of the sonata, the chronology of his revisions can be securely determined. But before considering the sonata's evolution, we must first familiarize ourselves with the composition's final form.

---

[4] DkB: Gade saml. C II 6, 4°. This sketch has sixteen continuously numbered pages. Format: 35.5 cm x 26.5 cm.

[5] DkB: Gade saml. C II 6, 4°. This set contains eighteen pages. Format: 34.5 cm x 24.5 cm.

[6] DkB: Gade saml. C II 6, 4°. This set contains four pages. The cover sheet was not intended for the piano sonata (the paper has a smaller format than sketch sets B and C). When writing the cover sheet Gade left the title blank. The sheet reads: 'componirt und seinem lieben Freunde M. WIEHÉ gewidmet von NWGade – d. 23ene Januar 1841.'

[7] Leipzig, Staatsarchiv der Stadt: Breitkopf und Härtels Archiv Nr. 6646. This manuscript contains thirty consecutively numbered pages. The title page carries a dedication to Franz Liszt, and the final page is dated June 1854.

Table 4
Gade's program for the Piano Sonata

(September 1839)   <u>Sonata for Piano. E minor</u>.

1) <u>E minor</u> (Allegro)   O Herz, sey endlich stille,
Was schlägst du so unruh(e)voll?
Es ist ja des Himmels Wille,
daß ich Sie lassen soll!

2) <u>E major</u> (Adagio)   Wir wollen es muthig ertragen,
Solang nur die Träne noch rinnt,
Und träumen von schöneren Tagen
die lange vorüber sind.

3) <u>E minor</u> (Finale)   Kühne Wogen, wildes Leben.
Laß den Sturm nur immer brausen,
Frischen Sturm im Herzen sausen.

Table 5
Gade's sketches for the Piano Sonata

SKETCH SET A

(1)	20–22 November 1839	Allegro appassionato	E min. *
(2a)	29 November 1839	Allegretto grazioso, quasi andantino	E maj.
(3)	9–16 December 1839	Scherzo	B min. *
(4)	3 January 1840	Finale	E min. *

SKETCH SET B (undated)

(1)		E min. *
(2a)	Andantino	E maj.
(2b)		E maj. *

SKETCH SET C

(3)	Intermezzo	B min./B maj. *
(1)	Fragment of development on discarded title page dated 23 January 1841.	A min. *

* = sketches to version found in published score.

The published version of the E-minor Sonata contains four contrasting movements: *Allegro con fuoco, Andante, Allegretto* and *Molto allegro e appassionato*. Table 6 shows the first movement's sonata-form structure. A descending triadic motive written in octaves begins this movement (ex. 5:1).

Example 5:1. Piano Sonata in E minor, Op. 28, first movement, measures 1–9.

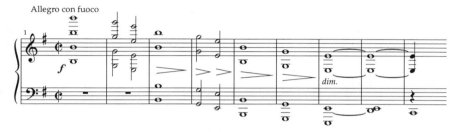

Appearing at least once in each of the four movements, this motive serves as the sonata's cyclical glue. In the first movement the motive appears in various forms (ex. 5:2a–e). In measure 59 the motive is expanded by six measures and marked *risoluto*. In measure 147 it is compressed to a mere five measures. It appears in the dominant minor (B minor) in measures 183–85, with the right and left hands moving in contrary motion. In measures 309–11 the motive is confined to the left hand, and in measures 333–37 it appears in imitation.

Example 5:2. Piano Sonata in E minor, Op. 28, first movement.

a) measures 59–64.

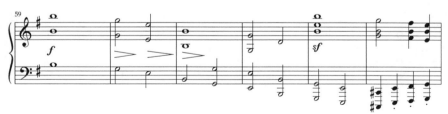

b) measures 147–51.

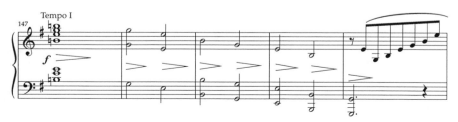

c) measures 183–86.

d) measures 308–11.

e) measures 333–37.

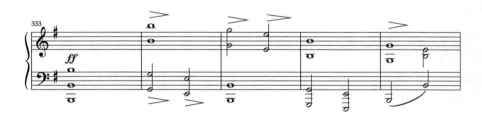

Table 6
Structural outline of the first movement

Measure number	Structural section
	INTRODUCTION
1–8	Descending triadic motive
9–22	Introductory theme (E minor)
	EXPOSITION
23–41	Primary theme (E minor)
42–58	Transition with ornamental passage in right hand
59–62	Return of descending triadic motive
63–96	Transition based on primary theme
97–127	Secondary theme (C major)
128–46	Transition with ornamental passage in right hand
147–51	Return of descending triadic motive
	DEVELOPMENT
152–206	Development of Primary theme
207–26	Transition based on secondary theme (C-sharp minor)
	RECAPITULATION
227–67	Return of secondary theme (E major)
268–72	Transition
273–87	Return of introductory theme (E minor)
288–308	Return of primary theme (E minor)
309–33	Transition with ornamental passage in right hand
334–65	Coda based on descending triadic motive

Following the opening statement of the cyclical motive, Gade presents an introduction of fifteen bars that leads directly to the primary theme in measure 24. Fervent and restless, this theme continues until measure 41 and then concludes with a transition section containing a long, ornamental passage in the right hand and a restatement of the cyclical motive. After this second statement of the cyclical motive, another transition section, again based on the primary theme, leads to the pianissimo entrance of the secondary theme in measure 97. Marked *un poco lento e sostenuto*, this lyrical, C-major melody serves as the perfect antithesis to the impassioned primary theme. The secondary theme ends with a long ornamental passage in the right hand followed by a restatement of the cyclical motive in the tonic key of E minor.

The following seventy-four measures contain the development section. Measures 152–206 present material derived from the primary theme, and measures 207–26 contain music based on the secondary theme. An E-major version of the secondary theme in measures 227–67 marks the beginning of an inverted recapitulation – this section is no more than a transposed repetition of the exposition's measures 97–127. This is followed by a return of the introductory material found in measures 9–22 and a restatement of the primary theme.[8] The movement concludes with a virtuosic coda derived from the primary theme followed by an extended statement of the cyclical motive.

Table 7 shows the ternary song form of the second movement. Written in G major, this work begins with a twelve-measure cantabile melody (A), which is then repeated and re-harmonized (A^i). The B section begins in measure 28. Written in the key of E-flat major and labeled *energico*, the animated phrases of this contrasting section serve to complement the vocal-like melody of section A. Measure 48 marks a return to the tonic key of G major and a final statement of the opening melody. A single reappearance of the cyclical motive brings the movement to a conclusion.

The structural layout of the third movement is of particular interest (table 8). The first half (mm. 5–49) presents a straightforward theme and variation; in contrast, the second half (mm. 54–112) contains a fantasy-like elaboration of the theme. As in the first movement, Gade uses distinct motives as a means of defining the structural outline. The movement opens with a syncopated rhythmic motive derived from the central theme. This theme, perhaps best described as a symmetrically-balanced waltz, occupies measures 5–20 and is followed by the first variation – a less symmetrical paraphrase of the theme. Here Gade modulates from F-sharp minor to D major and back to F-sharp minor. A restatement of the opening rhythmic motive marks a return to the tonic and the conclusion of variation one.

---

[8] As in the exposition, the primary theme closes with a long ornamental passage in the right hand and a statement of the cyclical motive.

Table 7
Structural outline of second movement

Measure	Structural section	Key
1–12	A	G major
13–27	A^i	
28–47	B	E-flat major
48–62	A	G major
63–67	CYCLICAL MOTIVE	

Table 8
Structural outline of third movement

Measure	Structural section
1–4	Syncopated motive (based on central theme)
5–20	Central theme (B minor)
21–49	Variation 1 (F# min. – D maj. – F# min.)
50–53	Syncopated motive
54–65	Central theme (B minor)
66–97	Variation 2 (Expansion of central theme)
98–112	Transition (B min. – B maj.)
113–16	Syncopated motive
117–19	CYCLICAL MOTIVE

Variation two opens with the first twelve measures of the central theme. It then branches off, like a fantasy, into a virtuosic improvisatory section. Using the opening three notes of the central theme as motivic material, measures 98–112 serve as a transition from the key of B minor to B major. This transition is then followed by a final statement of the syncopated motive (mm. 113–16). As in the second movement, the cyclical motive appears at the end; but here the motive serves the special purpose of confirming the key of B major. In this way, it prepares the listener for the beginning of the final movement.

The final movement suggests a rondo structure: A A^i B A A^i B C A (table 9). Section A (mm. 1–18) contains a driving neighbor-note theme in the key of E minor. This theme could be interpreted as a subtle cyclical link – its melodic structure appears to parallel that of the first movement's secondary theme. A pronounced statement of the cyclical motive in B major concludes this section (mm. 19–22). In section A^i the neighbor-note theme returns. Here, however, it is relegated to the middle voice; the upper voice introduces a trumpet-like fanfare. Again the section concludes with a statement of the cyclical motive (mm. 39–44), this time in F-sharp major. Section B (mm. 45–96) begins with a slow, stately theme in B minor that eventually evolves into a series of complex virtuosic passages. A transition to the tonic key prepares the listener for the return of section A in measures 97–114. A restatement of A^i directly follows (mm. 122–38), this time in the subdominant key of A minor. A third statement of the cyclical motive (B major) emerges in measures 139–44 and is followed by a restatement of section B in the tonic key. Measure 187 marks the beginning of section C – a virtuosic cadenza lasting twenty-four measures. A final return of section A appears in measure 222. This is followed by an extensive coda beginning in measure 252. The composition ends with a final statement of the cyclical motive (mm. 279–86) and a brief echo of the neighbor-note theme (mm. 287–95).

Returning to Gade's composition diary, we see that the restless heart and fated parting described in the first stanza of the program were originally to be realized through an impassioned *Allegro* in E minor. Sketch set A indicates that Gade began composing music for the first movement on 20 November 1839. The initial twenty-one measures of this first version are remarkably similar to the movement as we know it today; opening with the distinctive, descending triadic motive, the movement continues with a series of rapid scalar passages. In the final version, these scalar passages serve as the introduction. But in sketch set A they function as part of the primary theme.[9]

---

[9] The twenty-two measures preceding the final version's second statement of the opening motive are also present in sketch set A. Joined together with the running scalar passage these measures serve as the second part of sketch set A's primary theme.

Table 9
Structural outline of fourth movement

Measure	Structural section	Key
1–18	A	E minor
	(Interweaving neighbor-note theme)	
19–22	CYCLICAL MOTIVE	B major
23–38	A^i	E minor
39–44	CYCLICAL MOTIVE	F# major
45–80	B	B minor
81–96	Transition	B minor
		E minor
97–114	A	E minor
115–22	Transition	B major
		E major
123–38	A^i	A minor
139–44	CYCLICAL MOTIVE	B major
145–86	B	E minor
187–210	C (cadenza)	G–e–F#–d#
211–21	Transition	D# minor
		B major
222–51	A	E minor
252–78	Coda	E minor
279–86	CYCLICAL MOTIVE	E minor
287–95	A^{ii}	E minor

The transition sections leading into the secondary themes of sketch set A and the final version are of relatively equal length. But sketch set A is based on the scalar passages of its primary theme while the final version uses material from the opening triadic motive. A comparison of the final version's secondary theme to that of sketch set A reveals that although they are different in rhythm and character, their melodic profiles are remarkably similar (ex. 5:3a and b). As in the final version, the secondary theme of set A closes with a long ornamental passage in the right hand and a third statement of the opening triadic motive. A comparison of both versions' development sections reveals that although they begin and end in a similar manner, their use of different thematic material leads, unsurprisingly, to dissimilar results.

Example 5:3. Piano Sonata in E minor, Op. 28, first movement.

a) secondary theme in final version.

b) secondary theme in sketch set A.

The recapitulation in sketch set A opens with a return to the exposition's opening scalar passages. Once again, however, sketch set A shows no trace of what would later emerge as the final version's primary theme. Also absent from A is the virtuosic coda we know today. In its place appears a brief transition section leading to a short coda based on the opening triadic motive. This coda is important because it reveals a possible model for the sonata: Robert Schumann's C-major Fantasy for Piano, Op. 17 (1839). Like Schumann, Gade appears to have concluded his first movement with an allusion to Beethoven's song cycle *An die ferne Geliebte*. Whereas Schumann quoted the cycle's final piece, Gade adumbrated a section from the opening song 'Auf dem Hügel' (ex. 5:4). Gade's quotation of this song is appropriate: its lyrics echo the sentiments expressed in the first stanza of his program and thus allude to Gade's poetic inspiration,[10] and his use of the melody pays homage to Schumann and Beethoven, figures Gade then considered the foremost masters in piano literature (ex. 5:5).

---

[10] Text to Beethoven's 'Auf dem Hügel,' written by Alois Jeitteles: 'Auf dem Hügel sitz' ich, spähend in das blaue Nebelland, nach den fernen Triften sehend, wo ich dich, Geliebte fand. Weit bin ich von dir geschieden, trennend liegen Berg und Tal zwischen uns und unserm Frieden, unserm Glück und unsrer Qual. Ach, den Blick kannst du nicht sehen, der zu dir so glühend eilt, und Seufzer, sie verwehen in dem Raume, der uns teilt. Will denn nichts mehr zu dir dringen, nichts der Liebe Bote sein? Singen will ich, Lieder singen, die dir klagen meine Pein! Denn vor Liedesklang entweichet jeder Raum und jede Zeit, und ein liebend Herz erreichet, was ein liebend Herz geweiht!'

Example 5:4. Beethoven's 'Auf dem Hügel,' measures 1–10.

Example 5:5. Piano Sonata in E minor, Op. 28, first movement, conclusion.

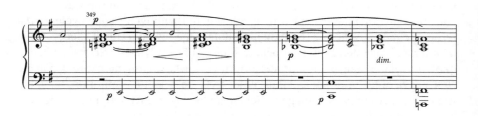

Gade's program indicates that he originally envisioned the sonata's second movement as an *Andante* in E major based on a single poetic stanza:

Wir wollen es muthig ertragen,
Solang nur die Träne noch rinnt,
Und träumen von schöneren Tagen
die lange vorüber sind.

(We will endure courageously,
As long as the tears still flow,
And dream of happier days,
That now are long past.)

Similar to the 'Fruhlingstraum' text from Schubert's *Winterreise*, this stanza expresses bittersweet emotions aroused by memories of a happier past. Like Schubert, Gade chose to express the text's sentimentality through the use of a major key.

Gade began composing music for the second movement on 29 November 1839. Written in 6/8 and labeled *Allegretto grazioso, quasi Andantino*, this E-major movement, with its lilting melody and undulating accompaniment, resembles an instrumental barcarolle (see appendix 5).

Gade was undoubtedly familiar with the barcarolle. Schubert used the style in his songs 'Auf dem Wasser zu singen' (D774), 'Des Fischers Liebesglück' (D933) and 'Der Gondelfahrer' (D808-9); and there are two Venetian Gondollieder which predate Gade's sonata among Mendelssohn's *Songs without Words*: Op. 19, no. 6 in G minor (1830), and Op. 30, no. 6 in F-sharp minor (1835). Mendelssohn also wrote a Gondollied in A major which was published in 1837. In addition, Edvard Helsted, Gade's closest friend in the Copenhagen Davidsbund, published a Barcarolle for Piano and Voice entitled 'Natten er saa stille' in *Melodier til Danske Sange* (1838).

No program is given for the third movement, but we know from sketch set A that Gade began composing the music for this movement on 9 December 1839. He originally structured this movement as a common scherzo-trio (table 10). The scherzo is divided into two parts: a central theme (A) and a variation of this theme (A^i). Measures 46–65 contain a transition which leads to the opening of a trio in F-sharp major. The trio is also divided into two parts: a secondary theme (B) and its expansion (B^i). A transition resembling the one found in measures 46–65 precedes the return of the scherzo section in measure 141. Here section A appears as it did in the opening, and it is followed by A^{ii} – a variation of the first scherzo's A^i. A comparison of these two sections shows that while A^i modulates from F-sharp minor to D major and back again, A^{ii} modulates from F-sharp minor to B major.

Table 10
Structural outline of Scherzo-Trio movement

Measure	Structural section	Key
1–16	A	B minor
17–45	A^i	F# min. – D maj. – F# min.
46–65	Transition	
65–81	B	F# major
82–134	B^i	F# major
135–40	Transition	
141–56	A	B minor
157–80	A^{ii}	F# min. – B maj.
181–228	Coda*	B minor

* Measures 181–214 are an expansion of A, and mm. 215–28 contain a motivic section based on the dotted rhythm in A.

The movement concludes with a B-minor coda that begins with the opening twelve measures of section A and then branches off into a virtuosic improvisatory section.

Gade's plan for a restless finale in E minor is clearly expressed in the last stanza of his program.

Kühne Wogen, wildes Leben.
Laß den Sturm nur immer brausen,
Frischen Sturm im Herzen sausen;

(Bold waves, wild life.
Let the storm thunder forever.
Let the fresh storm roar in the heart.)

Sketch set A shows that Gade began composing the music for this movement on 3 January 1840. Gade obviously struggled with the opening of this movement; after composing approximately seventeen measures he crossed out various sections, leaving only vague indications for an additional sixteen measures. He then scrapped this version completely and started over. Gade's second attempt begins with the neighbor-note theme known today and continues with an appearance of the descending triadic motive from the opening of the first movement. The presence of this motive is important – it reveals that in the earliest stages of composition Gade intended to link thematically the sonata's first and final movements.[11] Unfortunately, this is all that can be said of the fourth movement's evolution; the final pages of sketch set A are lost, and these scant twenty-three measures are all that remain of Gade's earliest version of the finale. Gade appears to have abruptly stopped work on the sonata in January 1840. Perhaps his frustration with the work was compounded by a second article on the sonata, published by Schumann in December 1839.

In this second article, Schumann presented a decidedly pessimistic view of sonata writing. He discussed the current French and German attitudes toward the genre and concluded that the sonata is 'a class of music that is only smiled at sympathetically in France and scarcely more than tolerated in Germany.'[12]

Later in the same review, Schumann expressed a general opinion related to him by Stephan Heller, a contributor to the *Neue Zeitschrift für Musik* and a fellow *Davidsbündler*. Heller had been working on his Piano Sonata, Op. 9 for several years, and as Schumann explains:

> The composer mailed it to me in quarterly installments, not because he wished to create suspense, but rather because, as he said himself, he had pondered over it slowly and wasted much time, and 'what more is a sonata, anyway, if not a great waste of time?'[13]

Gade's interest in his own sonata quickly waned after the appearance of Schumann's article. He struggled with the finale in early January and then set the sonata aside for over a year. Gade did not return to it until late January 1841. Curiously, this renewed interest in the sonata and his eventual revisions, as found in sketch sets B and C, coincide with the publication of a third sonata article by Robert Schumann.

In January 1841, in his preface to a review of recent sonatas, Schumann noted that few sonatas had been published within the last year and proposed a reason for their disappearance:

> Our last sonata review was published in December 1839. Only a few successful examples of this noble genre have appeared since then, and it appears that the sonata now struggles with three strong enemies: the public, the publishers, and the composers themselves. The public buys reluctantly, the publisher prints reluctantly, and the composers, perhaps for personal reasons, refrain from writing

---

[11] This cyclical link could be evidence of another model for Gade's sonata: Mendelssohn's Piano Sonata in E major, Op. 6. Published in 1826, this sonata displays a protocyclic form: the finale concludes quietly with an unexpected reminder of the first movement.

[12] Schuman, 'Sonaten für Pianoforte,' *Neue Zeitschrift für Musik* (10 December 1839): 185.

[13] Ibid., 186.

such 'old-fashioned' things. Therefore, those [composers] who do [write sonatas] nevertheless, should be worth twice as much to us.[14]

Schumann referred to the sonata as a noble genre and praised young composers willing to attempt such compositions. Apparently, these words of encouragement were all Gade needed; shortly after 23 January he returned to the piece.

When Gade wrote the first draft of his piano sonata (sketch set A) in 1839/40, he used his original, poetic program as a source of inspiration. But when he returned to the sonata in 1841 and began revisions, he slowly distanced himself from some of his original ideas. Table 11 shows the correlations between the first movement's first and second versions (sketch sets A and B respectively) and the movement's final, published version. After writing the second draft of his sonata, sketch set B, Gade altered the draft substantially in black ink and pencil. B2 reflects the structural changes engendered by these revisions.

Sketch set B shows that although Gade originally duplicated the opening of the exposition found in sketch set A, he later revised this section (B2) by inserting, in black ink, a new theme – the primary theme as we know it today. Using a pencil Gade eventually labeled this insertion 'theme' (figure 8). He rejected the secondary theme in sketch set A and replaced it with the present version. In addition, he revised the transition leading to the third statement of the descending triadic motive: whereas sketch set A uses material based on the opening scalar passages, sketch set B, like the final version, is built from the descending triadic motive.

The only additional sketch for the first movement appears as a fragment in sketch set C. Corresponding to mm. 207–27 in the final version, this fragment serves as a transition between the second appearance of the primary and secondary themes. As mentioned previously, this addition must have been made sometime after 23 January 1841.

Looking at the overall evolution of the first movement, we notice that, from the beginning, Gade envisioned the descending triadic motive as a structural device. The placement of this motive at the beginning of the movement, between the primary and secondary themes of the exposition, at the beginning of the development, and in the coda appears exactly the same in sketch sets A and B as it does in the final version. I stress this point, because as we shall see in the discussion of movements two and three, Gade's eventual adoption of this motive as a cyclical device played an important role in the overall evolution of the sonata.

---

[14] Schumann, 'Neue Sonaten für das Pianoforte,' *Neue Zeitschrift für Musik* (22 January 1841): 27.

Table 11
The different versions of the first movement
(Final version and sketch sets A and B)

P = material is present   A = material is absent
S = material is similar   D = material is different

mm.	Final version	Sketch set A	Sketch set B
1–8	CYCLICAL MOTIVE	P	P
9–22	Introductory theme	P	P
23–41	Primary theme	A	A, (B2) P
42–58	Transition (w/RH ornamental passage)	P	P
59–62	CYCLICAL MOTIVE	P	P
63–96	Transition (based on primary theme)	D	P
97–127	Secondary theme	S	P
128–46	Transition (w/RH ornamental passage)	P	P
147–51	CYCLICAL MOTIVE	P	P
152–206	Development (primary theme)	D	D
207–72	Development/Recap. (secondary theme)	D	P
273–87	Introductory theme (same as mm. 9–22)	P	P
288–308	Primary theme	A	A
309–33	Transition (w/ RH ornamental passage)	P	P
334–65	Coda based on CYCLICAL MOTIVE	S	P

Figure 8 Piano Sonata in E minor, Op. 28. First page of sketch set B
(DkB: Gade Saml., C II 6)

Albeit sketch set A's original version of the second movement appears relatively complete, Gade later edited this version heavily in black ink. Sketch set C represents a clean-written copy of this edited version.[15] The majority of Gade's corrections to sketch set A are superficial (re-workings of broken-chord patterns and the removal of repetitive passages), but his inclusion of a new ending is important. Unlike the original ending, the revised conclusion in sketch set B contains a five-measure statement of the first movement's descending triadic motive (ex. 5:6). Thus by revising the final measures of sketch set A, Gade prominently established a cyclical link between the sonata's first and second movements.

The importance of this cyclical link becomes all the more obvious when we turn to the final folio of sketch set B. Here a cleanly written E-major piece in 3/4 time appears as an alternate second movement. Although completely different in style and structure, this replacement (2b) utilizes an ending similar to that of its predecessor (2a) (ex. 5:7).

This correspondence between the two distinct versions of the second movement indicate that although Gade eventually rejected the version in sketch set B (2a), he did preserve its revised ending with the descending triadic motive in order to create a large-scale, cyclical work. When Gade submitted the Stichvorlag for the piano sonata to Breitkopf und Härtel in 1854, version 2b, transposed to the key of G major, appeared as the second movement.

Turning to Gade's third movement we notice that it also underwent a number of major revisions. Although sketch set C contains much of the thematic material in sketch set A, Gade completely transformed the general character of the movement by ingeniously changing the original scherzo-trio layout into a fantasy-like theme and variations (table 12). Gade used the A and A^i sections of sketch set A as the theme and first variation in sketch set C. In a similar manner, he borrowed the coda from sketch set A and used it for sketch set C's second variation (note that sketch set C does not contain the trio and A^{ii} sections from sketch set A). Moreover, Gade added to sketch set C an opening motive based on the dotted rhythm of the central theme and used this motive as a tool for organizing the movement's new structure. This motive appears at the beginning of the movement and directly after each variation. Finally, Gade incorporated the third movement into the sonata's overall cyclical structure by concluding the piece with a single statement of the descending triadic motive.

---

[15] A transcription of this movement is found in appendix five.

Example 5:6. Piano Sonata in E minor, Op. 28, conclusion of second movement (2a) in sketch set B.

Example 5:7. Piano Sonata in E minor, Op. 28, Final measures of alternate second movement (2b).

Table 12
Structure of third movement in sketch sets A and C

mm.	Sketch set A	mm.	Sketch set C
		1–4	Syncopated motive (based on central theme)
1–16	A ---------------------------- 5–20		Central theme
17–45	Aⁱ ---------------------------- 21–49		Variation 1 (f# – D – f#)
46–65	Transition -------------------------- 50–53		Syncopated motive
65–81	B		
82–134	Bⁱ		
135–40	Transition		
141–56	A ---------------------------- 54–61		Central theme
157–80	Aⁱⁱ		
181–228	Coda mm.181–211:----------------62–92 (expansion of A)		Expansion of central theme
	mm. 212–28: (motivic section based on dotted rhythm of A)		
		93–112	Transition (b – B)
		113–16	Syncopated motive
		117–19	CYCLICAL MOTIVE

Gade put much effort into his revisions of the sonata in early 1841, but his renewed interest in the work was short-lived. Smaller projects – a set of character pieces for the piano,[16] a collection of Danish folk songs,[17] and a piano transcription of his *Echoes of Ossian* Overture – left little time for the sonata during the early months of spring. Gade might have returned to the work in summer, but it appears that an encounter with Franz Liszt affected Gade's perception of the piece, causing him to set it aside once again.

On 15 July 1841, Liszt traveled to Copenhagen for his first and only visit to the city. Having met J.P.E. Hartmann in Hamburg, Liszt returned with the composer and remained in Copenhagen for two and a half weeks. In this time he gave three public concerts at the Royal Theater and at least two private performances for the King.[18] In addition to his concerts, Liszt came in contact with a number of Copenhagen's well-known figures. He dined with Hans Christian Andersen at the home of J.P.E. Hartmann[19] and spent several afternoons in Frue Kirke with C.E.F. Weyse.[20] Letters from this period show that Gade served as Weyse's assistant during the summer of 1841, thus he might have met Liszt during the latter's meetings with Weyse. No direct evidence confirming a meeting between Liszt and Gade has yet emerged, but the young composer was nonetheless influenced by Liszt's extended visit. A letter dated 26 July 1841 shows that Gade attended Liszt's third concert (figure 9) and was quite shocked by the spectacle of his virtuosic performance:

> Franz Liszt has been here and has presented three concerts. [His playing] is a true beast as far as skill and mechanics go. Nonetheless, I really must exclude from this a few pieces that he played excellently, e.g. Beethoven's Pastoral Symphony.[21]

---

[16] *Foraarstoner* was first published in 1842 without an opus number. In 1873 it was revised and published as opus 2b.

[17] *Seks danske Sange* was dedicated to C.E.F. Weyse and first published in 1841 without an opus number.

[18] According to Bengt Johnsson, 'Liszt i Danmark,' *Fyens Stiftstidendes Kronik* (26 July 1986), Liszt arrived in Copenhagen on 15 July. He performed at The Royal Theater on 17, 21, and 24 July and for Christian VIII on 15 and 22 July. Liszt did not leave Copenhagen until 1 August 1841.

[19] H.C. Andersen relates in *Mit Livs Eventyr*: 'After I came into town, Liszt gave his last concert. I was there, and the next day we dined together at Hartmann's house.'

[20] Bengt Johnsson, 'Liszt og Danmark I,' *Dansk Musiktidsskrift* (1962/63): 81.

[21] Letter to Carl Helsted found in Behrend, 'Omkring Niels W. Gade,' 66: 'Franz Liszt har været her og giver 3 Koncerter. Det er et sandt Uhyre hvad Færdighed og Mekanik angaar 'sonst' – dog maa jeg herfra undtage enkelte Stykker f. Ex. Beethovens Pastoral-Simphonie som han spillede Exelent.'

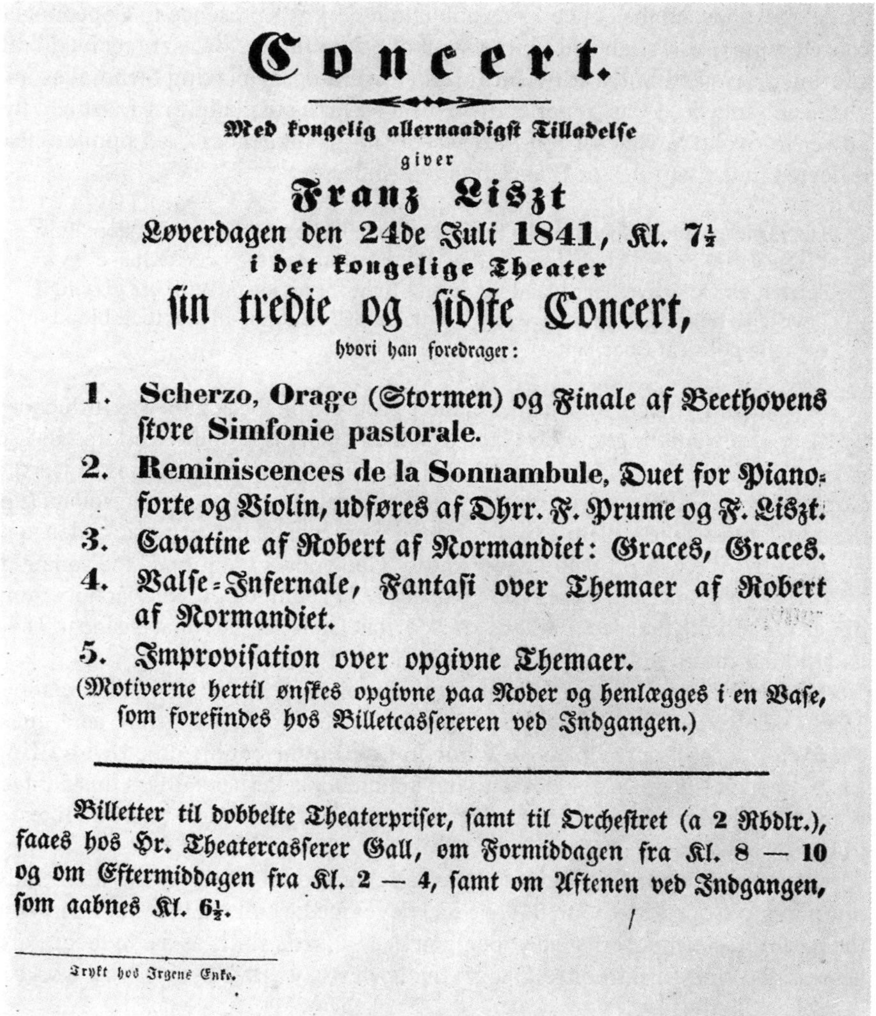

Concert.

Med kongelig allernaadigst Tilladelse

giver

Franz Liszt

Loverdagen den 24de Juli 1841, Kl. 7½
i det kongelige Theater

sin tredie og sidste Concert,

hvori han foredrager:

1. **Scherzo, Orage (Stormen) og Finale af Beethovens store Simfonie pastorale.**
2. **Reminiscences de la Sonnambule, Duet for Pianoforte og Violin, udføres af Dhrr. F. Prume og F. Liszt.**
3. **Cavatine af Robert af Normandiet: Graces, Graces.**
4. **Valse-Infernale, Fantasi over Themaer af Robert af Normandiet.**
5. **Improvisation over opgivne Themaer.**

(Motiverne hertil ønskes opgivne paa Nober og henlægges i en Vase, som forefindes hos Billetcassereren ved Indgangen.)

Billetter til dobbelte Theaterpriser, samt til Orchestret (a 2 Rbdlr.), faaes hos Hr. Theatercasserer Gall, om Formiddagen fra Kl. 8 — 10 og om Eftermiddagen fra Kl. 2 — 4, samt om Aftenen ved Indgangen, som aabnes Kl. 6½.

Trykt hos Irgens Enke.

Figure 9 Program for Franz Liszt's third public concert in Copenhagen.
(DkB: Musik Samling)

Gade's response to the concert was not unique. Liszt's presence in Copenhagen caused quite a stir. Labeled 'a true symbol of the future,'[22] Liszt received both adoring praise and bitter criticism for his revolutionary playing techniques and virtuosic fantasies. One reporter even went so far as to claim that Liszt had the power to evoke 'a state of political fervor' in his audiences,[23] an opinion also reflected in the writings of Hans Christian Andersen:

> I have met politicians who, under the influence of Liszt's playing, understood how the peaceful citizen could be so gripped by the sound of the 'Marseillaise' as to seize his rifle, leave hearth and home and fight for an idea. With his playing I have seen peaceful Copenhageners – with Danish Autumn mist in their blood – become political Bacchants.[24]

We can only speculate whether Gade's progress on the sonata was influenced by Liszt. It is tempting to view Gade's sudden disinterest in the work in 1841 as a response to performer's presence. Did the virtuosic improvisations in Liszt's Copenhagen concerts cause Gade to doubt his recent revisions to the sonata (i.e. the new fantasy-like structure of the third movement and the virtuosic cadenza in the finale)? We will probably never know. Gade never mentioned the sonata in his correspondence, and there is no evidence in his composition diary concerning his struggles with the piece. All we know is that Gade set the sonata aside in 1841 and did not return to it until thirteen years later.[25]

Gade's final revisions to the piano sonata took place in 1853/54. In December 1852 Gade traveled to Leipzig with his new wife, Sophie, to serve as a guest conductor at the Gewandhaus.[26] While in Leipzig the couple dined with 'King Liszt' and kept in close contact with the Schumanns. Perhaps it was this contact with colleagues in Germany that served as a catalyst for Gade's renewed interest in the sonata.

Gade's opinions about Liszt's music had changed substantially by 1852. Since returning to Copenhagen in 1848, he had developed a collegial relationship with the performer/composer. Gade openly praised Liszt's skills as a conductor, and he was the first to introduce Danish audiences to Liszt's symphonic works.[27]

---

[22] *Fædrelandet* (19 July 1841).

[23] *Corsaren* Nr. 39 (30 July 1841).

[24] H.C. Andersen, *A Visit to Germany, Italy and Malta 1840-1841 (A Poet's Bazaar I-II)*, translated by Grace Thornton, (London: Peter Owen, 1985), 35. It should be noted that although this translation is good, the editor often tacitly omits sections of the text concerning music.

[25] Gade refrained from composing piano music while living in Leipzig (1843–48). Although he resumed writing for the piano upon his return to Copenhagen in 1848, he did not work on the sonata, but instead concentrated on character pieces.

[26] Gade married his first wife, Sophie Hartmann (daughter of J.P.E. Hartmann) in 1852.

[27] Gade conducted the Danish premier of Liszt's symphonic poem, *Orfeus*, at a Music Society concert in 1859.

Perhaps Gade's new appreciation for Liszt motivated him to return to the sonata a final time. Whatever the case, Gade's respect for Liszt is a documented fact: when Gade submitted the Stichvorlag to Breitkopf & Härtel in 1854, it carried a hand-written dedication to no one other than Liszt himself.

But Liszt was probably not the only inspiration behind Gade's return to the sonata in the 1850s. The composer's admiration for Schumann was equally strong during this period, and Schumann's direct influence on Gade's work is revealed in a manuscript now housed in Copenhagen's Royal Conservatory. Written about the same time as the final version of the sonata, this piano work bears a strong resemblance to Schumann's *Papillons*. In fact, the title page reads:

> Butterflies
> (who fly back to their home)
> to my sweet Sophie
> 2 July 1854 Niels W. Gade[28]

Butterflies was published in 1854 under the title *Arabeske* – yet another title borrowed from Schumann. Like the piano sonata, this piece was composed over a number of years, eventually evolved into a cyclical work, and was revised and published in 1854.[29]

As we have seen in the preceding pages, studying the evolution of Gade's Piano Sonata in E minor offers important insights concerning his compositional process. We know from evidence in Gade's composition diary and sketch sets that he initially found inspiration in a literary program but was not bound to the text in later stages of composition. Indeed, sketch sets B and C reveal that Gade eventually sacrificed his program for the sake of creative development. The evolution of Gade's Piano Sonata in E minor clearly shows how the composer was affected by the masters of his age. The influence of figures such as Schumann,

---

[28] 'Sommerfugle (som flyve tilbage til deres Hjem) til min søde Sophie, d. 2 Juli 1854 Niels W. Gade.'

[29] The first sketches to music appearing in *Arabeske* date from winter 1849. At this time Gade composed a small set of character pieces containing three works: 'Allegro grazioso' (E major, 6/8, 36 measures, dated: 'Novbr. 49') 'Allegro vivace' (F major, 9/8, 46 measures, dated: 'December 49') and 'Andantino cantabile' (C major, 4/4, 33 measures, undated). The 'Allegro vivace' and 'Andantino cantabile' appear on either side of a single sheet of oblong manuscript paper measuring 25 cm x 35 cm now housed in DkB: Gade Saml. C II 6, 4°. The 'Allegro grazioso' is written on a matching sheet of manuscript paper now found in Washington, DC: Library of Congress, Music Collection. Both sheets of paper contain identical tears and fold marks indicating that the three works were originally a set. However, Gade eventually separated these three pieces. The 'Allegro grazioso' was first published in *Julehilsen til Store og Smaae fra danske Componister* 2 (1850) and then later appeared in 1852 as the second piece in *Tre Albumblade* (Fog no. 108). The 'Andantino cantabile' was first published in 1854 as the second part of *Arabeske*, Op. 27. The 'Allegro vivace' was never published.

Beethoven, Schubert, Mendelssohn, and Liszt appear at every stage of the compositional process.

Gade's sonata represents his initial struggle with large keyboard works. In an effort to move away from the character pieces and folk-song settings of his earlier years, Gade experimented, for the first time, with complex structures and cyclical devices. The E-minor Piano Sonata stands as Gade's first and last attempt at the genre. Although it is not his most celebrated work for piano, it nonetheless represents the finest example of the sonata genre in early nineteenth-century Denmark.

Chapter Six

Agnete and the Merman
(1839–43)

Gade's interest in the story of Agnete and the Merman resurfaced in October 1839. Approximately one year after his tour through Norway and Sweden and his first attempt at a musical work based on the ill-fated Agnete, Gade recorded in his composition diary a second program based on Agnete and the Merman. For this program Gade envisioned a five-movement symphony. As shown in the following transcription of this program (table 13), only the second, fourth, and fifth movements were supplied with detailed outlines. Gade left a good deal of empty space after the headings for the first and third – undoubtedly planning to develop the programmatic details of these movements at a later date.

Unfortunately, no musical realization of the 1839 program exists. Nevertheless, a comparison between this program and the overture sketches from 1838 reveals several similarities: both works were originally conceived in the key of A minor, both open with a depiction of Agnete's yearning by the sea, and both represent Agnete with a clarinet solo.

Despite these similarities, however, the programs are noticeably different. Gade substantially expanded his original 1838 idea. In addition to changing the form to a five-movement symphony, he enlarged the program's narrative by borrowing texts from the *Evangelist-Christian Psalmbook* (1798) and Jens Baggesen's ballad, *Agnete from Holmegaard* (1808). As a reading of *Agnete from Holmegaard* reveals, Gade apparently utilized this text when structuring his 1839 program.

Baggesen's ballad begins with a restless Agnete staring into the sea. A beautiful Merman appears and begins to sing. He pledges his love to Agnete and asks her to join him below the waves. She accepts his proposal and eventually bears him two sons. All is well, and Agnete is quite happy until one day the sound of church bells interrupts her while she is singing a lullaby. She becomes alarmed and suddenly feels compelled to visit her childhood church. The Merman allows her to go, but only on the condition that she return before daybreak. Agnete hurries towards the church and upon entering the graveyard comes face to face with her mother. When the mother discovers where Agnete has been for the past two years, she reminds her of the husband and daughters she abandoned and tries to convince her to forget the Merman and his two sons. But Agnete is firm; she renounces her family and remains true to the Merman. Then, she enters the church. Everyone turns their back to her. Agnete looks down at the floor and to her horror discovers that the gravestone before her bears the name of her mother.

Table 13
Program for *Agnete and the Merman*
as found in Gade's composition diary

October 1839

Agnete and the Merman (A ʍíʍ.)
Symphony

1.) Agnetes Longing by the sea. (Moderato) C A

2.) The Song of the Mermaids. (F-sharp-minor Andante
with Choir of women's voices.)
'Agnete. Agnete come!' ///[1]
tó ʍáj.(3 Choirs: various.) (íʍ ʍíʍ. ʍ/ ʋíʍś & ćéíʋóś)
(F-sharp major)

3.) Agnete's Wedding. (Scherzo E major. 3/4.)

4.) Lullaby. (C major Moderato or Andantino.)
(Clarinet solo.) interrupted by
Chorale, Who does not allow Our Lord to prevail[2] – or
pp   All Our Deeds shall be done in the Name of Jesus[3] –
sung by Men's Choir completely pianissimo –
(Dies irae, dies illa solvet saecla in favilla).

.................................page break.......................................

---

[1] /// indicates illegible, crossed-out material.
[2] Chorale text from *Evangelist-kristelig Psalmbog, til Brug ved Kirke og Huus-Andacht*, Copenhagen: Carl Frid. Schubart, 1798, # 301, p. 167.
[3] Ibid., # 135, p. 81.

(Table 13 cont.)

Allº agitato and Recitative (Clarinet solo.) –
Continuation of the Chorale –

x   <u>attacca</u>
5.) Finale.   <u>Agnete's Church entrance and Death</u>. (A minor)

             And all the small pictures, they turned around –
C major. 'O Lord Jesus, Forgive my Sins' –
             And the altar table turned, and the altar with it –
             Everything turned around –
             Wherever she turned her eye
             within the church. –

             Then the heart of the poor girl broke,
             Then her blood froze.[4]

(?)Chorale: A major. '<u>Dear Redeemer, forgive
                  every penitent Sinner</u>' –

x   <u>Fine</u>
5.) Finale. – – – – – –
             Song of the Mermaids (Women's voices) and
             Chorale singers (Men's voices) call Agnete.

---

[4] These seven lines come from Jens Baggesen's *Agnete fra Holmegaard* (1808).

The shock of this realization breaks Agnete's heart. She falls to the floor and dies. Now all her children, sons and daughters alike, long for their mother.

Familiarity with Baggesen's text greatly aids in the task of deciphering the many enigmatic details of Gade's program. In the fourth movement Gade interrupts Agnete's lullabye with a sacred chorale. This chorale, undoubtedly serving as a substitute for Baggesen's church bells, not only reminds Agnete of the life she abandoned, but also expresses, through its text, the moral struggles of Agnete's conscience: 'Who does not allow Our Lord to Prevail' and 'All our deeds shall be done in the name of Jesus.'

Similar in style is Gade's employment of the *Dies Irae* theme as a means of foreshadowing the deaths of both Agnete and her mother.[5] Finally, the *allegro agitato* clarinet solo toward the end of the movement represents Agnete's distraught reaction to the chorale and sudden compulsion to visit her childhood church.[6]

Gade's program for the final movement revolves around a quote from the ultimate scene in Baggesen's ballad:

And all the small pictures,
they turned around –

And the altar table turned,
and the altar with it –
Everything turned around –
Wherever she turned her eye
within the church. –

Then the heart of the poor girl broke,
Then her blood froze.[7]

---

[5] Finn Matthiassen, 'Niels W. Gade og troldtøjet,' *Festskrift Søren Sørensen* (Copenhagen: Dan Fog, 1990), 82, concludes that Gade's employment of the *Dies Irae* was probably influenced by Berlioz's earlier employment of the theme in the fourth movement of *Symphonie fantastique*. This conclusion is probably correct. Gade's interest in Berlioz is confirmed by a letter to Carl Helsted dated 26 July 1841 (for complete letter see Behrend, 'Omkring Niels W. Gade,' 65–6). Here Gade states: 'come death and torture, don't forget Berlioz, and tell us soon how his compositions actually hang together' (Død og Pine husk paa Berlioz og siig os snart hvordan det egentlig hænger sammen med hans Kompositioner).

[6] An *agitato* section with clarinet solo also appears in the 1838 sketches to Gade's *Agnete and the Merman* overture as the representation of Agnete's struggle with good and evil (see chapter two, music example 2:4).

[7] 'Og alle de smaa Billeder, de vendte sig omkring – /Og Altertavlen vendte sig og Alteret med den – /Alt med den – /Sig vendte, hvor hun Øiet/I Kirken vendte hen. – /da brast den Armes Hjerte,/da iisned hendes Blod.'

As in the previous movement, Gade uses a chorale text to reflect the state of Agnete's conscience: 'O Lord Jesus, Forgive my Sins.' He then ponders two options for the conclusion of the symphony. The first reflects a message of Christian salvation and centers around the chorale 'Dear Redeemer, Forgive Every Penitent Sinner.' In contrast, the second option reflects more closely the feeling of Baggesen's romantic text by using choirs of mermaids and humans to express the tragic longing caused by Agnete's death.

Some details in Gade's 1839 program, however, do not coincide with Baggesen's text. In his outline for the second movement Gade cites a 'Choir of women's voices' who sing 'Agnete, Agnete come!' as well as an additional three choirs described as 'various.' These vocal groups, not mentioned by Baggesen, are more than likely related to the four choirs who attempt to lure Agnete into the sea in the 'Song of the Waves' from H.C. Andersen's dramatic poem *Agnete and the Merman* (1836). In addition, Gade's third movement, 'Agnete's Wedding,' is undoubtedly based upon 'The Merman's Wedding,' also from Andersen's poem. Here Andersen describes Agnete's marriage to the Merman, an event not found in Baggesen's *Agnete from Holmegaard*.[8]

Gade's familiarity with Andersen's text is not surprising. The two men became friends toward the end of the 1830s[9] and collaborated on an 'Agnete and the Merman' project in the early 1840s. Labeled 'a dramatic poem in two acts' by Andersen, this project is based on an abridged version of *Agnete and the Merman* and features a series of songs and melodrama composed by Gade (table 14).

Agnete and the Merman displays many of the characteristics associated with the Singspiel tradition. Dialogue and/or melodrama link the various musical numbers, and motifs are used as a means of identifying various characters. On the whole, the songs in *Agnete and the Merman* utilize the strophic forms commonly found in the early-nineteenth-century Danish ballad tradition.[10] Often characterized by syncopated triplet rhythms, symmetrical phrasing and a limited vocal range, the melodies appear to be inspired by traditional folk models. In fact, as one scholar

---

[8] In addition to its more involved plot, Andersen's dramatic poem employs a larger cast of characters. These include Hemming, Agnete's forlorn, mortal fiancé; Hintze, a wealthy butcher; a group of hunters; and a little fisher boy. Unlike previous versions of the story, Andersen's rendition introduces a more compassionate Agnete – she does not abandon husband and children, only a fiancé she never agreed to marry.

[9] Gade knew Andersen from their contact at the Royal Theater. Andersen occasionally attended meetings of the Copenhagen Davidsbund, and he lived in the same building on Vingaardstræde as Gade's close friends, Carl and Edvard Helsted.

[10] For a complete discussion of the ballad in early-nineteenth-century Denmark see Niels Martin Jensen, *Den danske romance 1800–1850 og dens musikalske forudsætninger* (Copenhagen: Gyldendal, 1964).

Table 14
Musical numbers composed by Gade for Andersen's Dramatic Poem
Agnete and the Merman

Act I

1. Hemming's Song – 'Der voxed' et Træ.'
2. Choir of Mermaids – 'Jeg veed et Slot.'
   Merman and Agnete – Melodrama (seduction scene).

Act II

3a. Agnete's Lullabye – 'Sol deroppe ganger under Lide.'
3b. Choir of Huntsmen – 'Trara! Trara! Trara!'
4. Hemming – 'Agnete var elsket.'
5. Choir of Huntsmen – continuation of no. 3b.
6a. Repetition of no. 4, but without orchestral introduction and coda.
6b. Choir in Church – 'Barn Jesus, Brudgom faux og fiin.'
7a. The Fisherboy's Ballad – 'Lærken synger sin Morgensang.'
7b. Choir in Church – continuation of no. 6b.
8. Merman and Agnete – Melodrama (Agnete's death).

has previously noted, the melody of 'Agnete var elsket' offers a minor-keyed variation of the folk song 'Agnete hun stander på højlofts bro' (ex. 6:1a and b).[11]

Example 6:1. *Agnete and the Merman.*

a) Gade's 'Agnete var elsket.'

b) the folk tune 'Agnete hun stander på højlofts bro.'

In composing *Agnete and the Merman* Gade relied to some extent upon Weber's *Der Freischütz*. Weber's opera was not unfamiliar to Copenhagen audiences. On 8 October 1820 Claus Schall conducted the première of *Der Freischütz* Overture at the Royal Theater, and in later years the opera was performed numerous times.[12] Gade borrowed Weber's technique of key symbolism, associating C major with the powers of good ('Barn Jesus, Brudgom faux og fiin') and D major with the robust, natural world of the hunters ('Trara! Trara! Trara!'). He then continued by

---

[11] Ibid., 169. Gade would have known this folk-song from volume 5 of *Udvalgte danske Viser fra Middelalderen* (Copenhagen: Abrahamson, Nyerup & Rahbek, 1812–14), no. 50a.

[12] As John Warrack explains in the second edition of his book, *Carl Maria von Weber* (Cambridge: Cambridge University Press, 1976), 244 fn. 2: 'Max Maria evidently knew nothing of this, for he describes a subsequent Dresden performance as the première.' For further documentation of Weber's visit to Copenhagen see: Erik Abrahamsen, 'Carl Maria von Weber in Copenhagen,' *The Chesterian* (June 1926).

representing the characters of Agnete and the Merman with the keys of F and A-flat major respectively. Only Hemming, Agnete's forlorn fiancé, is represented by minor tonalities ('Der voxed' et Træ' in D minor, 'Agnete var elsket' in A minor).

Reinforcing this tonal structure is a carefully constructed pattern of instrumentation. Like Weber, Gade devised distinct tone-colors for the principal characters. Agnete is the only character given the honor of a full, orchestral accompaniment ('Sol deroppe ganger under Lide'). Hemming is represented by the oboe and strings, and his antithesis, the Merman, is accompanied by the winds and harp. As might be expected, horns are associated with the hunters, and an organ identifies the church choir. Even the fisher boy is given an unique ensemble: clarinet, cello, and contrabass. Melodrama is reserved for the immortal character, the Merman. Like Samiel in *Der Freischütz*, the Merman never sings – representing the personification of sin and temptation, he uses passion and wealth to tempt Agnete and eventually persuades her to 'forsake her Saviour.'

It is not known when Andersen and Gade first began their collaboration on *Agnete and the Merman*, but a letter from Andersen shows that the project was well under way by the summer of 1842:

Bregentved – 17 July 1842

Dear Friend!

Since I haven't seen a single word about our maiden 'Agnete' in the newspapers, [I assume] she still will not be in service this summer, the French Count[13] has taken her place. Still, it seems best to me that we attend to our maiden, and that is why I am writing this short epistle.

Will you get the clean-written manuscript from Mr. Holst[14] and send it – along with a couple of words saying that you have composed the music and will now complete an overture to the piece – to the board of directors. In all probability we will receive an answer from the censor at the beginning of the season, and then Agnete can be presented in September or October. You might also bring it to conference advisor Collin and talk with him about what the music involves. I will then write about the piece.[15]

---

[13] This refers to a three-act comedy *Grev Létorières Proces* by Bayard and Dumanoir. Performed at the Royal Theater on 1 and 8 July 1842.

[14] Wilhelm Holst played the role of the Merman in the premiere of *Agnete and the Merman*. Agnete and Hemming were played by Johanne Luise Heiberg and Christian Hansen.

[15] The original letter is housed in DkB: Ny kgl. Saml. 1716 4°. (Kjære Ven! Da jeg endnu ikke i Aviserne seer et eneste Ord om vor Jomfru 'Agnete,' saa kommer hun nok ikke i Tjeneste i Sommer, den franske Greve har nok faaet hendes Plads. Det forekommer mig imidlertid bedst om vi tog os lidt af Jomfruen og derfor skriver jeg dette korte Epistel. Vil de have det reenskrevne Manuscript, af Hr. Holst og da indsende dette til Direktionen, med et Par Ord at De har componeret Musikken og vil nu fuldende en Ouverture til Stykket; vi ville altsaa rimeligvis erholde Svar fra Censoren ved Saisonens Begyndelse og Agnete kan da gives i September eller Oktober. De kan ogsaa bringe det til Conferentsraad Collin og tale med ham hvad Musikken

Andersen was hoping for a premiere at the Royal Theater in September or October 1842. Nonetheless, *Agnete and the Merman* did not appear until 20 April 1843. The autograph score for this performance contains musical emendations as well as performance indications – in its present state it opens with the song 'Der voxed' et Træ.'[16] A close study of the manuscript reveals that the page numbers have been changed – pages one through five were originally numbered four through eight. One could assume that a musical number was eliminated from the dramatic poem. But an examination of the prompt book used for the premiere reveals that 'Der voxed' et Træ' had always been conceived as the work's opening song.[17] Thus, the altered page numbers must be due to the elimination of some other type of music.

A hint as to what this music might have been is revealed in Andersen's letter. After commenting on the unexpected delay of the *Agnete and the Merman* premiere, Andersen asks Gade to write the director of the theater and explain that he 'will complete an overture for the piece.' But the final score contains no overture, and the question arises: could the altered page numbers in the *Agnete and the Merman* score be evidence of Gade's second failed attempt to compose an overture? Such a conclusion seems plausible when we consider the evolution of *Agnete and the Merman*. From the beginning Gade appears to have struggled with the task of creating a large programmatic composition. His first project, an overture, never progressed beyond preliminary sketches. In his second project, a symphony, Gade added choirs and texts as a means of facilitating the musical expression of the program, but to no avail. Finally, after abandoning all plans for an instrumental work, Gade resorted to writing the musical numbers to Andersen's dramatic poem. Andersen was hoping for a premiere in autumn 1842, but his plans were delayed due to Gade's failure to write an overture. When the dramatic poem finally did appear in April 1843, no overture was included – like the other programmatic works, Gade's second *Agnete and the Merman* overture never came to fruition.

Andersen and Gade spent many months preparing for the premiere of *Agnete and the Merman*. Despite these efforts the production itself was short-lived; it closed after two performances.[18] According to the contemporary critic J.L. Heiberg, *Agnete and the Merman* failed for various reasons:

---

angaar, jeg skal da skrive om Stykket.)

[16] DkB: Musik saml., C II 108, 4°.

[17] DkB: Handskrift afdeling, Kongelige Teaters Sufflørbog saml. no. 17. Although the prompt book's copyist has not yet been identified, both Andersen and Gade appear to have entered corrections. The text for *Agnete and the Merman* was first submitted to the Royal Theater on 2 September 1842 (Annotated edition of H.C. Andersen, *Mit Livs Eventyr*, Copenhagen: Gylendale, 1951, Vol. II, p. 100).

[18] 20 April and 2 May 1843.

It is understandable why the story has not grown better, but actually worse, with this abridged version of the poem which has been transported from the bookstore to the stage. Yet with this it must be remembered what has been noted publically before, namely that the author did not decide to present the work on stage himself, but instead solicited an actor who was already swamped with summer performances.[19] Certainly it would have been better if his [the actor's] willingness to do a favor had not induced him to sacrifice himself, and if the composer Herr Gade had not wasted his characteristic, emotion-filled music on a work which it was easy to predict could not bear it.[20]

Edvard Collin expressed a similar opinion about the dramatic poem in a letter to Andersen dated 23 April 1843. Like Heiberg, Collin appears to have found Gade's music the most redeemable part of the production:

It is always my fate to write to you about the works of yours that bring you no comfort. This is also the case now with Agnete; it was performed for the first time on Thursday the 20th,... Both Gottlieb and I had a presentiment of its outcome; a strange chill and state of boredom covered the entire [presentation]. Mrs. Heiberg's performance pleased a certain few, [but] myself and many others disliked it. Hansen was tolerable, Holst [was] very good. The adaptation [was] mediocre – in the conclusion, even incredibly bad. The scene where the fisherman buries Agnete and puts up a cross that he has lying ready was so poorly arranged, that I waited to hear laughter from the passive mob at every moment. The music was delightful and left nothing to be desired.[21]

---

[19] When Andersen first moved to Copenhagen, he was hoping to become an actor/singer at the Royal Theater. These plans never truly came to fruition, but he did occasionally appear in dramatic performances.

[20] Johan Ludwig Heiberg, *Intelligensblade*, no. 30 (1843). 'At Sagen ikke er blevet bedre, men snarere være ved det Udtog af Digtet, som man har transporteret umiddelbart fra Bogladen op paa Scenen, forstaaer sig af sig selv. Men herved maa erindres – hvad allerede offentlig er bemærket – at Forfatteren ikke af egen Drift har bestemt sig til at bringe sit Arbeide paa Scenen, men anmodet derom af en Skuespiller, som var i Forlegenhed med sin Sommerforestilling. Rigtignok havde det været bedre, om hans Tilbøielighed til at gjøre en Tjeneste ikke havde forledet ham til at opoffre sig selv, og om Componisten Hr. Gade ikke havde ødslet sin characteristiske, følelsesfulde Musik paa et Arbejde, hvorom det var saa let at forudsige, at det ikke kunde bære den.'

[21] *H.C. Andersens brevveksling med Edvard og Henriette Collin*, Copenhagen: Levin & Munkgaards Forlag, 1933, vol. 1, 339-40. 'Det falder altid i min Lod at skrive Dem til om de af Deres Arbejder, som De ingen Glæde har af. Dette er nu ogsaa Tilfældet med Agn[ete; den] gik første Gang i Torsdags d. 20de, ... Baade Gottlieb og jeg havde hele Tiden Forudfølsen af denne Skjebne; en forunderlig Kjølighed og Kjedsommelighed var udbredt over det Hele. Fru Heibergs Spil behagede vist Adskillige; mig og mange Andre mishagede det; Hansen var jevn, Holst meget god. Arrangementet maadeligt, i Slutningen endog fabelagtigt slet; Scenen hvor Fiskeren begraver Agnete og sætter et Kors, som han liggende færdigt, var saa dumt arrangeret, at jeg hvert Øieblik ventede at høre Latteren fra den villige Pøbel. Musiken var yndig og lader

After the failure of *Agnete and the Merman*, Andersen abandoned the project and relinquished all hopes of publishing it.[22] Gade, on the other hand, maintained an interest in the work and eventually arranged six of its songs for voice and piano. This set, entitled *Songs from Agnete and the Merman*, Op. 3 was dedicated to A.P. Berggreen and published in 1845 by C.C. Lose & Hansen (table 15).

Table 15
Songs from *Agnete and the Merman*, Op. 3

1. Song of Hemming the Minstrel
   'Der voxed' et Træ'

2. Choir of Mermaids
   'Jeg veed et Slot'

3. Agnete's Lullabye
   'Sol deroppe ganger under Lide'

4. Choir of Huntsmen
   'Trara! Trara! Trara!'

5. Ballad about Agnete and the Merman
   'Agnete var elsket'

6. The Fisherboy's Ballad
   'Lærken synger sin Morgensang'

---

intet tilage at ønske.'

[22] In a letter to Edvard Collin dated 27 November 1843 Andersen wrote, 'Agnete is shelved [abandoned] forever.' (Agnete er for evigt skrinlagt.) Cited from *H.C. Andersens brevveksling med Edvard og Henriette Collin*, 347.

Six years after the publication of *Songs from Agnete and the Merman*, Op. 3, Gade wrote a choral piece entitled *Agnete and the Mermaids*. Composed for soprano, women's choir, and orchestra, this work is little more than a revised version of two songs from *Agnete and the Merman* ('Jeg ved et Slot' and 'Sol deroppe ganger under Lide'). Performed for the first time in 1858 by Copenhagen's Music Society, *Agnete and the Mermaids* was later arranged for voice and piano and then published, posthumously, in 1891.

Gade's various *Agnete* compositions are not among his most notable efforts, but they are nonetheless important to any study of his development as a composer. Gade's early programs for the 1838 overture and five-movement symphony reveal his broad knowledge and treatment of literary sources. Intrigued by 'Agnete and the Merman,' Gade did not limit himself to a single telling of the story, but rather created his own unique version by drawing on various sources, especially Baggesen and Andersen. In addition, the evolution of *Agnete and the Merman* – from overture, to symphony and dramatic poem – reveals the composer's struggle toward an individual, 'poetic' style and his willingness to experiment with various compositional techniques. Finally, Gade's continued interest in the Agnete and the Merman theme (despite the failure of his first orchestral attempts and Andersen's dramatic poem) illustrates his perseverance and unyielding self-confidence – characteristics that would later become trademarks of his public image.

Chapter Seven

The Concert Overtures (1840–41)

Gade's true breakthrough as a composer took place on 30 March 1841, when Copenhagen's Music Society announced that his *Echoes of Ossian* Overture had won first place in its annual competition for new compositions. *Echoes of Ossian* soon came to be recognized as Gade's most innovative work, and today it is described as Denmark's first 'nationalistic' composition – an odd attribute considering it was originally designed according to German, not Danish, tastes.

On 3 April 1842 Gade's second complete overture, *St. Hans' Evening Play*, was premiered at a concert in the Royal Theater. This time Gade designed his overture with Danish audiences in mind. *St. Hans' Evening Play* received rave reviews from critics, but the overture was never published during Gade's lifetime and has never been included as one of his early, nationalistic works. Does the varied reception of these two overtures seem illogical? Perhaps, but as this chapter will explain, Gade's success as a composer depended on his ability to appeal to a broad, international audience, not local listeners. Orchestral works designed for Danish audiences offered little hope for financial success and consequently were ignored by publishers, whereas works designed for a broader audience received instant recognition and were often viewed as examples of Gade's finest music. By comparing the evolutions of Gade's *Echoes of Ossian* and *St. Hans' Evening Play* Overtures, we witness the power that commercial viability held over Danish composers in the early nineteenth-century.

***

In a memo dated 21 August 1839, the Administration of Copenhagen's Music Society proposed that 20–25 ducats be set aside as prize money for 'the best composition of an overture for full orchestra.'[1] Advertisements for the competition began to appear in March. These explained the entry requirements for the competition and noted that the judges were being chosen from 'Germany's most recognized musicians.'[2] On 28 March it was announced that Louis Spohr,

---

[1] DkB: Musikforeningens Arkiv, kapsel 4, Forhandlingsprotocol 1836–49, tilæg 57. This proposal was unanimously accepted by the board of representatives on 8 September 1839 (kapsel 4, Forhandlingsprotokol 1838–56, 8r.), and on 25 January 1840 J.P.E. Hartmann announced the competition at a general meeting of the society (kapsel 89, Forhandlings Protokol 1836–46, 89v).

[2] Ibid., 93r. On 28 March this advertisement was placed in *Adresse-Avis, Den Berlingske Tidene* and *Altonær Merkur*. The rules were: 1) Only Danes, or composers living in Denmark

Friedrich Schneider and Felix Mendelssohn had been asked to serve as judges.[3] All three accepted with pleasure.

In order to keep the quality of the entries at a high level, the administration repeatedly stressed that the prize would only be awarded to a work 'of recognizeable worth;' and as Schneider stated in a letter to the society dated 15 August 1840, 'a work that is only tolerable' would not be considered.[4] Perhaps such warnings initially discouraged Gade from entering the contest. Whatever the reason, when the 31 October deadline arrived Gade still had not submitted a composition. As Dagmar Gade explained:

> Gade had not thought about competing, but one day when he was walking across Kongens Nytorv he unexpectedly met Concertmaster Frøhlich, and they began to talk with each other. During the conversation [Frøhlich] enthusiastically invited him to participate and added: 'We indeed are waiting for something from you!'[5]

As shown by his composition diary, Gade did not begin composing *Echoes of Ossian* until November 1840. Indeed, Gade's overture was the tenth and final entry. The minutes of the Music Society meetings unfortunately do not mention the dates on which each overture was submitted. In fact, the first mention of the overtures after the 31 October deadline does not occur until 16 January 1841. On this date Hartmann opened a general meeting of the society by announcing that he had recently received a letter of resignation from one of the judges: 'A letter dated 30 December 1840 has come in from Mendelssohn, wherein he explains that his time will not allow him to serve as a judge for the overture prize.'[6]

---

and its territories, could compete. 2) The contestants could choose, if they so wished, a specific topic for their compositions. 3) The winning overture would become the Society's property and would be published at the Society's expense. 4) The composer to whom the prize was awarded was required to make a 2- or 4-hand piano reduction of his/her work. 5) The compositions must be submitted by the end of October. 6) The entries must be supplied with a motto, written on a sealed envelope containing the composer's name.

[3] Ibid., 95r.

[4] Ibid., 97r-98v. Schneider's letter was read aloud at the 26 August meeting.

[5] Dagmar Gade, *Niels W. Gade*, 22. 'Gade havde ikke tænkt paa at konkurrere, men en Dag, da han gik over Kongens Nytorv, mødte han tilfældigvis Concertmester Frøhlich, som gav sig i Snak med ham og i Talens Løb spurgte, om han indleverede en Ouverture til Musikforeningens Konkurrence, og efter det benægtende Svar, opfordrede han ham ivrig dertil og tilføjede: "vi venter os jo netop noget af Dem!"'

[6] Minutes for this meeting begin on 103v of kapsel 89. 'Fra Mendelssohn var indkommet et Br. dat. 30 Decbr. 1840, hvori han erklarede at hans Tid ikke tillod ham at overtage Dommerarbeidet med "Pris-Ouverturen."' The original Mendelssohn letter is now in DkB: Musikforeningens Arkiv. Responses from Hartmann and the Society are found in volumes XI and XII of Mendelssohn's Correspondence in the Bodleian Library, Oxford. For a complete transcription of Mendelssohn's letters to the Music Society see appendix four.

Hartmann responded immediately (16 January), and in the hope of changing Mendelssohn's mind, assured the composer that all the overtures would be in the mail shortly.[7] Hartmann then informed Mendelssohn that it would be impossible to find a replacement judge at such a late date. He tried to convince Mendelssohn that his resignation would be unfair to the contestants – they had been informed of his acceptance as judge and had submitted their overtures accordingly.

Judging from the mottos accompanying the ten overtures, which apparently were submitted without titles, we may surmise that Hartmann was correct; the majority of the contestants chose German mottos, undoubtedly with the hope of winning favor with the judges:

1) Hoch lebe die Musik!
2) J'aimis mon bonheur dans mes chants.
3) Irrthum verläßt uns nie; doch zieht ein höher Bedürfniß immer den strebenden Geist leise zur Wahrheit hinan.
4) Cet essai vous demande l'indulgence.
5) Wie auch der Erfolg, nicht ohne Nutzen wird mein Streben seyn. (Composer: C.F. Hauch)
6) Träume sind Schäume.
7) Und Noah ließ eine Taube von sich ausfliegen, auf daß er erführe – da aber die Taube nicht fand, da ihr Fuß ruher konnte, kam sie wieder zu ihm in den Kasten – 1. Buch Mose VIII, 9.
8) Nur ein Traum. (Composer: Carl Helsted)
9) Und wirst Du's auch nimmer erreichen das Ziel, befleiß'ge doch stets dich, mit redlichem Streben, des Guten.
10) Formel hält uns nicht gebunden, Unsre Kunst heißt Poesie. (Composer: Niels W. Gade)

But Gade went one step further; in addition to using a motto from a popular poem by Uhland entitled 'Freie Kunst,'[8] he chose a programmatic title for his

---

[7] A copy of Hartmann's letter is recorded in the minutes for this meeting (DkB: Musik-foreningens Arkiv, kapsel 89, Forhandlingsprotokol, 103v-104r). In this letter Hartmann states: 'Im Ganzen sind etwa 10 Ouvertüre eingekommen ... Daß die Arbeiten überhaupt so spät an die Richter gelangen, mußen wir bedauern, das fängst von zufalligen Umständen.' Hartmann never explains what these 'zufalligen Umständen' are, but his vagueness concerning the number of overture entries – 'etwa 10' – leads me to believe that he was still waiting for the final entry (Gade's overture). This suspicion is strengthened by Hartmann's letter to Schneider dated 22 January. Here Hartmann states that 'as of today's date, 10 overtures have been submitted' (DkB: Musikforeningens Arkiv, kapsel 89, 107r). Thus it appears that Gade submitted his overture sometime between 16 and 22 January – three months after the deadline!

[8] Oechsle, *Symphonik nach Beethoven*, 135–36, discusses the importance of this poem in relation to the aesthetics behind the creation of Gade's overture.

overture, *Nachklänge von Ossian* (*Echoes of Ossian*),[9] which he knew would pique the judges' interest. Ossian was extremely popular among early 19th-century German composers, both Spohr and Mendelssohn had composed Ossianic or related works. Although Gade was probably unfamiliar with Spohr's Scene for soprano and orchestra, *Oscar*,[10] he definitely knew Mendelssohn's *Fingalshöhle* overture, which would have been understood to carry Ossianic allusions. As R. Larry Todd has noted, Gade's overture was heavily indebted to Mendelssohn's *Fingalshöhle.*[11] Even Schumann later noticed a connection between Mendelssohn and the *Echoes of Ossian.*[12]

Gade's *Echoes of Ossian* Overture divides into three major parts: prologue, middle section and epilogue. The prologue opens with a slow, circular succession of chords: i VI III III VI i (ex. 7:1). These initial chords are important in that they not only foreshadow the closing measures of the epilogue, but also allude to the general harmonic outline of the entire overture (table 16).

---

[9] In a letter to Carl Helsted dated 15 October 1841, Gade states: 'First of all, I am waiting for the upcoming performance of my Overture in A minor in the Music Society's concert on 11 November. For the record, it is called *Nachklänge von Ossian* and moves in the romantic sphere.' (Jeg venter med det første at faae min Ouverture a moll at høre i Musikforeningens Koncert d. 11. November. Til behagelig Efterretning tjener, at den hedder *Nachklänge von Ossian* og bevæger sig i den romantiske Sphære.) This letter is found in DkB: Ny kgl. Saml. 1716, Gades efterladte papirer. Although the first edition of the overture (the four-hand piano version) carried the Danish title *Efterklange af Ossian*, Gade's original competition entry was labeled with two titles: *Gjenklange af Ossian* (Danish) and *Nachklänge von Ossian* (German).

[10] According to Folker Göthel, *Thematisch-Bibliographisches Verzeichnis der Werke von Louis Spohr* (Tutzing: Hans Schneider, 1981) *Oscar* was written in the Fall of 1805 for the chamber singer, Elisabeth Scheidler. It was premiered in Gotha and performed at the Gewandhaus in Leipzig on 16 December 1805. Reviews found in *Berlinische musikalische Zeitung* (1805): 412 and *Allgemeine musikalische Zeitung* 8 (1806): 230ff. Autograph manuscript now in Kassel: MBLB Partitur.

[11] See R. Larry Todd, 'Mendelssohn's Ossianic Manner, with a New Source – *On Lena's Gloomy Heath,*' *Mendelssohn and Schumann: Essays on Their Music and Its Context* (Durham: Duke University Press, 1984), 146–49.

[12] R. Schumann, 'Niels W. Gade,' *Neue Zeitschrift für Musik* 20 (1 January 1844): 2. 'Von neuern Componisten ist namentlich ein Fluß Mendelssohn's in gewissen Instrumental-combinationen sichtbar, namentlich in den *Nachklange aus Ossian.*'

Example 7:1. *Echoes of Ossian*, measures 1–10.

Table 16
Harmonic outline of *Echoes of Ossian*

Section		Key
Prologue ------------- i/I ------------		A
Middle section		
1st theme ----------- i -------------		A minor
Transition	V	E major
	III	C major
2nd theme ---------- VI ------------		F major
Development ------- III ------------		C major
	VII	G major
	IV	A major
Recap. 1st theme --- i --------------		A minor
2nd theme ----------- I -------------		A major
Epilogue -------------- i/I -------------		A

Similar in function to the opening chords of Mendelssohn's *A Midsummer Night's Dream* Overture, Gade's chordal introduction transports the listener into the dream-like world of the overture's dramatic framework.

In the main, the music of the prologue (mm. 13–78) offers a parallel to the opening paragraph of the program:

> An ancient melody! Presents the great achievements of the day!
> O Lora, your rippling waves recall memories from the past –
> Three old spruces lean from the crown of the hill;
> Green are the narrow plains at their feet. –
> Two Stones half-sunken in the earth show their moss-clad backs. –
> An ancient melody! Presents the great achievements of the day!
>   – Such were the Bard's words. –
> Memories of the past often come to my soul with the
> evening sun. – Suddenly the songs of our Bard break
> through: The warriors strike their shields. –

The 'ancient melody' mentioned at the beginning of the paragraph is undoubtedly related to the prologue's opening theme in measures 13–20. This theme is possibly an adaptation of a folk song entitled 'Ramund var sig en bedre mand,' which Gade knew from *Udvalgte danske Viser fra Middelalderen* (ex. 7:2a and b).[13]

The references to Lora's rippling waves is musically represented by the undulating eighth-note violin passages in measures 21–31 and 48–54 and by the rising scales in the violas and cellos in measures 40 and 44. In a similar manner the 'three old spruces' leaning 'from the crown of the hill' are apparently represented by the descending line played by the clarinet in measures 23–26 and the flutes and bassoon in measures 27–30 (ex. 7:3).

The return of the phrase 'An ancient melody! Presents the great achievements of the Day!' coincides with the second statement of the prologue's central theme in measures 32–39. Only the antecedent phrase of Gade's adapted folk song appears in measures 13–20 (cellos) and 32–39 (clarinet and bassoon). Not until measures 59–76 do we finally hear the prologue's central theme in its entirety. This version undoubtedly relates to the closing lines of the program's first paragraph: 'Suddenly the songs of our Bard break through: The warriors strike their shields' (ex. 7:4).

---

[13] *Udvalgte danske Viser fra Middelalderen*, 5 vols (Copenhagen: Abrahamson, Nyerup og Rahbek, 1812–14).

Example 7:2. *Echoes of Ossian.*

a) the folk song 'Ramund var sig en bedre mand.'

b) the opening theme to Gade's overture.

Example 7:3. *Echoes of Ossian*, measures 22–26.

Example 7:4. *Echoes of Ossian*, measures 59–76.

As Oechsle observed, Gade substantially transformed the character of this folk-song melody before using it in his overture – the melodies are only analogous in the opening measures. But if we interpret the falling third g^1–e^1 (m. 4) in the folk tune as a modulation to C major, then the second phrase of the overture's theme (m. 67) also can be related to the melodic structure of the folk tune.[14] The accompaniment built from arpeggiated chords in measures 59–76 continues the archaic flavor of the prologue's opening chord sequence. Thus it appears that the relatively weak harmonic function of the prologue's central theme reflects Gade's attempt to imitate the tonal flavor of the original Scandinavian folk tune.[15]

---

[14] Oechsle, *Symphonik nach Beethoven*, 139.
[15] Ibid., 140.

The overture's middle section is in sonata form and begins in measure 78. Here Gade realizes musically the remainder of his program. The primary theme of the middle section refers to the program's second paragraph:

– The battle's terrifying, rumbling dark sky tumbles
forth far and wide, like fog that streams out over the
x   valley when a storm envelopes the tacit sun of Heaven.
(a.) The commander advances in front (trumpet) like the angry
(forte) spirit in front of the cloud. – Carril sounds the battle
horn on a distant heath. –

Gade realizes the above battle scene with piercing fanfares and racing string passages. The near frenetic quality of the primary theme imitates the flooding forth of 'the battle's terrifying, rumbling dark sky' (ex. 7:5). The fanfare for horn and trumpet preceding this theme (mm. 77–79) illustrates the underlined text: 'The commander advances in front (trumpet),' while the horn calls in measures 90–93 and 100–104 refer to the sound of the warrior, Carril, sounding 'the battle horn on a distant heath.' Gade uses the opening measures of the prologue's central theme in measures 86–89 and 96–98. Here the altered folk melody not only acts as a symbolic battle cry, but also serves as a cyclical link to the preceding section.

The secondary theme of the middle section begins in measure 115. Characterized by the tranquil sound of a lone oboe, this lyrical, F-major melody functions as the perfect antithesis to the turbulent nature of the overture's primary theme (ex. 7:6). Looking at the next paragraph in Gade's program, we realize that this new theme represents Selma's evening song:

– I lay in safety at night. – My eyes were half closed.
Luscious tones came to my ear, like the rising breezes
(F.) that fly over the dark, clouded meadow. Selma was the
one who sent up the evening chorus; for she knew that my
soul was a stream that flows with luscious tones. – Sing, you
sweet voice, for you are luscious, and let my night pass
in peace.

The overture's development corresponds to the fourth paragraph of Gade's program:

– Spirits fly on clouds and ride on wind
They repose together in their caves and
talk about the dead. –

Example 7:5. *Echoes of Ossian*, measures 78–85.

Example 7:6. *Echoes of Ossian*, measures 115–26.

Here Gade uses the fervent string passages from the primary theme to represent the clouds and wind of the spirits, while strains of the folk theme from the prologue are interspersed with the horn calls of the primary theme and the dramatic strumming of Ossian's harp (ex. 7:7). This symbolic mixture of themes is then carried through a circle of fifths which eventually ends in the tonic.

Example 7:7. *Echoes of Ossian*, measures 155–63.

The program's closing paragraphs describe the overture's recapitulation:

x – Again, the battle's terrifying, rumbling dark sky
(a.) tumbles forth, like fog that streams out over the
        valley – – – – – –
     My days are with the departed spirits, no morning will
     shine forth before me. – They shall search for me in
     Temora, but they will not find me. – Draw the arrow from
     my side, and lay Cuchullin under that Oak; – The clouds of
     night come rolling down, and rest upon Cromla's dark-
(a.) brown field. – The distant wind whispers in the forest,
     but the prairies of death are silent and dark. – Finally
(Ap)Selma's luscious voice sounds in my ears on Lena's heath.

The stormy skies of the exposition's battle scene return. This time, however, the battle ends in defeat. A final return of 'Selma's luscious voice' (now in A major), comforts the dying warrior.

In the epilogue we encounter the most imposing rendition of the 'ancient melody.' This is followed by a return of the chordal sequence from the first ten measures of the prologue. The work closes with an echo of the folk tune's ancient melody and a final invocation of Ossian's primeval harp.

In considering Gade's choice of an Ossianic topic for his overture, some scholars have been impressed by a romanticized image of the young composer, struck with inspiration while reading the fervent poetry of the ancient bard. Others have assumed that Gade's choice reflected the literary taste of his homeland. In truth, neither explanation accurately illuminates why Gade chose Ossian. His reasons were calculated, and based on German, not Danish, taste.

Numerous twentieth-century studies have revealed that nineteenth-century Ossian reception differed greatly from country to country.[16] While Ossian reception in England and Scotland was often fueled by political issues, French

---

[16] For further information about Ossian reception outside Great Britain see the three fine articles by Howard Gaskill, 'Ossian at Home and Abroad,' *Strathclyde Modern Language Studies* 8 (1988): 5–26; 'German Ossianism: A Reappraisal?' *German Life and Letters* 42 (1989): 329–41; 'Introduction' to *Ossian Revisited* (Edinburgh: Edinburgh University Press, 1991); as well as Rudolf Tombo, *Ossian in Germany*. Originally published in 1902. Reprint ed. (New York: AMS Press, 1966); Paul van Tiegham, *Ossian en France*. 2 vols. reprint ed. (Geneva: Slatkine reprints, 1967); Q.W.J. Daas, *De Gezangen van Ossian in Nederland* (Nijmegen: Gebr. Janssen, 1961); *'Ossian' den svenska dikten och litteraturen* (Malmö: Aktieboglagets Boktrykkeri, 1895); Frederic I. Carpenter, 'The Vogue of Ossian in America: A Study in Taste,' *American Literature* 2 (1931): 405–17; Glynn R. Barrat, 'The Melancholy and the Wild: A Notice on Macpherson's Russian Success,' *Studies in Eighteenth-Century Culture* (1973): 125–35; Karl Weitnauer, 'Ossian in der italienischen Litteratur bis etwa 1832, vorwiegend bei Monti,' *Zeitschrift für vergleichende Literaturgeschichte, Neue Folge* (1906): 251–322.

interest was little more than a fashion following Napoleon's admiration for Ossian's tragic-heroic characters. In Italy Ossian was viewed as the Northern foil of classical antiquity, and in Germany he was claimed as a national hero – the father of Germanic literature. In the past, scholars have mistakenly assumed that Denmark's enthusiasm for Ossian equaled that of their German neighbors.[17] Although several Danish poets, artists and musicians did treat Ossianic topics, these experiments were conducted, for the most part, outside Denmark and/or under the influence of foreigners. In Denmark itself, the vogue for the Ossian myth was relatively short-lived, controversial, and disconnected with ideas of national identity. There was no link between Ossian and Danish nationalism: in literature Ossian represented the ancient epics of a neighboring nation, while in art it simply served as one of several sources for historical genre paintings. In addition, the only Danish composition based on Ossian that appeared before Gade's overture had been designed and performed for German audiences. In fact, when Gade began composing his overture in 1840, the zenith of Denmark's brief interest in Ossian had well passed.[18] So why did Gade choose Ossian? Because he knew it would appeal to the literary tastes of the German judges. While the Germans enthusiastically accepted Ossian as the champion of their glorious past, the Danes simply viewed him as a curious foreign fancy. Gade did not choose Ossian for nationalistic reasons – such a connection never would have been understood in Denmark. Instead he selected Ossian because he knew it was a topic that would appeal to the tastes of the German judges.[19]

---

[17] Hamburg Kunsthalle, *Ossian und die Kunst um 1800* (Munich: Prestel-Verlag, 1974); Charlotte Christensen, 'Ossian-Illustrationer i Danmark,' *Fond og Forskning* 19 (1972): 7–32; Henry Okun, 'Ossian in Painting,' *Journal of the Warburg and Courtald Institutes* 30 (1967): 327–56. Charles Kjerulf, *Niels W. Gade, til Belysning af hans Liv og Kunst* (Copenhagen: Gyldendalske Boghandel, 1917), 59. Niels Martin Jensen, 'Niels W. Gade og den nationale tone,' *Dansk Identitetshistorie 3, Folkets Danmark 1848–1940*, ed. Ole Feldbæk (Copenhagen: C.A. Reitzel, 1992), claims that Denmark's reading public showed great enthusiasm for Ossian and regarded these tales as remnants of the nation's ancient past: 'Kunsterne og det læsende publikum blev begejstrede for denne særprægede digtning, der tilsyneladende vakte en røst fra en fjern nordisk fortid til live' (p. 244); and 'Disse digte kom således for mange i samtiden til at stå som udtryk for en gammel nordisk digtning' (p. 245).

[18] The last Ossian illustration appeared in 1828, the last performance of an Ossian composition took place in 1811, and the most recent Ossianic literary work was published in 1808. For a complete history of Ossian reception in Denmark see my article '*Efterklange af Ossian*: The Reception of James Macpherson's *Poems of Ossian* in Denmark's Literature, Art, and Music,' *Scandinavian Studies* 70 (1998): 359-96.

[19] Indeed, the cantata *Comala* (Gade's 'sequel' to the Ossian overture) was not as enthusiastically received in Denmark as it was in Germany. Although the libretto for this work appeared in both German and English, it was never translated into Danish. For a more thorough discussion of the reception of Comala in Denmark and Germany see Jensen, 'Niels W. Gade,' 259–62.

We know from contemporary accounts Gade was an ambitious composer who vowed to achieve greatness before his twenty-fifth birthday. Regarding the competition as his best chance for fame, Gade apparently did everything possible to appeal to the judges. On 30 March 1841 the young composer's dreams were fulfilled when the Music Society announced him as their winner. After hearing these results a thrilled, and obviously relieved, Gade placed a small crown over the Ossian program preserved in his composition diary and then entered this passage:

> The 30th of March 1841: the preceding overture was found (according to Spohr and Schneider's judgement) to be the one worthy of the competition's selected prize. So, then, here is the wished for sign – *Glory to God!*[20]

***

After winning the Music Society's competition, Gade began working on a piano arrangement of his overture for publication.[21] In a letter to Carl Helsted dated 28 July 1841, Gade related, with great relief, the completion of this tedious project, and then described his newest musical undertaking:

> I have begun an overture to Oehlenschläger's *St. Hans' Evening Play* which will be in a light and more cheerful tone; except for that I haven't done anything this summer.[22]

Turning to Gade's composition diary, we see that he worked on the overture throughout the month of August and finished it in September 1841. The musical subject of the overture was Oehlenschläger's *St. Hans' Evening Play*, a literary topic that was familiar and well-loved by readers in Denmark.

Written in one long act with a prologue and epilogue, Oehlenschläger's *St. Hans' Evening Play* combines a wide variety of poetic forms, moods and perspectives in a richly textured portrayal of contemporary bourgeois society.[23]

---

[20] 'd. 30te Marz: 1841 fandtes foregaaend Ouverture (efter Spohr og Schneiders bedømmelse) at være værdig den med Koncurencen udsette Pris. Saa, saa heri det ønskede Wink. Deo gloria.'

[21] In a letter to Edvard Collin dated 12 April 1841 (DkB: Collin Saml. nr. 314) Gade states that he has begun working on the four-hand piano arrangement of the overture.

[22] Behrend, 'Omkring Niels W. Gade,' 65–66. The original letter is in the Helsted family's private collection. 'Jeg har begyndt paa en Ouv: til St. Hansaften-Spil af Øhlenschläger som skal være i en let og heater Tone, Firestone har jeg ikke bestilt noget I Sommer.'

[23] The immediate model for Oehlenschläger's *St. Hans' Evening Play* was Goethe's youthful shrovetide farce, *Das Jahrmarktsfest zu Plundersweilern* (See Wilhelm Dietrich Lippstadt, *Oehlenschlägers 'Sankt Hansaftenspil' im Abhängigkeitsverhältnis zur deutschen Literatur*, Borna-Leipzig, 1916). Yet as Kathryn Shailer Hansen, *Adam Oehlenschläger and Ludwig Tieck: A Study in Danish and German Romanticism* (Ph.D. diss. Princeton Univ. 1978), 78–79, explains, although 'both evoke a bustling carnival atmosphere and make use of similar stock

Intending to capture, as had Shakespeare,[24] the magical atmosphere of Midsummer Night (i.e. St. Hans' Evening in Denmark[25]), Oehlenschläger sets his play in Copenhagen's Dyrehave (Deer Park)[26] and alternates scenes of a raucous midsummer carnival and enchanted forest, and episodes from the touching love story of Ludvig and Maria.

The prologue opens with a speech by an old vagabond. Acting as the prologus he climbs an ancient burial mound and greets the audience:

> Welcome to the red hour of daybreak,
> each of you who now has gathered here
> to follow us with persevering, healthy feet
> from the sluggish fog of the city to
> yonder forest, which arches green and cool ...[27]

In awe of nature's beauty, the vagabond then breaks into a rhapsodical morning song. At the song's conclusion Harlequin appears.[28] Claiming to be 'the genuine prologus,' he dismisses the vagabond and then continues, much in the style of a Märchenkomodie, by insulting the audience and taking stabs at figures such as

---

characters, in terms of actual setting, scope and purpose, the two bear little relationship.'

[24] Oehlenschläger was quite familiar with Shakespeare's play; he published a Danish translation of the work entitled: *En Skiærsommernats Drøm. Lystspil af Shakespeare. Oversat af Adam Oehlenschläger* (Copenhagen: Brünnich paa Oversætternes Forlag, 1816).

[25] Rooted in the traditions of pre-Christian Denmark, St. Han's Evening (June 23) marks Denmark's observance of the summer solstice. According to popular legend, the powers of nature are especially keen on this evening, thus a number of raucous activities and superstitions have become associated with the holiday. Celebrated on hills or along the coast, these festivities often include sacrifices to holy springs, the plucking of magical herbs, and the construction of large bonfires, upon which are burnt effigies of witches and evil spirits. For a complete history of this holiday during the eighteenth and nineteenth centuries see Eiler Nyström, *Offentlige Forlystelser i Frederik den Sjettes tid*, volume I (Copenhagen: Gyldendalske Boghandel, 1913).

[26] The Dyrehave comprises the grounds surrounding Ermitagen, a rococo palace belonging to the royal family. Located approximately fifteen miles north of Copenhagen in Klampenborg, this wooded area (originally the royal hunting grounds) was opened to the public by Frederik V in the mid-eighteenth century. Shortly thereafter an amusement park, Bakken, was opened on the grounds surrounding Kirsten Pil's Spring. To this day the Dyrehave serves as a favored retreat for Danes.

[27] Adam Oehlenschläger, 'St. Hansaftenspil,' *Poetische Skrifter*, vol. 1 (Copenhagen, Det Nordisk Forlag, 1857), 3. (Velkommen i den røde Morgenstund/ Enhver, som tidlig now har samlet sig,/ For snart med ufortrodne, raske Fied/ At folge os fra Byens dorske Taage/ Til Skoven hist, som grøn og sval sig hvælver.)

[28] A figure originally from the Italian tradition of commedia dell'arte, Harlequin became a popular theatrical character in early nineteenth-century Danish literature. Holberg was the first Dane to make use of the Harlequin figure (De Usynlige) and Harlequin still appears in present-day performances of Casorti's Pantomime in Copenhagen's Tivoli. For a study of the Harlequin see Otto Driesen, *Der Ursprung des Harlekins* (Berlin: A. Duncker, 1904).

Shakespeare, Homer, and various dramatic critics.[29]   Toward the end of Harlequin's speech, the rural setting for the prologue is transformed into the living room of a middle-class, urban home, and the audience is prepared for the commencement of the play:

> Now we have all been dragged to the city.
> Yet the unity of the play has not been observed exactly;
> So those who are not partial to change,
> can stay behind when we next rearrange.
> We are now in the home of a common man.
> None other than Hillemænd! See, he is approaching.
> It would be best for me to yield to this person,
> I do not want to spoil the illusion.[30]

The home belongs to Maria's foster parents; the man approaching is her foster father. He tells the audience her tragic story: Maria has fallen in love with a handsome young count named Ludvig. But her mother feels the relationship is futile, for he is 'well above her station.' So the poor girl has been sent away so that time and distance will lessen her distress. Naturally, just the opposite has happened: time has only increased her love for Ludwig, and their separation has caused her great sorrow. In an effort to lift the young girl's spirits, her foster parents decide to take her to the Dyrehave. Maria is comforted by the idea of escaping the city. While her foster parents prepare for the journey, she enlists the help of a servant girl and plans a secret rendezvous with Ludvig.

A brief lyric interlude, 'De Kiørende' (The Driving Ones), provides the transition from the city to the country, and the travelers soon arrive at the carnival-like setting of the Dyrehave, where Maria's foster father meets a 'young man from Langeland.' Unaware that the lad is in fact Ludvig, he introduces him to Maria and his wife, and the four spend the day together. They visit several attractions, including a glass-blower, puppet show, pantomimes, exotic animals, tight-rope walker, dog act, and a public drinking house. At the close of the scene the crowd thins as evening approaches.

A second lyric passage, 'Gyngesang' (Swing song) transports the audience deeper into the forest, and Ludvig and Maria again become the focus of attention. As the night scene opens, Ludvig sits alone and sings a lament while Maria slowly

---

[29] For a discussion of Oehlenschläger's allusions to these figures see Aage Kabell, 'Sanct Hansaften-Spil,' *Danske Studier* 76 (1981): 32–44.

[30] Oehlenschläger, 'St. Hansaftenspil,' 7–8. 'Nu er vi alle til Staden draget./ Stykkets Eenhed er just ei iagttaget;/ Men de, som ei lide Changement,/ Kan blive, naar vi flytte næste Gang./ Her er vi i Huus hos en Borgermand./ Men, Hillemænd! see, der kommer han./ Jeg faaer da vel at tage for Personen,/ For ei at forstyrre Illusionen.'

makes her way toward him. Finally the lovers are reunited – the fantasy begins as Maria sings a hymn that resounds through the forest:

Magical Harmony
in earth's midnight darkness!
Blessed Sympathy!
Holy Poetry
without words!
Amalgamation of grove and sea
and stars, and a youth and maiden locked in an embrace!
Arm in arm
the whole of Nature interprets the name of Love.[31]

The forest takes on magical overtones: an ancient oak tree and a tiny glow-worm (St. Hans' worm) compare life experiences, Death frolics through the trees singing a macabre song, and St. Kirsten approaches her sacred spring and, much to the delight of the personified waves, sheds fresh tears.[32] Throughout these fantastic happenings Maria and Ludvig remain entwined in one another's arms. At midnight, however, they are awakened from their dream by the chimes of a distant clock tower. They realize that their reunion can only be temporary. But just as they are about to depart the 'Genie of Love' appears and tells them of an enchanted place where they can escape. Without a word, the lovers abandon their responsibilities and retire to their blissful retreat.

At the play's conclusion a hunter wanders through the forest and delivers an epilogue about universal love and nature. He then blows his horn and departs, leaving a flock of small birds behind to sing the closing chorus:

---

[31] Ibid., 61. 'Tryllende Harmonie/ I midnatsdunkle Jord!/ Salige Sympathie!/ Hellige Poesie/ Uden Ord!/ Sammensmelting af Lund og Sø/ Og Stierner og omsynget Yngling og Mø/ Favn mod Favn/ Tolker hele Naturen Kiærligheds Navn.'

[32] Discovered in 1583 by a maiden named Kirsten Pils, St. Kirsten's Spring (a.k.a Kirsten Pils' Spring or Brinkman's Spring) is a natural spring in the Dyrehave. This spring is often incorrectly referred to in popular literature as one of Denmark's 'sacred' springs – i.e. a spring created through the miraculous actions of a saint. Little mention was made of the spring before the mid-eighteenth century, but in 1732 a dancer for the royal court named Brinkman re-discovered the spring and erected a small monument at its source. The spring is renowned for its healing qualities, and when Frederik V opened the Dyrehave to the general public, the spring became a popular attraction. According to legend, the medicinal powers of St. Kirsten's Spring are especially potent on St. Hans' Evening. To this day St. Kirsten's Spring is one of the Dyrehave's most popular attractions.

In the moonlight
behind a latticework of branches,
we birds so small
peep at each other and sing:
Thank God, we are united
on our small little branch!
Only when it is safe
for us to hop around free,
oh, then we are so happy,
so happy, so happy!
Kweereeleet, Kweereeleet![33]

Turning to Gade's overture we readily recognize several scenes from Oehlenschläger's play.[34] Gade begins his composition with a morning scene. Whereas Oehlenschläger describes 'the red hour of daybreak' through the words of his vagabond prologus, Gade uses the arpeggiated melody of a solo horn for the same purpose in his slow introduction (ex. 7:8a). An echo of the horn is heard in measure 22, and in measure 25 the bassoon and violins repeat the arpeggiated theme, again followed by a horn echo in measure 34. The dawn of a new day is further characterized by a gradual thickening of the texture and twittering bird calls played by the flute (mm. 38–44).

A transition marked *stringendo poco a poco* begins in measure 51 (ex. 7:8b). Foreshadowing the arrival of the primary theme, this section grows in dynamics and rushes headlong until, in an explosion of rhythmic activity, it yields to the *Allegro con viverra* in measure 71. Here we meet the exposition's vibrant primary theme. This theme, played in unison by the upper strings and woodwinds and accompanied by full and arpeggiated chords in the brass, lower strings, and bassoon, depicts the carnival-like setting of Oehlenschläger's Dyrehave (ex. 7:8c).

At the end of the primary theme, a second transition section appears (mm. 93–123). Depicting the forest setting from Oehlenschläger's play, the first nineteen measures of this section are characterized by rippling eighth-note passages in the strings (St. Kirsten's spring), a tranquil neighbor-note motive in the third horn, and bird calls in the upper woodwinds (ex. 7:8d). Toward the end of this section (m. 112) the carnivalesque primary theme returns; but like the crowd of revelers in Oehlenschläger's Dyrehave, the texture of this section thins (m. 120) and the theme fades away (mm. 121–23).

---

[33] Oehlenschläger, 'St. Hansaftenspil,' 67. 'I Maaneskin titter/ Vi Fugle saa smaae/ Bag Grenenes Gitter/ Til hinanden, og slaae./ Gudskeelov, vi er ene/ Paa vore smaae Grene!/ Naar kun vi har Ro/ Til at hoppe frit,/ O, da er vi saa froe,/ Saa froe, saa froe!/ Quirilit, quirilit!'

[34] For the only published version of the overture see my edition: *Niels W. Gade. St. Hans' Evening Play Overture* (Middleton, Wisconsin: A-R Editions, 2001).

The secondary theme begins in measure 124. Soaring above the gentle, syncopated accompaniment of the strings, marked 'dolce,' this E-major melody reflects the interminable love of Ludvig and Maria (ex. 7:8e). As in his previous overtures (e.g. *Agnete and the Merman* and *Echoes of Ossian*), Gade chose an upper-woodwind instrument to play this stirring love theme. Occasional chromatic tones in the strings (for ex., mm. 132–33 and 137–40) add a certain poignancy to the music, recalling Maria's impassioned hymn during the climax of the play: 'Magical Harmony in earth's midnight darkness! Blessed Sympathy! Holy Poetry without words!' A repetition of the secondary theme begins in measure 156; this version of the theme contains running eighth-note passages similar to those in the carnival music of the primary theme (mm. 156–69, first violins).

Example 7:8. *St. Hans' Evening Play* Overture.

a) Prologus' morning song/Epilogus' hunting horn.

b) transition to Dyrehave (De Kiørende).

c) carnival at Dyrehave.

d) the enchanted forest.

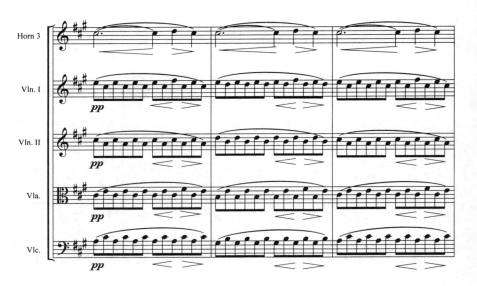

e) love theme of Ludvig and Maria.

Example 7:9. *St. Hans' Evening Play* Overture.

a) original secondary theme.

b) folk tune 48b from *Udvalgte danske Viser*.

In the opening of the development (m. 170), motives from the previous two transitions are presented simultaneously: the strings play the characteristic rhythmic motive first encountered in the *stringendo poco a poco* section (mm. 51–70), while the horn and upper woodwinds repeat the tranquil neighbor-note motive and bird calls from the forest scene in measures 93–123. These motives are soon joined by an echo of the secondary theme in the clarinet and cello (mm. 173–78). A treatment of the primary theme dominates the development from measure 186 and progresses through several modulations: E major (mm. 170–84), A minor (mm. 185–94), C major (mm. 195–206). Variants of the secondary theme in the key of E major return in measure 207, but soon yield to a return of the primary theme in C major (m. 227). Further harmonic development includes modulations to A minor (m. 239), G major (m. 245), C minor (m. 251), C major (m. 260), and E major (m. 272).

Toward the end of the development an animated transition similar to measures 51–71 leads to the recapitulation. Here Gade takes special care to avoid merely retracing the thematic course of the exposition. A return of the forest music in the tonic key prepares the way for a final presentation of the primary theme (m. 304). Ludvig's and Maria's love theme returns in measure 336, and after several repetitions closes with a slight ritard leading to the coda. Marked *tempo primo*, the coda features a return of the horn melody from the slow introduction. The return of this theme is significant; in addition to supplying the work with a sense of thematic closure, it refers to the horn call played by the hunter in the epilogue of Oehlenschläger's play. The overture concludes with a faint echo of the midsummer carnival in the key of F major (mm. 434–39, violins) and a hint of Ludwig's and Maria's love theme (mm. 442–46, oboe). A plagal cadence announces the overture's final resolution.

The earliest sketches for *St. Hans' Evening Play* confirm that, from the beginning, Gade intended to use the intricate complex of thematic ideas found in the final version.[35] Written in piano reduction with full details of scoring and dynamics, these sketches present almost exactly the overture's final form. Except for the omission of several minor repetitive passages, the only revisions involve a slight remodeling of the secondary theme. In the sketches this theme is symmetrical and more folk-like in character. In fact, it appears that an actual folk tune, melody 48B of *Udvalgte danske Viser*, may have served as the theme's original model (ex. 7:9a and b).

Gade did not draw on folk music alone. His primary musical models for *St. Hans' Evening Play* appear to have been Mendelssohn's *The Fair Melusine* (1833) and *A Midsummer Night's Dream* (1826) Overtures. Gade was well acquainted with *The Fair Melusine*,[36] and it appears that the overture's lyricism

---

[35] DkB: Gade Saml. C II 6.

[36] In 1838 he alluded to its 'beauty' in a letter to A.P. Berggreen (see chapter two).

and sanguine opening influenced the creation of *St. Hans' Evening Play*. But these are only superficial similarities. In terms of thematic structure and form, Gade's primary model was Mendelssohn's *A Midsummer Night's Dream*. Although this overture was not premiered in Copenhagen until 1843,[37] parts of it were used in 1835 as a prelude to the Royal Theater's productions of J.L. Heiberg's *Alferne*.[38] No great leap of faith is needed to imagine the young Gade somehow gaining access to the score, as a member of the Royal Chapel he played violin in the theater orchestra from 1834 to 1838.

In addition to a similarity in programs (the magical happenings of midsummer night), *St. Hans' Evening Play* and *A Midsummer Night's Dream* display a similar approach to thematic content, motivic development, and formal construction. In his most recent discussion of *A Midsummer Night's Dream*, R. Larry Todd draws attention to the 'especially rich thematic content' displayed in the overture: 'Animated by no fewer than six sharply delineated figures,' the exposition presents the listener with an array of dramatic scenes and characters.[39] Impressed by Mendelssohn's use of distinctive themes as a means of relating the various dramatic parts of a program, Gade adopted a similar procedure in the *St. Hans' Evening Play* Overture. Like *A Midsummer Night's Dream*, this work's exposition contains several themes representing scenes and characters from the play (ex. 7:8a–e).

As Todd explains, although each of Mendelssohn's six motives enjoys its own special character, they are all the product of a series of metamorphoses that traces its development from a common source – the four wind chords of the overture's opening motto.[40] Gade used a similar method of motivic transformation in the various themes for *St. Hans' Evening Play*. Whereas Mendelssohn concealed the motivic germ of his overture in its opening chords, Gade chose to present it prominently in his overture's initial horn call. Outlining a major triad, this melody generates the basic building block for the overture's subsequent thematic ideas (table 17). Themes *b* and *c* frame the triad in their leaps and scalar passages, and *e* plainly displays a triad in the love theme of Ludvig and Maria. At first glance theme *d* might appear free from the influence of this device, but close inspection of the accompaniment reveals a triadic structure in the strings and bassoon. Even the general harmonic structure of the overture is affected by the triad: its principal tonal areas – tonic, mediant, and dominant – reflect a major/minor triad.

---

[37] According to Angul Hammerich, *Musikforeningens Historie 1836–1886* (Copenhagen, Musikforeningen, 1886), 84, Franz Glæser premiered the overture at a Music Society Concert in 1843.

[38] Nils Schiørring, *Musikkens Historie i Danmark*, vol. 2, 303, reports that *Alferne* was premiered in 1835 and soon became part of the Royal Theater's standard repertoire.

[39] R. Larry Todd, *Mendelssohn: 'The Hebrides' and Other Overtures* (Cambridge: Cambridge University Press, 1994), 53.

[40] Ibid., 53–56.

Table 17
General harmonic structure of *St. Hans' Evening Play*

Structural section	Key	Tonal area	Measure number
Introduction:	A	I	1
Exposition:	A	I	51
Primary theme	A	I	71
Secondary theme	E	V	124
Development:	E	V	170
	a	i	185
	C	III	195
	E	V	207
	C	III	227
A minor:	a	i	239
	G	VII(V/iii)	245
	c	iii	251
	C	III	260
	E	V	272
Recapitulation: *A major*	A	I	288
Primary theme	A	I	304
Secondary theme	A	I	336
Coda:	A	I	400
Primary theme (echo)	F	(♭VI)	434
	A	I	439

In the formal plan of *St. Hans' Evening Play* Gade avoided a routine, sequential ordering of the various thematic elements in the development and recapitulation.[41] By mixing the diverse thematic ideas and varying their order of appearance, Gade succeeded in his attempt to create an intricate and subtle composition (table 18).

Table 18
Thematic structure of *St. Hans' Evening Play*

Introduction/Exposition:

THEME:	a	b	c	d	(c)	(b)		e	(c)
KEY:	A--E------------								
MEASURE #:	1	51	71	93	112	116		124	156

Development:

d(b)	(e)	b	(c)	c	b	(e)	e	d	(b)	c		b
E-----------a-----------C---------------E-----------------C-a-G-c-C-E-												
170	174	185	187	195	199	201	207	215	224	227		275

Recapitulation: Coda:

d	c	(a)	e	(d)		a(e)		c	e	
A--F------A-------------------										
288	104	330	336	368		400		434	441	448

---

[41] For a thorough description of Mendelssohn's ingenious manipulation of motivic material in *A Midsummer Night's Dream* overture, see Todd, *'The Hebrides' and Other Overtures*, 54, 56–58.

When Gade completed *St. Hans' Evening Play* in September 1841, he was quite pleased with the work. In a letter to Carl Helsted dated 15 October he wrote:

> Dear Brother and Friend!
> ... After a fraternal greeting and salute I hereby inform you that I find myself in the best of health, fresh as a fish.... I have written a new ditto to Oehlenschläger's *St. Hans' Evening Play* in A major that I will have performed at a concert in the Theater. Very merry and also erotic (a pretty piece).[42]

The performance mentioned above was none other than Clara Schumann's first concert at Copenhagen's Royal Theater (3 April 1842).[43] In a letter to her husband Clara commented on Gade's overture: 'At my concert Gade will present a new overture that is quite different from the first; it is completely cheerful in character.'[44] In addition to Clara's approving words, Gade's overture received glowing reviews from the press. A critic for the paper *Fædrelandet* wrote:

> Last evening the public was given the opportunity to enjoy a new work by the talented, young composer, Herr Gade – an overture to Oehlenschläger's *St. Hans' Evening Play*. Like his previous [overture], this composition distinguished itself by beautiful ideas, originality in treatment, and a prize-worthy detachment from all pursuits after external effects. The composer received a warm and honorable recognition from all those knowledgeable in music.[45]

---

[42] Behrend, 67. The original letter is in the Helsted family's private collection. 'Kjære Broder og Ven!/ ... Næst broderlig Hilsen og Salut melder jeg dig herved, at jeg befinder mig i bedste Velgaaende, frisk som en Fisk.... Jeg har lavet en nye ditto til Øhlenschlägers 'St. Hansaftenspil' i A Dur som jeg vil lade opføre i Theatret ved en Koncert. Meget lystig og tillige erotisk (peent Stykke).'

[43] Clara Schumann gave three concerts in Copenhagen – two at the Royal Theater (3 and 10 April) and a third at the Angleterre Hotel.

[44] Berthold Litzmann, *Clara Schumann. Ein Künstlerleben. Nach Tagebüchern und Briefen* (Leipzig: Breitkopf und Härtel, 1905), vol. 2, 48. 'Er [Gade] wird in meinem Konzert eine neue Ouverture von sich aufführen, die ganz verschieden von der ersten ist, sie ist ganz heiteren Charakters.' The letter is dated 31 March 1842. Naturally Clara's mention of 'der ersten' overture is a reference to the *Echoes of Ossian* overture, which Schumann would have known from the published four-hand arrangement (1841) and from performances in Leipzig by the Euterpe orchestra on 18 January 1842 [*Der Musikverein Euterpe zu Leipzig 1824–1874. Ein Gedenkblatt* (Leipzig, C.F. Kahnt, 1874), 34] and the Gewandhaus orchestra on 5 February 1842.

[45] *Fædrelandet* (4 April 1842): 6724. 'Publikum havde denne Aften Leilighed til at glæde sig ved et nyt Arbeide af den unge talentfulde Componist, Hr. Gade, en Ouverture til Øehlenschlägers "St. Hans Aftenspil." Denne Composition udmærkes sig ligesom hans forrige, ved smukke Ideer, Originalitet i Behandlingen og en prisværdig Forsmaaen af al Jagen efter ydre Effect, og erhvervede Componisten en varm og hædrende Anerkjendelse hos alle Musikkyndige.'

A similar review appeared in another Copenhagen paper, *Det Berlingske Tidene*:

> Among the other numbers on the concert we especially must emphasize our talented *Capelmusicus* N.W. Gade's new overture to Oehlenschläger's *St. Hans' Evening Play*, which was received with lively applause.[46]

When Gade first presented his overture to the Royal Theater in 1841, its cover page contained the following inscription:

Overture to Oehlenschlägers 'St. Hans' Evening Play'
(op?) (September 1841)[47]

As the opus marking on the title page reveals, Gade originally intended to publish the overture, but his plans never came to fruition. Despite the positive reviews from Clara Schumann and Copenhagen's critics, Gade's *St. Hans' Evening Play* was never performed outside Denmark. This might seem strange at first, given the international attention received by Gade's *Echoes of Ossian* Overture just one year before. But a brief investigation of Danish and German publishing practices reveals that the overture's failed publication was likely due its distinctly Danish program.

During the first half of the nineteenth century, music publishers in Denmark and Germany tended to print compositions that would appeal to an international, amateur market. Chamber music was favored, especially works for keyboard, flute, and/or violin.[48] Orchestral works were published less often due to expensive production costs; and keyboard arrangements of these works had a better chance at publication if they carried titles and/or programs familiar to a large portion of the consumer population. Simply stated, composers in Denmark had to write music for an international market if they hoped to get published; and Oehlenschläger's *St. Hans' Evening Play* was not familiar to readers outside Scandinavia.

---

[46] *Det Berlingske Tidene* (4 April 1842). 'Blandt de andre Numere, hvoraf denne Concert bestod, maae vi især fremhæve vor talentfulde Capelmusicus N. W. Gades nye Ouverture til Oehlenschlägers "Sanct Hans Aftenspil," hvilken modtages med levende Bifald.'

[47] This manuscript is found in DkB: Gade saml. C II 6. 'Ouverture til Øhlenschläger's "St. Hansaftenspil"/ (op. ?) (September 1841).'

[48] See Dan Fog, *Musikhandel og nodetryk i Danmark efter 1750*, 2 vols. (Copenhagen: Dan Fog, 1984).

Oehlenschläger's play was hailed as a literary milestone in Denmark,[49] but it failed to gain international acclaim. Although the majority of the poet's works were translated and published by foreign publishers shortly after their appearance in Denmark, such was not the case with *St. Hans' Evening Play*.[50] Consequently, music publishers found little hope for financial profit in Gade's overture. The limited consumer market of Oehlenschläger's play, combined with the expense of printing an orchestral work, dissuaded publishers from investing in Gade's overture.

After the 1842 premiere and failed attempt at publication, Gade set *St. Hans' Evening Play* aside and did not return to it until sometime during the 1860s, when he made an inventory of his manuscripts and sketches. We can tell from comments added to the title page that Gade was uncertain about what he should do with the manuscript:

> Overture to Oehlenschläger's 'St. Hans' Evening Play'
> (op?) (September 1841)
> Cast out (?)
> Must be 'reworked.'[51]

He considered throwing the manuscript out, but on second thought decided to keep it and return to it in the future.

Gade began revising *St. Hans' Evening Play* in the summer of 1870. At this time he returned to the original 1841 score and entered various changes. Gade's musical corrections were minor. In fact, his most dramatic revision appeared on the score's title page (fig. 10). In an attempt to make the overture more accessible to non-Danish audiences, Gade veiled the original connection to Oehlenschläger's play by changing the title of his overture to *A Summer Day Love-Idyll*:

---

[49] Especially appealing to mid-nineteenth-century Danish readers was Oehlenschläger's unprecedented use of a rich blend of literary genres. According to K. Hansen, 'Adam Oehlenschläger and Ludwig Tieck,' Oehlenschläger incorporated a wide variety of verse forms into his play, some of which were entirely new to Danish poetry (i.e. the Italian canzone and ottave). In the case of more traditional forms, Oehlenschläger often presented them in an unorthodox manner so as to produce a specific effect – for example blank verse in the vagabond's prologue, hexameter in the highly satiric Idyll, and doggerel in the segment entitled 'A man with a perspective case.'

[50] In fact, the first German translation of this work did not appear until 1853: *St. Johannis-Abend-Spiel. Dichtung von A. Oehlenschläger frei übergesetzt von Heinrich Smidt* (Berlin: Verlag von C. Grobe, 1853). As the title indicates, this edition of the play was a free translation. Consequently, many of the distinctive Danish characteristics in the original version were either omitted or altered considerably.

[51] Ouverture til Øhlenschlägers/ 'St. Hansaftenspil'/ (Op ?) (September 1841)/ Kassert (?)/ MUSICAL SIGNATURE./ Skal 'Omarbeides.'

Originally Overture to Oehlenschlägers 'St. Hans' Evening Play'
(op?) (September 1841)
Cast out (?)
Must be 'reworked.'
A Summerday
Love-Idyll Overture (1870)[52]

Unfortunately, no fair copy of *A Summer Day Love-Idyll* exists. Thus we can only assume that Gade abandoned this project shortly after its undertaking in the summer of 1870.[53]

---

[52] Oprindelig Ouverture til Øhlenschlägers/ 'St. Hansaftenspil'/ (Op ?) (September 1841)/ Kassert (?)/ MUSICAL SIGNATURE./ Skal 'Omarbeides.'/ En Sommerdag Idylleib Ouverture (1870).

[53] In 1886 Gade began work on a secular cantata entitled 'St. Hans' Evening Play,' but it was left incomplete at the time of his death. The composer Rued Immanuel Langgaard completed the orchestration for Gade's piece and added the hymn, 'Tryllende Harmoni.' This revised version was published as: 'Sanct Hansaften Spil af Adam Oehlenschläger. Fragment af Slutningsscenen komponeret for Sopransolo, Kor og Orkester' (Copenhagen: Samfundet, 1916).

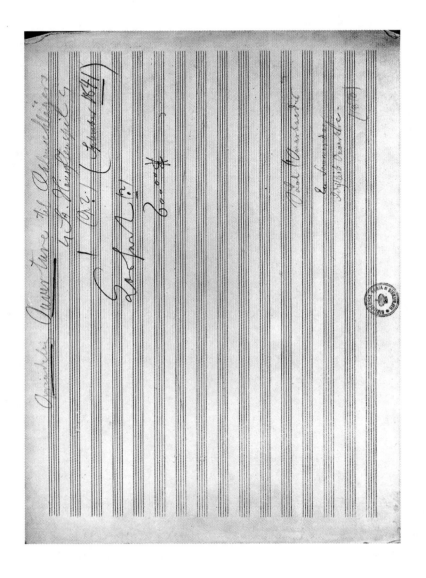

Figure 10 St Hans' Evening Play, title page of the autograph score.
(DkB: Gade Saml., C II 6)

Chapter Eight

Symphony No. 1 in C Minor, Op. 5 (1841–42)

Perhaps the fate of *St. Hans' Evening Play* influenced the creation of the final work in Gade's composition diary, the Symphony No. 1 in C Minor, Op. 5. On the whole, Gade's first symphony reflects a tension between German and Danish sources. Gade's musical sketches verify the influence of German models: i.e. Beethoven, Mendelssohn, and Schubert, but his original program was pieced together using excerpts of Danish folk ballads (table 19).

For the first movement, an Allegro in C minor, Gade selected the opening stanza to a battle song entitled 'Turneringen' (The Tournament). Composed of sixty-six stanzas, this ballad tells the story of a duel between two warriors. Gade's source for the ballad was *Udvalgte Danske Viser*, the folk-song anthology he consulted when composing the dramatic music *Agnete and the Merman* and the concert overtures *Echoes of Ossian* and *St. Hans' Evening Play* (see chapters two, six, and seven). We can only speculate why Gade chose 'Turneringen' as his musical inspiration. Perhaps he was struck by the powerful visual imagery of the opening stanza:

> They numbered seven plus seven-times-twenty,
> those who marched out from the field,
> and who came to Brattingsborg.
> where they set up their tents.
> It thundered under horses –
> the Danish noblemen, they rode out.[1]

The history of 'Turneringen' might have also interested Gade. According to the editorial comments in *Udvalgte Danske Viser*, 'Turneringen' was believed to be one of Denmark's oldest and most well-known ballads.[2] In addition to referring to a famous duel in 1284 between the Kings of Denmark and Sweden (verse 34), the text presents a detailed description of many of the North's most famous ancient heros.

---

[1] 'De vare syv og syvsindstyve/ Der de droge ud fra Hald,/ Og der de komme til Brattingsborg/ Der sloge de deres Tjald/ Det donner under Ros, de danske Hofmænd/ der de udride.'

[2] *Udvalgte Danske Viser* (Copenhagen: Abrahamson, Nyerup & Rahbek. 1812–1814), vol. 1, 360–67, 'det er fast den ældste Kjæmpevise, som af Arildstid herindtil haver været meget brugt i Danmark.'

Table 19
Original program for Symphony No. 1 in C minor

	Symphony (based on battle-song texts)
C minor	

1.   <u>Introduction</u>

2. All°.   They numbered seven plus seven-times-twenty,
                those who marched out from the field,
                and who came to Brattingsborg.
                where they set up their tents.
                It thundered under horses –
                the Danish noblemen, they rode out.

x
(2)(3)   Herr Olaf, he rides far and wide
(C Maj.)   To invite everyone to his wedding.
                Four are dancing, Five are dancing.
(A-flat Maj.)   The Elf King's daughter stretches out her hand.

x
(2)(3) Andantino. (E-flat Maj.)
                Svend Vonved,
                he played ornaments on the Golden Harp.
chorus: The summer and the meadow go so well together.
(<u>Viol. w/ chorus</u>)

                I went out one summer day to hear
Duet between   birdsong, which touched the heart,
Fl. and Cl.   in the deep valley,
w/ Harp accomp. among the nightingales.

Wind inst. in   The moment my dear sweetheart was found,
choral refrain. on all sides of the forest
                song and blossoms emerged
                from both the deep valley
                and the nightingales. (<u>Legend</u>)

Turning our attention to the program for the second movement, we recognize an abrupt change in mood – instead of borrowing stanzas from a battle song, Gade quoted excerpts from the first and second stanzas of the love ballad, 'Elveskud' (Elf-shot):

> Herr Olaf, he rides far and wide
> To invite everyone to his wedding.
>
> Four are dancing, Five are dancing.
> The Elf King's daughter stretches out her hand.[3]

Composed of twenty-five stanzas, this ballad, also found in *Udvalgte Danske Viser*, relates the tragic story of Herr Olaf and his encounter with the Elf-King's daughter.

The program for the third movement initially contained excerpts from two ballads: the battle song 'Svend Vonved,' concerning an idle Prince forced to go out into the world to prove his worth; and the love ballad 'Asbjørn Snares Frieri til Kongens Datter' (Asbjørn Snare's proposal to the King's daughter), a humorous account of a young man's courting methods. Gade no doubt knew both these ballads from *Udvalgte Danske Viser*. Eventually, however, he became disenchanted with the third movement's program. Crossing out the excerpts from *Udvalgte Danske Viser*, he replaced them with the first and last verses of a contemporary love song entitled 'Jeg gik mig ud en Sommerdag at høre' (I went out one summer day to hear):

> I went out one summer day to hear
> Birdsong, which touched the heart,
> In the deep valley,
> Among the nightingales.
>
> ———
>
> When you, my heart's dearest, were found,
> On all sides of the forest
> Song and blossoms emerged
> From both the deep valley
> And the nightingales.[4]

---

[3] 'Hr Olaf han rider saa vide./ Alt til sit Bryllup at byde./ Der dandse fire, der dandse fem/ Elvekongens Datter rækker Haanden frem.'

[4] 'Jeg gik mig ud en Sommerdag at høre/ Fuglesang, som Hjertet monne røre,/ I de dybe Dale,/ Blandt de Nattergale./ – Da nu min Hjertenskjæreste var funden,/ Sang og blomstrede det rundt i Lunden,/ Baade dybe dale,/ Og de Nattergale.'

'Jeg gik mig ud en Sommerdag at høre' was written by Henrik Hertz (1798–1870), and Gade no doubt knew the work from Hertz's anthology, *Samling af danske Sange. Udgivet af Selskabet for Trykkefrihedens rette Brug* (*Collection of Danish Songs. Published by the Society for the Correct Use of Freedom of the Press*).[5]

When Hertz compiled his *Samling af danske Sange* in 1836, he borrowed a number of songs from previously published sources, often rewriting them in accordance with his own German-romantic tastes. 'Jeg gik mig ud en Sommerdag at høre' is one such example. The original version, entitled 'Den danske Kjæmpevise' (The Danish Battle Song), was written by N.F.S Grundvig (1783–1872), the nineteenth century's foremost representative of Danish nationalism. Gade no doubt knew this version from its appearance in volume five of *Udvalgte Danske Viser*.

In its original form, 'Den danske Kjæmpevise' served as an ode to the beauty of Denmark's land and language. In the hands of Hertz, however, the ballad took on quite a different character. Eliminating Grundvig's nationalistic sentiments and political ideals, Hertz transformed the work into a naturalistic love ballad.

Gade's selection of the Hertz text is important. Not only does it inform us of the composer's literary preferences, but it also reveals important insights concerning his programmatic intentions. Gade's use of Hertz's text indicates that his initial motivation came from the lyrics, not the melodies, of the various folk songs. *Udvalgte danske Viser* served as the source for all the excerpts in Gade's program, excepting 'Jeg gik mig ud en Sommerdag at høre.' Yet the original version of this song, 'Den danske Kjæmpevise' was set to the same melody in *Udvalgte danske Viser*. If Gade had been considering only the melodies for inspiration, there would have been no need to quote Hertz's text. In addition, his rejection of Grundvig's patriotic 'Den danske Kjæmpevise' suggests that nationalistic sentiments were not the primary inspiration behind his program for the C-minor Symphony.

It is difficult to determine when Gade began composing the music to his symphony. Evidence shows that progress was slow. A letter written by Clara Schumann to Robert during her concert stop in Copenhagen describes the piece as no more than a 'work in progress' in March 1842.[6] In later letters Clara mentions numerous meetings with Gade and briefly remarks on the compositions they played for one another. The symphony is not mentioned. This is not surprising; Gade was only in the primary stages of composition at the time. In fact,

---

[5] Henrik Hertz, *Samling af danske Sang. Udgivet af Selskabbet for Trykkefrihedens rette Brug* (Copenhagen: Qvist, 1836).

[6] 'Er hat jetzt eine Symphonie in Arbeit – ich will mir etwas daraus vorspielen lassen.' The letter is dated 24 March 1842. Litzmann, *Clara Schumann Ein Künstlerleben nach Tagebüchern und Briefen*, vol. 2, 48.

the sketches for the work show that a rudimentary score of the first three movements was not finished until 1 August 1842.[7] There is no trace of the fourth movement; it must have been completed at an even later date.

Sketches show that Gade began formalizing the general layout of the symphony in July 1842, and even at this early stage, we see that he had already begun to stray from his original program. The second movement, initially planned in C major and A-flat major, was written instead in C major and A minor, and the third movement was changed from E-flat major to F major. In addition, Gade expanded his program to include another battle song, 'Kong Valdemars Jagt' (King Valdemar's Hunt). Based on a text by B.S. Ingemann, this ballad tells the story of Valdemar IV (1340–74) and his insatiable lust for hunting. The ballad first appeared in 1816,[8] but it was not set to music until 1838, and then by Gade himself (ex. 8:1). It was published in 1840 in A.P. Berggreen's *Melodier til de af 'Selskabet for Trykkefrihedens rette Brug' udgivne fædrelands-historiske Digte* (Melodies to historic national poems published by the *'Society for Freedom of Press'*).[9]

Example 8:1. Gade's 'Kong Valdemars Jagt.'

---

[7] DkB: Gade Saml. C II 6.

[8] B.S. Ingemann, 'Kong Valdemars Jagt' (Et sjællandsk Folkesagn), *Julegave, en Samling Digte* (Copenhagen, 1816), 37–42.

[9] A.P. Berggreen, *Melodier til de af 'Selskabet for Trykkefrihedens rette Brug' udgivne fædrelandshistoriske Digte* (Copenhagen, 1840).

Gade used the melody to 'Kong Valdemar's Jagt' as the basis for the cyclical structure of his symphony. In the first movement, the melody appears twice in its original form: first as the slow introduction and then as the primary theme (ex. 8:2a). An A-flat-major version of the tune's opening triadic motive serves as the secondary theme (ex. 8:2b). This triadic motive then reappears in the scherzo, first in C major and then in A minor (exx. 8:2c-d), and in the fourth movement's primary theme (ex. 8:2e). Finally, the original tune reappears briefly in the C section of the fourth movement rondo (ex. 8:2f).

Example 8:2. Symphony No. 1 in C minor.

a) first movement, measures 1–8.

b) first movement, measures 124–26.

c) second movement, measures 9–12.

d) second movement, measures 37–40.

e) fourth movement, measures 17–19.

f) fourth movement, measures 90–104.

Previous scholars have claimed that Gade's quotation of 'Kong Valdemar's Jagt' reflects a national tone; the minor tonality, 6/8 time signature, open fifths and octaves, and phrygian cadence on the fifth all could be viewed as elements of a Danish style.[10] But grasping the musical substance of a national tone is often difficult. Dahlhaus explains:

> The open fifths of a bagpipe drone, the Lydian fourth, a rhythmic-agogic pattern – how often have these been claimed as attributes of Polish music only to appear Scandinavian in other contexts.[11]

In addition, we must remember that 'Kong Valdemars Jagt' was not a popular folk song in the early 1840s, but rather a contemporary composition written by Gade and published in a single anthology. In 1843, the year the symphony was first performed, few Danes would have recognized the tune or associated it with nationalist sentiments. Consequently, Gade must have had another reason for using the melody.

Closer study of the symphony's first movement reveals that Gade's interest in 'Kong Valdemars Jagt' was not limited to its melody; the text also served as a source of inspiration. 'Kong Valdemar's Jagt' is similar in mood to the battle song, 'Turneringen,' used by Gade for the first movement's original program. But 'Kong Valdemar's Jagt' contains a greater array of visual imagery. The ballad opens with a romantic description of the landscape surrounding the ruins of Valdemar's castle:

On Zealand's fair plains
Along the Baltic shore,
Where woodlands form a wreath
'Round the meadow's flowerbeds,
Where silver springs now drift
By the base of ancient ruins,
There, in olden times,
Proudly stood a royal home.[12]

---

[10] Niels Martin Jensen, 'Niels W. Gade,' 248–49. Oechsle, *Symphonik nach Beethoven*, 65–73.

[11] Carl Dahlhaus, *Nineteenth-Century Music*, trans. J. Bradford Robinson (Los Angeles: University of California Press, 1989), 38.

[12] 'Paa Sjølands fagre Sletter,/ Ved Østersøens Bred,/ Hvor Skoven Krandse fletter/ Om Engens Blomsterbed,/ Hvor Sølverkilden glider/ Nu ved Ruinens Fod,/ Der stolt, i gamle Tider,/ En Kongebolig stod.'

Gade appears to have reproduced this tranquil atmosphere in his slow introduction. The piece opens with a gentle, rolling melody in the lower strings. This is followed by a soft echo in the violins and a plaintive hunting call played by a lone horn.

As Ingemann's text continues, we are transported into the past. The castle is intact, and King Valdemar and his men terrorize the countryside:

> (stanza four)
> Horn and bow were taken up,
> The stallion leapt forth with the king
> And snorted in the blaze of the sun
> And swung himself towards the forest;
> With a jovial crowd of hunters
> flying on white steeds,
> The King often rode without caution
> Over stumps and hillocks.[13]

Once again, Gade appears to have been inspired by Ingemann's text (ex. 8:3). The tranquility of the slow introduction is shattered by an outburst of hunting horns (mm. 40–44), followed by the tempestuous primary theme, whose dotted rhythms in the strings and bassoons bring forth images of raging horses, leaping and snorting across the landscape.

In Ingemann's text, Valdemar and his men are compared to the strong north winds of a blustry storm:

> (stanza five)
> Like strong north winds
> The Hunters rode forth;
> Then Roe deer and buck flew
> Like leaves in the trail of a storm;
> But at the sound of the hunting horn
> Their fervent joy
> Caused them to forget to pray
> And honor the song of the Mass.[14]

---

[13] 'Da rørtes Horn og Bue,/ Med Kongen Hengsten sprang, Og fnøs i Solens Lue,/ Og sig mod Skoven svang;/ Med lystig Jægerskare/ Paa hviden Ganger fløi/ Den Konge tit med Fare/ Henover Stub og Høi.' Ingemann's leaping stallions and mighty hunters evoke a visual image similar to that of the Danish noblemen and their thundering horses in 'Turneringen.'

[14] 'Som stærke Nordenvinde/ De Jægere henfoer,/ Da flyede Raaer og Hinde/ Som Løv i Stormens Spor;/ Men i den raske Glæde, Ved Jægerhornets Klang,/ De glemte tit at bede,/ Og høre Messesang.'

Example 8:3. Symphony No. 1 in C minor, first movement, measures 50–60.

Example 8:4. Symphony No. 1 in C minor, first movement, measures 81–88.

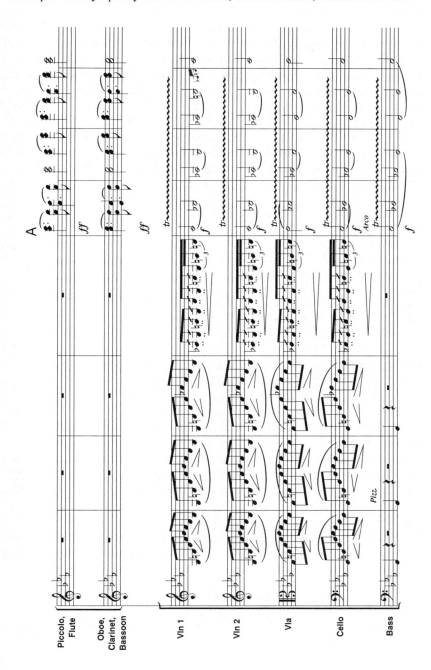

Gade captures this image in measures 81–100 (ex. 8:4). Here rolling arpeggios mirror roaring northern winds (mm. 81–84), and a tremolo string accompaniment (mm. 85–99) echos the turbulence of a storm. Gade foreshadows this scene in measures 28–44 with rumbling thunder rolls played on the tympani.

Whether Gade took any additional inspiration from Ingemann's text is unclear. The narrative continues by describing the turmoil caused by Valdemar and his men: they disrupt church services, destroy property, and terrorize the local peasants. Finally, a bishop confronts the King and threatens excommunication if the hunts do not stop. In a fit of anger, Valdemar determines his fate by replying: 'If I could spend eternity hunting, I wouldn't need our heavenly father!'[15] Could Gade's alternation of the folk tune's character from slow and peaceful to savage and fierce be a metaphor for Valdemar's conflict with the Bishop and peasants? It is difficult to say. But the stormy conclusion of the first movement was likely inspired by the last stanza of Ingemann's text:

> On horses of white,
> One sees the King ride,
> So pale in the Night,
> With a host of ethereal huntsmen.
> Thus it is said
> That he must pay for his malice
> And wait for the Kingdom of God
> And the Day of Final Judgement.[16]

Gade's second movement, a scherzo in C major, also appears to have been inspired by a popular narrative – in this case, the love ballad 'Elverskud.' As Herr Olaf rides into the countryside to distribute invitations to his wedding, he is suddenly confronted by the Elf-King's daughter and her entourage. She tries to seduce him, offering expensive gifts in exchange for his affection. But he resists her advances and remains true to his future bride. Enraged by Herr Olaf's rejection, the Elf-King's daughter curses him with 'disease and illness' and sends him away. Once home, Herr Olaf retires to a nearby grove to die; his bride-to-be joins him there. The next morning two corpses are carried away alongside the lifeless body of Herr Olaf: that of his bride, and that of his mother, who has died of a broken heart.

Gade's scherzo is constructed of two contrasting themes. I have labeled these A and B. Theme A, an *Allegro risoluto* in C major, no doubt represents the

---

[15] 'Fra Paven Troen bragtes,/ Den kan han faae igjen;/ Hvis her jeg evig kunde/ Ved Jagten fryde mig,/ Jeg vilde ei misunde/ Vor Herre Himmerig.'

[16] 'Paa Gangeren den hvide,/ Med luftig Jægerhær,/ Man seer da Kongen ride/ Saa bleg i Natten der;/ Saalunde, mon man sige,/ Han bøde maa med Nag,/ Og vente paa Guds Rige,/ Og Dommens store Dag.'

spirited character of Herr Olaf (ex. 8:5). Note the galloping triplets in the strings – an obvious reference to the ballad's first line: 'Herr Olaf, he rides far and wide.'

Theme B, *Meno Allegro*, represents the Elf-King's daughter and her dancing entourage (ex. 8:6). Here Gade was obviously influenced by Mendelssohn's *A Midsummer Night's Dream* Overture: the long, evocative tones in the upper woodwinds (mm. 87–94) and animated dance in the first violins (mm. 95–106), bears a strong resemblance to Mendelssohn's spirited fairy music.

Turning our attention to the thematic layout of the movement, we see that it parallels the narrative structure of the ballad (table 20). The alternation of themes A and B in measures 1–260 mirrors Herr Olaf's dialogue with the Elf King's daughter. She tries to seduce him (theme B in A minor), but Herr Olaf stands firm (theme A in C major). Measures 261–64 (again theme A, this time in A minor) foreshadow Olaf's death. The Elf-King's daughter's curse is portrayed in measures 265–96 (theme B in E major). This is followed by Herr Olaf's fatal illness (mm. 297–308), signified by the return of the A theme in a slowed tempo and minor tonality. A final statement of the Elf-King's daughter's theme (B) is heard in measures 309–28 and is followed by Herr Olaf's death (theme A in A minor) in measures 329–40. The movement concludes with an allusion to theme A in the key of C major, a symbol of Herr Olaf's triumphant reunion with his bride after death.

As mentioned earlier, Gade had trouble defining the program for his third movement. After discarding excerpts from two different folk ballads, he finally decided on the first and last stanzas of a contemporary love song. He then added these notes concerning orchestration: 'duet between flute and clarinet with harp accompaniment. Wind instruments in choral refrain.' But he never realized these plans in the music: the movement has no harp part, and the only duets involve cello, flute, oboe, and/or violin.[17]

At the bottom of his program Gade added a cryptic memo: 'Legend.' Perhaps this refers to the nightingales mentioned in the ballad's refrain. The bird was a popular topos in nineteenth-century literature, and many legends arose concerning its melancholy song and magical powers.[18] Although we can only conjecture about the inspiration behind Gade's third movement, it seems likely that the lyrical, principal theme is a reflection of the ballad's 'Birdsong, which touched the heart' (ex. 8:7).

---

[17] The closest Gade comes to realizing this orchestration is in theme B of the scherzo: Here a duet between the flute and clarinet is accompanied by broken arpeggio patterns in the strings.

[18] We know from other compositions that Gade was intrigued by the nightingale; in December 1848 he published a song entitled 'Die Nachtigall' in *Julehilsen til Store og Smaae fra Danske Componister* (Copenhagen: Lose & Delbanco). The text to this song is similar to Hertz's, in both the song of the nightingale brings young lovers together.

Example 8:5. Symphony No. 1 in C minor, second movement, measures 1–12.

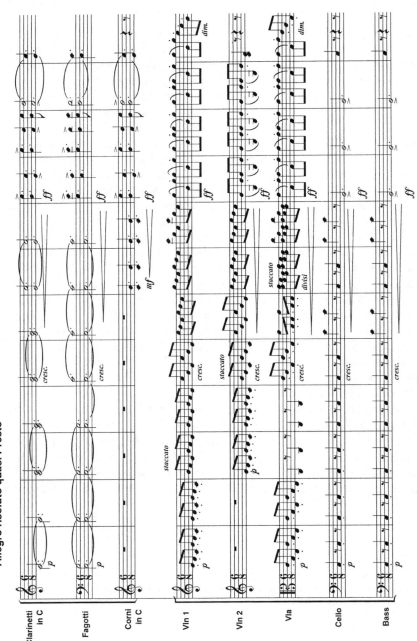

Example 8:6. Symphony No. 1 in C minor, second movement, measures 87–98.

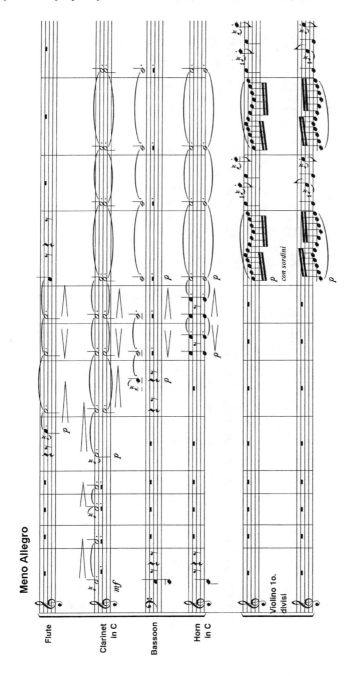

Table 20
Outline of Scherzo (second movement)

SECTION:	A	B	A	B	A	B	A¹	B	A
MEASURE #:	1–86	87–139	140–97	198–230	231–64	265–96	297–308	309–28	329–87
KEY:	C	a	C	a	C a	ECB	e	a	a C
NARRATIVE:	Dialogue between Olaf and Elf-King daughter					The curse	Olaf's illness		Death & Reunion

Example 8:7. Symphony No. 1 in C minor, third movement, measures 1–8.

No doubt in the finale of his symphony Gade had Beethoven in mind. No program survives for this movement, but the C major tonality and triumphant character of the opening theme conjures up Beethoven's Fifth Symphony. The second theme, entering in measure 90, resembles a battle hymn or chorale (ex. 2f). Could this be an homage to Beethoven's Ninth? As Jensen notes, the theme's common opening – step-wise motion down a fifth – brings various musical models to mind: the final phrase of 'Kong Valdemar's Jagt,' Gade's folk-song setting of 'Tordenskiolds Vise,'[19] and Johan Crüger's chorale *Jesu, meine Freude*.[20]

But the strongest influence on this theme was likely the first movement of Schubert's 'Great' C-major symphony.[21] Gade appears to have been influenced by Schubert's use of mediant relationships. In Schubert's first movement, the shift to the dominant G major is thwarted by the entry of the E-minor oboe melody in parallel thirds. In the second theme of Gade's finale, a similar mediant relationship is found: the second theme wavers between the mediant E minor and dominant G major. Schubert's symphony was discovered by Schumann in 1839, and it was premiered at the Gewandhaus by Mendelssohn on 21 March the same year. Although the extent of Gade's knowledge of Schubert's symphony before 1841 is not known, he likely came in contact with the piece through his close friend, Carl Helsted, who was traveling through Germany in 1839. Helsted visited Schumann shortly after the symphony's discovery and attended the premiere in March. He made a habit of keeping his friends in Copenhagen abreast of the latest musical news. No great leap of faith is needed to imagine that Helsted described the events surrounding the discovery of Schubert's symphony in his letters home. It is even possible that he sent excerpts and/or detailed descriptions of the work to his

---

[19] Published in volume four of Berggreen's *Folke-Sange og Melodier*.

[20] Danish title: *Gud skal alting mage*. As Jensen, 'Niels W. Gade,' 251 notes, a reference to Robert and Clara Schumann might also lie behind this theme; similarities can be found in both the opening theme of Robert's C-Major Fantasy, Op. 17 and Clara's theme in the slow movement of Robert's *Concert sans Orchestre*, Op. 14.

[21] Schumann noticed the influence of Schubert on Gade's C-minor Symphony. In an article about Gade he wrote: 'in der Symphonie erinnert manches an Franz Schubert.' *NZfM* 20 (1 January 1844): 2.

friends in the Copenhagen Davidsbund. News of Schubert's symphony no doubt also reached Gade through the *Neue Zeitschrift für Musik*.[22]

On the whole, the musical tone of Gade's first symphony reflects a tension between Danish and German elements. Gade used Danish ballad texts as inspiration for the symphony's various movements, but he fell under the sway of German-Romantic models – i.e. Beethoven, Mendelssohn and Schubert – when fashioning the work's music. In addition, Gade based his symphony on 'Kong Valdemars Jagt' – a folk ballad dating from 1816, which was first set to music in 1838 by Gade himself. Previous scholars have viewed Gade's quotation of this tune as proof positive of his intention to create a national tone. But this hypothesis begins to crumble when we realize that when Gade composed the symphony in 1841/2, few Danes would have recognized this tune or associated it with nationalistic sentiments. In short, Gade's use of a literary program and his quotation of 'Kong Valdemars Jagt' more than likely reflect the creation of a personal style, not a national tone.

We know from records in the archives of Copenhagen's Music Society that Gade submitted a score of his symphony to the Society in late August 1842. On 1 September, the symphony was brought up for review at a meeting of the Society's board of administrators. It received a cool reception. On the whole, the administrators felt that 'everything' about the work 'was too German.'[23] Nonetheless, the symphony was included on a list of possible selections for the upcoming concert season. Two weeks later, 15 September, the Society's administrators met again to determine the program for the next concert. After deciding on Spontini's *The Vestal Virgin* and Haydn's *The Seasons*, the members were asked to select a symphony. According to the minutes for this meeting, the vote was tied between Beethoven's *Pastoral* Symphony and the symphony by Gade. Consequently, the final decision was left to the discretion of the Society's president, J.P.E. Hartmann. In the end, Gade's symphony was passed over.[24] Frustrated by this decision, Gade tried to get the Society to agree on a later concert date – but to no avail. The premiere of Gade's symphony was repeatedly postponed.[25]

Around this time, during the autumn of 1842, one of Gade's childhood acquaintances, C.C. Lose (the Younger), returned to Copenhagen after an extended stay in Leipzig.[26] Lose had been working in the music publishing

---

[22] Schumann published a review of the symphony in *Neue Zeitschrift für Musik* (1840): 1.

[23] DkB: Musikforeningens Arkiv, kapsel 89, 138r.

[24] This concert was later cancelled due to C.E.F Weyse's unexpected death.

[25] Gade tried to have his symphony performed at Weyse's memorial concert, but the society viewed Beethoven's *Eroica* as a more appropriate choice. In autumn 1842 the Society started a new concert series. Four concerts were planned, but, once again, no place was found for Gade's symphony.

[26] H.V. Schytte, 'Gades Ossian-ouverture,' *Programmet* (1902/03): 14.

business there for several years, and he told the disgruntled Gade that an interest in his compositions had begun to take root in Germany.[27] Leipzig was already well-acquainted with the *Echoes of Ossian* Overture – it had been received enthusiastically by both Euterpe and Gewandhaus audiences [28] – and according to another Dane at Breitkopf and Härtel, H.V. Schytte, Gade's works had piqued the interest of Felix Mendelssohn, who had begun to inquire about more recent compositions.

No doubt encouraged by this turn of events, Gade allowed his symphony to be sent to Conrad Schleinitz, an influential member of the Gewandhaus board of directors, and shortly thereafter it was passed on to Mendelssohn. Enraptured by the work, Mendelssohn wrote to Gade on 13 January 1843:

Honorable Sir!
    Yesterday we had the first rehearsal of your C-minor Symphony, and although you and I don't know each other personally, I can not resist the wish to address you and tell you what an extraordinary delight you have given me with your splendid work, and how grateful I am from my heart for the great pleasure that it has provided me. No work has made a more vivacious, lovely impression on me in quite a long time. With every bar I became ever more astonished and felt all the more at home. That is why I today feel the need to express my thanks for so much pleasure and to say to you how much I admire your marvelous talent, and how much this symphony – the only one of yours of which I am presently familiar – makes me greedy for all earlier and later works! And since I hear you are so young, I look forward to the later works, with the same expectation that I greet in such a lovely [symphony], for which I can now already thank you, just as I did for the pleasure you gave to me yesterday.
    We will have more rehearsals of your symphony, and in just 3–4 weeks we will perform it.... Herr Raymund Härtel told me that rumor has it that you will be coming here yourself this winter. Would that such is the case, and that I could personally express my thanks and deep respect in a manner that is better and clearer than these empty, written words! Whether we get to know one another or not, I ask you to please look to me as one who will follow all your work with devotion and interest, and as one to whom the encounter with an artist such as you and an artwork such as your C-minor Symphony is the greatest and most

---

[27] Lose assured Gade that his name 'would soon be a brilliant name outside Denmark.'
[28] Gade's overture was premiered in Leipzig by the Euterpe Orchestra on 18 January 1842 under the direction of J. Verhulst. After hearing reports of this concert's success, Mendelssohn decided to perform the work at the Gewandhaus. This second concert took place on 5 February 1842.

delightful joy. So, receive my thanks once again and permit the absolute, deep respect with which I am respectfully yours,

Felix Mendelssohn Bartholdy[29]

Gade quickly responded:

Copenhagen. 28 January 1843

With what extraordinary pleasure, with what inner, energetic thanks, with what deep-felt admiration, did I read your precious letter. [I feel] joy for having pleased a master, thanks for the rare goodness with which this master has written to an unknown youngster, and admiration for the man who is just as great a person as he is an artist. If I should describe the full extent of my thankfulness, then I must also describe to you the full significance of your letter to me.

I do not need to tell you that my strength and my self-confidence was surely strengthened by such – perhaps all too praiseworthy – recognition; and you certainly must have suspected that a letter from you could not go unacknowledged, and that all would follow the master's opinion.

Indeed, that is just what has happened. You have done me a favor for which I will be eternally grateful. I feel so strong and cheerful, in a way that I have never felt before; and the public has pleased me just as much, as if they are excited about a man who feels so beautiful, so artistic, and so human.

I would like to come to Leipzig soon so that I may say to you, in a deeper and better way, what I have written here. Unfortunately, I cannot show you my gratitude as much as I would like. As a weak sign of my thanks, however, I have given myself permission to dedicate to you my symphony, which has gained worth through your goodness. It is not much, but it is the best that I have. In a short while, I will take the liberty of sending you my other things. You will grant these a benevolent reception. Once again, I offer you my deepest thanks for a letter that has provided me with such a rare pleasure, and [for] the joy of being allowed to show my deepest admiration and devotion to a master from whom I have learned so much.

Niels W. Gade[30]

As we can see from Mendelssohn's next letter, the premiere of Gade's symphony was an overwhelming success:

---

[29] *Briefe aus den Jahren 1833 bis 1847 von Felix Mendelssohn Bartholdy* (Leipzig: J. Rietz, 1865), 369–70. Also published in Dagmar Gade, 27–28. See appendix three for original German.

[30] Dagmar Gade, 29–30. See appendix three for original German.

Leipzig. March 3, 1843

Honorable Sir!

Yesterday, at our 18th subscription concert, your C-minor Symphony was premiered to the lively, undivided joy of the entire audience, who broke into the loudest applause after each of the four movements. After the Scherzo, people were filled with true excitement, and there seemed to be no end to the shouts and hand-clapping. The same happened after the Adagio, and after the finale, and after the first movement – after all the movements! To see the musicians so unanimous, the audience so delighted, and the performance so successful – that was a true joy, as if I had composed the work myself! Actually it was better, for one always sees the mistakes and failures in one's own work most clearly, while in your work I sense nothing but joy over all the delightful beauty. Through last night's performance you have made lasting friends with the entire Leipzig public, who really does love music. From now on no one will speak of your work with anything but the most heartfelt respect and love; and each of your future works will be received with open arms, studied with the most extreme care, and greeted cheerfully by all local music lovers. 'Whoever wrote the last half of the scherzo is a superb master, and we have the right to expect the greatest and most delightful things from him.' That was the general opinion of the orchestra and the entire concert hall yesterday evening – and we are not fickle here. So, you have acquired many life-long friends through your work. Fulfill our wishes and hopes by writing many, many more works of the same type, with the same beauty. And in doing that stimulate our beloved art, for Heaven has given you all that it can give.

Thank you for your kind letter and the good intentions you allow me to perceive there. But more than that, thank you for the joy that you yourself have given me through your work; and believe me when I say that no one can follow your career with more interest nor look forward to your future works with more hope or greater love than

Your respectfully devoted,
Felix Mendelssohn Bartholdy[31]

Gade's success in Leipzig caused quite a stir in Copenhagen. Local citizens wanted to hear the work, but the Music Society still refused to perform it. The situation came to a head on 16 May 1843, when *Fædrelandet* published an attack on the Music Society:

When 'the Music Society' was founded on 6 March 1836, its purpose was: to support the dissemination of superior *Danish* compositions.... Consequently, the society's primary provision is to protect the nation's art [and] to secure recognition for Danish composers by seeking the performance and publication of their works. And it is especially the younger composers – who are not yet famous

---

[31] *Briefe aus den Jahren 1833 bis 1847 von Felix Mendelssohn-Bartholdy*, 374–76. It is also printed in Dagmar Gade, 30–33. See appendix three for original German.

and therefore require encouragement, support, and references – who may expect to receive this from the Music Society.... We have already mentioned in passing that a symphony by Hr. Gade, which has received warm praises from Germany's highest musical authorities, has gone into exile because it was unable to find favor in the eyes of the Music Society's Aeropagus,...[32]

The Music Society refrained from publishing a response to this article, but a formal reply was written by one of the Society's administrators, Edvard Collin, and read at a meeting of the representatives on 2 June 1843. Collin began his reply by criticizing the reporter's quotation of the old 1836 statutes.[33] According to Collin, the society's present goal was to present works of the highest quality, Danish or otherwise. Collin then addressed the issue of Gade's symphony:

> In reference to the too much talked about *Symphony by Gade*,... Gade presented it to me, namely us, in August or September; it was delivered to the Administration to be examined by those who could judge it.... The music experts in the Administration recognized that the symphony was a deserving and promising work, but believed it was inferior to the overture *Echoes of Ossian* in terms of individuality and invention, and [that it] suffered from a certain breadth.[34]

---

[32] *Fædrelandet* 1236 (16 May 1843): 9917–18. '*Musikforeningen* satte sig, da den stiftedes 6te Marts 1836, til Øiemed: at befordre Udbredelsen af fortrinlige *danske* musikalske Arbeider. ... Selskabets Bestemmelse er altsaa først of fremmest at beskytte den indenlandske Konst, at skaffe danske Componister Anerkjendelse ved at søge for deres Arbeiders Udgivelse eller Opførelse, og det er da især de yngre Componister, der endnu ikke have vundet et berømt Navn, og altsaa trænge til Opmuntring, Understøttelse og Anbefaling, der maae vente at finde dette hos Musikforeningen.... I Forbigaaende have vi allerede tidligere omtalt, at en Symphoni af Hr. Gade, som Tydsklands første nulebende musikalske Autoriteter have ydet varme Lovtaler, var gaaet i Landflygtighed, fordi den ikke havde kunnet finde Naade for Musikforeningens Æropagus,...'

[33] The Music Society revised its constitution in 1839. Although the new statutes retained the goal of 'supporting the dissemination of superior Danish musical compositions,' the means through which this goal was attained were changed. Now the Society's central concern was simply the presentation of 'superior quality' music. Naturally this included the performance of works by foreign composers. The Society maintained that by presenting works of the highest quality, they would train the ears of their countrymen and, consequently, raise the nation's standard of music.

[34] DkB: Musikforeningens Arkiv, kapsel 89. 'Med Hensyn til den formeget omtalte *Symphonie af Gade*, ...Gade levered mig Symphonien, nemlig uns, i August eller September; den blev overleveret Adm. til Gjennemsyn af dem, som kunde bedømme den.... Musikkyndige i Administrationen erkjendte, at Symphonien var et fortjenstfuldt og talentfuldt Arbeide, men antage at den i Eiendommelighed og Opfindelse stod tilbage for Ouverturen, Efterklang af Ossian, og led af en vis Bredhed!'

In response to the Leipzig reception of the symphony, Collin came right to the point:

> We cannot rely on Leipzig's taste, which is undeniably one-sided and Mendelssohn-ish. It is not seldom that a composition which is raised to the heavens by Leipzig papers, later sinks into oblivion. That was the case not so long ago with one of Schumann's symphonies,[35] whose weaknesses are now generally recognized.[36]

Despite the Music Society's negative regard for Gade's Symphony, publicity about its success in Germany led to Gade's reception, in Autumn 1843, of a grant from the national foundation, *Ad usus publicos*. He arrived in Leipzig on 30 September and was warmly received by Mendelssohn. Four weeks later, on 26 October, Gade conducted the second performance of his C-minor Symphony at the Gewandhaus – once again to rave reviews:

> The Symphony by *Niels W. Gade* (from Copenhagen), which was greeted with general applause when it was first performed last winter at a Gewandhaus concert directed by *Mendelssohn-Bartholdy*, has experienced just as brilliant a success once again (this time under the direction of the composer himself). Such a success can be earned and received only by the best works. Never before has a composer's first work appeared before us that so clearly bears the stamp of a truly great talent as does this symphony. To judge from it, we can expect only the most excellent, soon perhaps the most masterful, from Herr *Gade*.[37]

The concert's success was even reported in local Copenhagen papers:

> Our countryman, the composer Gade, has now conducted his first symphony at a concert in Leipzig. Every movement was received with stormy applause, and at the end the composer was called forth again and greeted with enthusiastic

---

[35] Collin is probably referring to the first version of Schumann's Symphony in D minor.

[36] DkB: Musikforeningens Arkiv, kapsel 2. 'Vi kunne ikke ganske stole paa den Leipzigske-Smag, der unægtelig en særdeles ensidig og Mendelsohnsk. Det er ikke sjældent hændet, at en Komposition i Leipzigske Blade er bleve hævnt til Skyerenen senere er hedsunken i Forglemmelse. Dette har for ikke længe siden været Tilfælde med en Symphonie af Robert Schumann, hvis svage Sider nu almendelig erkjendes.'

[37] *AmZ* 45 (8 Nov. 1843): 815. 'Die Symphonie von *Niels W. Gade* (aus Copenhagen), welche zuerst *Mendelssohn-Bartholdy* in einem der Gewandhaus-Concerte des letztvergangenen Winters bei uns einführte, und die schon damals mit allgemeinem Beifall aufgenommen wurde, hat auch diesmal, unter Direction des Componisten, einem so glänzenden Erfolg gehabt, wie ihn nur die besten Werke verdienen und haben können. Uns ist noch kein Erstlingswerk eines Componisten vorgekommen, das den Stempel wahrhaft grossen Talents so entschieden an der Stirn trüge, wie diese Symphonie; nach ihr zu schliessen, haben wir von Herrn *Gade* nur Ausgezeichnetes, bald vielleicht das Meisterhafteste zu erwarten.'

fervor. According to reports, we also can expect to hear the symphony now in this country. It will be performed at the Music Society's first large concert, which will probably take place sometime this month.[38]

With the success of the second performance in Leipzig, the Music Society's hands were tied. There was no choice but to present the work in Copenhagen. This performance took place on 28 November 1843. No reviews of the concert were published.[39] But letters written by Gade's family and friends indicate that the performance was flawed.[40] A local paper requested an immediate public performance of the symphony, but to no avail.[41] A second performance did not take place until Gade returned to Copenhagen for a summer holiday in 1846.

Given this state of affairs, one begins to wonder how Gade's symphony attained its present reputation as a nationalistic work. As the next, and final, chapter of this book explains, the transformation of Denmark's reception of the symphony from 'too German' to 'nationalistic' was a long and somewhat convoluted process, controlled by a mixture of political misfortune, educational reform, and scholarly myth-making.

---

[38] *Ny Portefeuille*, 'Theater og Musik.' Volume 4, section 7 (Sunday, 12 November 1843). 'Vor Landsman, Componisten Gade, har nu ved en Concert i Leipzig dirigeret sin første Sinfonie. Hver enkelt Afdeling blev modtaget med stormende Bifald, og til Slutningen blev Componisten endnu fremkaldt og hilset med enthusiastisk Jubel. Efter Forlydende ville vi nu ogsaa herhjemme vente at faae denne Sinfonie at høre, idet den vil blive opført paa Musikforeningens første store Concert, der sandsynligvis vil blive afholdt endnu i indeværende Maaned.'

[39] A private organization, the Music Society could control which concerts received published reviews.

[40] On 28 November 1843 Frederik Høedt wrote: 'Above all I dare not exaggerate when I say that Glæser (the conductor) did not understand you at all.' (Fremfor alt tør jeg uden Overdrivelse paastaa, at Glæser aldeles ikke har forstaaet Dig.) Two days later (30 November) E. Helsted wrote Gade about the dreadful rehearsals that proceeded the concert and then said: 'As you see, dear friend, your symphony did not receive a performance that was what it should have been, or could have been, if the work had been properly rehearsed.' (Som Du ser, kjære Ven, fik din Symphonie ikke en Udførelse, der var, som den burde være, og kunde have været, dersom en virkelig Indstudering havde fundet Sted.) Finally Gade's parents wrote to him on 1 December: 'It [the symphony] went very well, without mistakes, but I heard from others that there were several places that should have been better.' (Den gik meget godt uden nogen Feil, men som jeg hører af andre, skal der dog have været nogle Steder, der kunde have været bedre.) Dagmar Gade, 57–67.

[41] A second performance, this time at the Royal Theater, was scheduled for 12 December 1843. But it appears this concert never took place. No announcements or reviews of this concert appear in local papers, and letters from this period show that Gade was eager to get the score and parts sent back to Leipzig.

Part Three

Gade and Danish Nationalism

Chapter Nine

Gade's National Roots

Paraphrasing Marx, one could say that nationalist ideology only becomes a social force when it manages to seize the beliefs of the masses. But under what conditions and/or circumstances does this seizure of beliefs take place? In truth, there is no set formula for the creation of national identity. Political instability, the weakening of organized religion, the rise of historical consciousness, interest in cultural uniformity and/or racial purity – since World War II all these conditions, and numerous others, have been described as essential ingredients of modern nationalism. But broad, sweeping definitions of nationalist ideologies should not be applied to the whole of Western Europe. Today, there is the danger of viewing nationalism through the lens of late-twentieth-century experience, applying modern ideologies to historical situations. The nation states and global communities so common today were not imaginable in the nineteenth century. Instead, the development of national identities emerged on the local level and was the result of historical and cultural changes specific to circumscribed regions and/or territories. National identity did not arise overnight, but rather evolved at varying rates of speed in different locations. The rise of nationalism in Germany, France and Italy was quite different from the development of nationalistic ideas in smaller, provincial countries. Consequently, the purpose of this chapter will be to look at Denmark specifically. By examining the social and cultural conditions that affected Denmark's national identity in the nineteenth century, I hope to describe, in at least a general manner, the influence Danish nationalism had on the reception of Gade's early orchestral works and the historical circumstances that eventually led to his identification as Denmark's first nationalist composer.

The rise of Denmark's national identity in the nineteenth century appears to have been the result of a shift in ideology from what is perhaps best defined as political patriotism in the first half of the century to cultural nationalism in the second half of the century. Because the terms patriotism and nationalism have taken on much baggage over the last few decades, I should define more accurately my interpretation of these terms in the context of the present study. My idea of patriotism is linked to Jaucourt's definition of *patrie* as it appeared in Diderot's *Encyclopédie*. As Jaucourt explained, *patrie*, often translated in English as country or homeland, originally indicated one's birthplace but was also understood to include the society to which one belonged and the rule of law that insured one's happiness and well-being.[1] Consequently political patriotism in the context of this

---

[1] Rousseau, on the other hand, believed that *patrie* referred to one's native land, irrespective of its political regime. In short, the terms *patrie* and nation often converged in the writings of

study refers to the type of national identity linked to geographic boundaries and political allegiance. In the beginning of the nineteenth century a citizen of Denmark was anyone who was born on Danish soil (this included present-day Denmark, Norway, sections of Northern Germany, the Faroe Islands, the North Atlantic Islands, Iceland, Greenland, and some minor colonies in Guinea and Tranquebar in India) and pledged his allegiance to Denmark's monarch.

Later in the century a second ideology, cultural nationalism, came to the forefront of Danish consciousness. Cultural nationalism is firmly rooted in theories concerning language and cultural heritage. The nation, as explained by Herder, was defined in terms of its ethnic and linguistic features. This ideology was transferred into Danish thought by N.F.S. Grundtvig, a theologian, philosopher, and poet who was the first to describe Denmark's national identity along cultural and linguistic lines.[2] According to Grundtvig, the Danish nation was not demarcated by political and/or geographical borders. Instead the Danish people were unified through a common language (Danish), a common land (the Danish-speaking regions of Denmark), a common history (the Vikings), and a common culture (Norse mythology, folk songs, etc.).[3]

Denmark's shift in ideology from political patriotism to cultural nationalism affected many artistic genres in the nineteenth century, but perhaps the most lucid reflections of Denmark's change in political outlook can be seen in the production of Danish songbooks. Singing was an important political tool in nineteenth-century Denmark, and as the country's national identity changed, the content and structure of Danish songbooks followed suit.[4] During the first decades of the nineteenth century, Denmark was a multi-cultural nation that acknowledged within its borders the use of various languages: Danish, Norwegian, German, Faroese, Frisian, and Icelandic. Political patriotism was paramount to the success of national unity. All regions of Denmark, despite their language and/or cultural heritage, were unified by their allegiance to a single, absolute monarch, and this ideology was reflected in the nation's songbooks.[5] Here Denmark's monarchy

---

Rousseau. For a more detailed description of the history of the term *patrie* see Joseph Llobera, *The God of Modernity: The Development of Nationalism in Western Europe* (Berg: Oxford and Providence: 1994), 151–54.

[2] For an in-depth study of Grundtvig see A.M. Allchin, *N.F.S. Grundtvig: An Introduction to his Life and Work* (Aarhus: Aarhus University Press, 1997).

[3] Grundtvig's ideas concerning Danish nationalism are discussed in: Uffe Østergård, 'Peasants and Danes: The Danish National Identity and Public Culture,' *Becoming National: A Reader* ed. by Geoff Eley and Ronald Grigor Suny (Oxford: Oxford University Press, 1996): 179–202.

[4] For an excellent study of Danish songbooks in the nineteenth century see Hans Kuhn, *Defining a Nation in Song: Danish patriotic songs in songbooks of the period 1832–1870* (Copenhagen: C.A. Reitzels Forlag AS, 1990).

[5] Ibid., 8–9.

served as a symbol of national unity. Pride in one's king represented pride in one's nation. As long as Denmark and its territories were blessed with financial prosperity and peace, political patriotism offered a secure sense of national identity for all citizens. But history has taught us that financial prosperity and military peace are never permanent, and in the first two decades of the nineteenth century, Denmark suffered military and economic crises that laid the groundwork for a shift from political patriotism to cultural nationalism.

Copenhagen was attacked by Great Britain in 1807, and Denmark's Navy, a symbol of national pride, was laid to waste. The following years were plagued by war and economic hardship. In 1813 Denmark declared bankruptcy, and in 1814 Norway seceded under the Treaty of Kiel. In seven short years the nation was brought to its knees. Grundtvig was shocked by these tragedies, and he reacted by producing a series of publications. Influenced by the works of Herder, Goethe, and Sir Walter Scott, Grundtvig sought to rejuvenate the spirits of his worn-torn compatriots through a rediscovery of their homeland's glorious past, when Vikings roamed the seas and Scandinavia was blessed with a pantheon of powerful gods and heroes.[6] For Grundtvig, the glory of Denmark was found in its history and language. With patriotic poems and hymns and publications such as *Udsigt over Verdens-Krøniken* (1812-1817), *Danne-Virke* (1816-1819), *Saxo og Snorre* (1818-1822), *Beowulf* (1820), *Nyaars Morgen* (1824), and *Nordens Mythologie* (1832) Grundtvig initiated an era of literary antiquarianism in Denmark. He believed in the rejuvenating power of folk poetry, and his work in this field inspired the writings of Adam Oehlenschläger and B.S. Ingemann, Denmark's 'Golden Age' poets.[7]

The production of Danish songbooks increased in the 1820s and 30s. This was likely influenced by three events: Denmark's economic recovery in the 1820s, Christian VIII's creation of the Provincial Assemblies in 1834,[8] and the founding of Selskabet for Trykkefrihedens rette Brug (The Society for the Proper Use of the Press) in 1835. Denmark's economic recovery sparked a rise in the production of patriotic songs. Inspired by folk tales and stories of Denmark's history, Danish poets focused on praising the common good (i.e. Denmark's monarchy) and opposed the pursuit of individual desires. With the establishment of the Provincial Assemblies in 1834, patriotic tunes increased again. Christian VIII was a rather enlightened ruler, and under his reforms Denmark was divided into four regional governments: Holstein, Schleswig, Jutland, and the rest of the kingdom. Most of

---

[6] Lorenz Rerup, 'N.F.S. Grundtvig's Position in Danish Nationalism,' *Heritage and Prophecy: Grundtvig and the English-Speaking World,* ed. by A.M. Allchin, D. Jasper, J.H. Schjørring and K. Stevenson (Norwich: The Canterbury Press, 1994), 241–42.

[7] Kuhn, 10.

[8] The king declared his intention to establish the four assemblies in 1831. The legal framework was approved in 1834, and in 1835 the Provincial Assemblies were put into practice.

Denmark viewed the establishment of the Provincial Assemblies as a positive change, but the German duchies of Schleswig and Holstein were displeased. Christian VIII's reforms placed the duchies in separate assemblies and consequently weakened their political and economic unity. With the establishment of the Provincial Assemblies, seeds of discontent were sown among Denmark's German-speaking citizens.

In 1835 Selskabet for Trykkefrihedens rette Brug was founded in reaction to the arrest of C.N. David, editor of the liberal Newspaper *Fædrelandet*. David was charged with criticizing the government, and although he was never prosecuted, many feared that Denmark's freedom of the press was under threat. The society attracted many members: almost 2000 by the end of 1835 and 5000 at its peak in 1840. Its goal was 'folkeoplysning' (educating the people), in this case through the printed word. The society published many works, among them translations of Tocqueville's *Democracy in America* and a life of Martin Luther. Curiously, a number of the society's publications were songbooks. In these collections revolutionary songs from various parts of Europe (i.e. the 'Marseillaise' and Ernst Moritz Arndt's 'Was ist des Deutschen Vaterland') were printed side by side with those by Grundtvig and Ingemann and apparently embraced with equal enthusiasm.[9]

One of the most famous song collections printed by Selskabet for Trykkefrihedens rette Brug was A.P. Berggreen's *Melodier til de af 'Selskabet for Trykkefrihedens rette Brug' udgivne fædrelandshistoriske Digte* (Melodies to National-Historic Poems Published by 'The Society for the Proper Use of the Press') (1840).[10] Of the forty melodies in this collection, twenty-two were composed by Berggreen, and several were written by Gade, the most notable being his setting of Ingemann's 'Kong Valdemars Jagt.'

The 1840s witnessed a renewed interest in traditional folk ballads and the publication of numerous anthologies, including C.E.F. Weyse's *Halvtredsindtyve gamle Kæmpevise-Melodier harmonisk bearbeidede* (A Hundred old Battle Song Melodies Harmonically Reworked) (1840) and Berggreen's *Folkesange og Melodier, fædrelandske og fremmede* (Folk Songs and Melodies: National and Foreign) (1842). Berggreen's anthology was typical for the period. As the title suggests, traditional folk ballads from Denmark were included along with songs from foreign lands, namely Norway, Sweden, Scotland, France and Germany.

---

[9] Kuhn, 12–13.

[10] This volume of melodies was designed as a companion volume to Frederik Fabricius' *Samling af fædrelandshistoriske Digte*, published in 1836 and containing 48 poems on subjects from Danish history, from Thyra Danebrog to King Frederik VI's creation of provincial assemblies in 1831. The poets are mostly contemporaries: Oehlenshläger and Ingemann being the most popular, and each poem is given a brief historical introduction. As Hans Kuhn explains (*Defining a Nation in Song*, 26–27), this collection is basically a gallery of historical figures honored by contemporary poets.

Berggreen's *Folkesange og Melodier* eventually expanded into an eleven-volume series, and in the nineteenth century it was considered the most authoritative Danish source of European folk song. Gade contributed several melodies to the series: a harmonization of the Swiss folk song 'Kuhreigen' for volume one, and arrangements of 'Tordenskiolds Vise' and 'Regnar Lodbroks Dødsang' for volume four. This last arrangement, however, was not used – Berggreen considered it 'too modern' and consequently published his own arrangement instead.[11]

This was the political atmosphere of Gade's formative years. Denmark's national identity was characterized by political patriotism, and there was little conflict between the nation's various cultural communities. Gade moved to Leipzig in 1843 and remained there until 1848. During this five-year period, Denmark's national identity was weakened by growing conflicts between Denmark's Danish- and German-speaking communities. In a relatively short stretch of time, political patriotism gave way to a growing interest in cultural nationalism.

The political unrest first initiated in the German-speaking duchies by the creation of the Provincial Assemblies in 1834 came to a head in the mid 1840s. Christian VIII died in January and was succeeded by his son, Frederik VII, who, although loved by his subjects, had a somewhat capricious temperament and only limited political sense. He had barely settled on the throne when the revolution in Paris engendered a chain of liberal revolts in Germany that sparked a similar political upheaval in Denmark's German-speaking duchies. In March, Schleswig and Holstein united and demanded a separate constitution for a Schleswig-Holstein state. The duchies wanted to abandon Denmark and enter into what appeared to be an emerging united Germany. The Danish government responded by declaring that a constitution would be drawn up for the monarchy and Schleswig, but that Holstein would be granted a separate charter. Displeased, the duchies took matters into their own hands. They formed a provisional government and called upon the German states to aid their cause. Soon German and Prussian volunteers reinforced the Schleswig-Holstein forces. What began as a civil war quickly escalated into an international struggle.

With the onset of the Schleswig-Holstein War, Denmark's Danish-speaking citizens rallied around their king in a great upsurge of national sentiment. Youthful volunteers from Denmark, Norway and Sweden banded together in a fight for Scandinavia's heritage. With their national identity threatened (an identity associated with political patriotism), many Danes looked to the teachings of Grundtvig for guidance and, consequently, found a new national identity in Denmark's language and culture. Grundtvig took an active role in the Schleswig-Holstein controversy and soon became an advocate for the pro-Danish forces. On 14 March 1848, he expressed his views concerning Schleswig and Holstein in a

---

[11] Niels Martin Jensen, 'Niels W. Gade,' 218.

lecture that was later published under the title *Frihed og Orden* (Freedom and Order). Here he defined Denmark's borders along cultural lines: 'The Danish land only reaches as far as Danish is spoken and basically not further than to the point where the people will continue to speak Danish.'[12] Grundtvig's goal was to revive, through literature and the arts, a strong faith in Denmark's culture. His dedication to the Danish language took on something of a missionary character in the 1840s, and soon Denmark's writers and artists became examples of the nation's worth.[13] As a byproduct of Grundtvig's ideology, figures such as Bertel Thorvaldsen, Hans Christian Andersen and Niels W. Gade came to be viewed as national heroes, and over the course of several decades some of their works were adopted as symbols of the Danish state.[14]

In the case of Gade, this process of nationalization was hastened by the composer's return to Denmark shortly after the outbreak of the war. Gade originally planned no more than an extended visit, but political unrest and the danger of traveling convinced him to resign from his posts in Leipzig and remain in Copenhagen.[15] The city embraced Gade – the prodigal son returned from the rancor of Germany – and he soon found himself entrenched in Copenhagen's musical life.

The first Schleswig-Holstein War ended in 1850 with a Danish Victory. Schleswig and Holstein were reclaimed by Denmark, but they would never be allowed to feel 'Danish' again. Grundtvig's promotion of Denmark's 'native' language and culture had acquired new meaning, a phenomenon reflected in the production of war-time and post-war songbooks.

During the Schleswig-Holstein War, Denmark's songbooks took on the duties of propaganda literature. Danish became the dominating language, and songs from previous publications were recycled and given new shades of meaning. For

---

[12] 'Tale i den Slesvigske Hjelpforening 14/3. 1848,' *Danskeren* I (Copenhagen, 1848): 84–96; G. Christensen and Hal Koch, eds. *N.F.S. Grundtvig, Værker i Udvalg*, vol. 5 (Copenhagen, 1842), 260–61.

[13] For an in-depth study of Grundtvig's participation in Danish politics see: Vagn Wåhlin, 'Denmark, Slesvig-Holstein and Grundtvig in the 19th Century,' in *Heritage and Prophecy: Grundtvig and the English-Speaking World,* ed. by A.M. Allchin, D. Jasper, J.H. Schjørring and K. Stevenson (Norwich: The Canterbury Press, 1994), 243–70.

[14] Curiously, all three artists were forced to leave Denmark in search of recognition early in their careers. Thorvaldsen lived twenty years in Rome and created many of his finest works there. Andersen received little praise from Danish critics during his early years, but was received warmly by Germany and England. Only after winning the approval of foreign readers did Andersen gain acceptance in Denmark. Similarly, Gade moved to Leipzig in 1843 when Copenhagen's Music Society refused to perform his first symphony.

[15] After receiving a draft notice from the *Communlgarden* in Leipzig on 24 June 1848 (DkB: Ny kgl. Saml. 1716, 4°, Gades efterladte papirer), Gade posted a letter on 12 August (stadtarchiv Leipzig: Bestand Gewandhaus, Nr. 207) and resigned from his posts at Leipzig's Gewandhaus and Conservatory.

example, Gade's famous setting of Ingemann's 'Kong Valdemars Jagt' appeared in two political songbooks published in 1849 and 1850. The first, *Viser og Sange for Danske*, was a small book of twenty songs published by Harald Erslev. The first eleven pieces in this collection were classical patriotic songs, including one Norwegian and one Swedish. Five topical songs followed, including an anti-German text by Grundtvig and Ingemann's 'Kong Valdemars Jagt.' The final three songs were based on pan-Scandinavian texts.[16] The 1850 publication, Peter Christian Koch's *Fædrelandske Vise-Bog*, contained twenty-seven songs, the majority of which were dedicated to the Schleswig-Holstein War.[17] In this context the original moralizing tale of 'Kong Valdemars Jagt' was transformed into an ode of Denmark's heroic past.

Conflict between Denmark's Danish and German provinces continued until 1864, when Prussia settled the problem by claiming Schleswig and Holstein in a brief, but demoralizing war. This is when the myth of Gade's promotion of Danish versus German ideals really took root. By this time, the folk-song settings Gade had written as a youth had become staples in the numerous folk-song anthologies published for Danish schools and social organizations. Gade's tunes were now part of the Grundtvigian educational system, and in that capacity they were infused with nationalistic sentiments that originally had not been there. Because Gade used simple folk-like melodies in his early orchestral works, they too came to be viewed as nationalistic. The transformation of Gade's early compositions from their original status as 'German' works to Danish nationalist pieces is perhaps best shown in the reception history of his most popular compositions: the *Echoes of Ossian* Overture, Op. 1 and the Symphony in C Minor, Op. 5.

Curiously, the reception of Gade's early orchestral works as nationalist music began in Germany. When Gade first traveled to Leipzig in 1843, Robert Schumann published a brief biography of the composer in the *Neue Zeitschrift für Musik*. After commenting on Gade's uncanny resemblance to the mature Mozart (the two men were thought to share a similar profile and characteristically thick head of wavy hair) Schumann described Gade's most recent orchestral compositions and commented on the Dane's interest in Nordic culture:

> Our young composer was brought up on the poets of his fatherland; he knows and loves them all. The old fairy tales and sagas accompanied him on his youthful wanderings, and from England's coast Ossian's enormous harp loomed over here. His music shows, especially in his Ossian Overture, a definite, pronounced Nordic character.[18]

---

[16] Kuhn, 46.

[17] Ibid., 49.

[18] R. Schumann, 'Niels W. Gade,' *Neue Zeitschrift für Musik* 20 (1 January 1844): 2. 'Auch unsern junger Tonkünstler erzogen die Dichter seines Vaterlandes; er kennt und liebt sie alle;

In a review of Gade's *Echoes of Ossian* one year later, Schumann discussed Gade's 'national' tone:

> The character, poetic coloring, and a certain somber *national* element make the present overture quite interesting. In reference to this last characteristic the listener admittedly must have a sensitivity for that sort of thing, as for everything national; for it presupposes a certain uniformity in expression and, I would like to say, a coolness in tone.[19]

It should be noted that Schumann's inclusion of these descriptions was not an attempt to distinguish a new national school of composition, instead it was a way of emphasizing Gade's musical genius and individuality. Indeed, Schumann praised Gade for his ability to capture a native spirit. But he also warned the composer against getting caught up in a national style:

> With this is only a wish that the artist does not give in to his nationality, his 'nordic-laden' fantasy, as someone described it, and that he also looks to other spheres of nature for inspiration. One would like that all artists first discover something original, and then shed themselves of it again – like a snake who sheds his skin when the old clothes become too tight.[20]

Clearly the interpretation of Gade's early works as nationalistic pieces originated in Germany. As one of the many rising stars under Mendelssohn's watchful eye, Gade was warmly embraced by German audiences, and his music became a topic of interest among critics. In search of a way to define Gade's fresh poetic style, journalists like Schumann looked to his 'nordic' heritage and eventually began describing his music as nationalistic. But several decades passed before a similar interpretation took root in Denmark. In an effort to track this development, let

---

die alten Märchen und Sagen begleiteten ihn auf seinen knabenwanderungen, und von Englands Küste ragte Ossians Riesenharfe herüber. So zeigt sich in seiner Musik, und zuerst eben in jener Ossians-Overture, zum erstenmal ein entschieden ausgeprägter nordischer Character.'

[19] R. Schumann, *Neue Zeitschrift für Musik* 16 (4 February 1842): 42. '...die vorliegende Ouverture ist durch ihren Charakter, ihre petische Färbung und ein gewisses düsteres *nationelles* Element im hohen Grade interessant. Für die letztere Eigenschaft muß der Hörer freilich, wie für alles Nationelle, den empfänglichen Sinn mitbringen, weil dieselbe eine gewisse Einförmigkeit des Ausdrucks, und ich möchte sagen, Kälte des Tones bedingt.'

[20] R. Schumann, 'Niels W. Gade,' *Neue Zeitschrift für Musik* 20 (1 January 1844): 2. 'Dabei ist nur eines zu wünschen: daß der Künstler in seiner Nationalität nicht etwa untergehe, daß seine "nordscheingebärende" Phantasie, wie sie jemand bezeichnete, sich reich und vielgestaltig zeige, daß er auch in andere Sphären der Natur und des Lebens seinen Blick werfen möge. So möchte man allen Künstlern zurufen, erst Originalität zu gewinnen und dann sie wieder abzuwerfen; schlangengleich häute er sich, wenn das alte Kleid zu verschrumpfen anfängst.'

us examine, in more detail, Denmark's reception of the *Echoes of Ossian* Overture and the Symphony No. 1 in C minor.

The reception history of Gade's *Echoes of Ossian* is fascinating. Although the work was originally designed for German audiences, its significance for Danish listeners began to change shortly after the first Schleswig-Holstein War. Upon Adam Oehlenschläger's death in 1850, Gade was chosen to arrange a memorial concert for the poet at the Royal Chapel. This was a singular honor for the young composer, and he put much effort into the assignment. In an act of reverence to Oehlenschläger's memory, Gade began the concert with his *Echoes of Ossian* Overture – a poignant gesture, linking the passing of Denmark's greatest bard with an illustrious bard from antiquity.

Descriptions of the concert appeared in several Danish papers, and for the first time, Gade was described as a 'national' composer. It should be noted, however, that at this point *Echoes of Ossian* was not considered a nationalist piece. In fact, the question of a national tone in Gade's work did not really enter discussions of his music until the late nineteenth-century.

In 1888 Gade was honored at the first Nordic Music Festival, and *Echoes of Ossian* was performed as one of the featured compositions (fig. 11). According to contemporary reports of the festival, Gade showed little interest in the idea of Danish nationalism. 'There is nothing more to make of it,' he said.[21] Nonetheless, attendees at the festival were moved when Gade mounted the podium and conducted *Echoes of Ossian*. One orchestra member reported:

> To see Gade's shifting facial expressions and to follow the look on his face as he waved the baton in his authoritative way was an experience I will never forget. His face was right above my head, and I had to do nothing more than follow his marvelous expressions. What gripped me in particular was to see his own excitement when the trombones sounded the Ossian motive; his eyes looked as though they beheld something distant and marvelous. There was no doubt that, at that moment, he felt at one with his work.[22]

---

[21] *Dags-Telegrafen*, 9 June 1888.

[22] 'Den store nordiske Musifest 1888: Et Par smaa Erindringer om Niels W. Gade.' *Musik* 1:4 (15 February 1917): 38. 'At se Gade's Minespil og følge hans Ansigtsudtryk, medens han paa sin myndige Maade svang Takstokken, var en Oplevelse, jeg aldrig glemmer. Jeg havde ikke andet at gøre end at følge dets vidunderlige Udtryk. Hvad der navnlig greb mig var at se hans egen Betagelse under Ossian Motivets Basunklange; hans Øjne fik et Udtryk, som skuede de ind I noget fjærnt og vidunderligt. Der var ingen Tvivl om, at han I det Øjeblik følte med og var med sit Værk.'

Figure 11 Niels W. Gade serving as conductor at the 1888 Nordic Music Festival.
(DkB: Photograph Collection)

The Nordic Music Festival of 1888 was the first of many musical events in the late nineteenth century dedicated to the celebration of Scandinavianism in music. Gade's direction of *Echoes of Ossian* was the highlight of the festival. And with this memorable performance, Gade's status as a national composer and his *Echoes of Ossian* Overture were resolutely united.

After Gade's death in 1890, the first scholarly studies of his life and music began to appear. In 1892 Dagmar Gade wrote a biography of her father, and Philip Spitta, the noted Bach scholar, published the first insightful study of Gade's music. Spitta noted a similarity between the primary theme of *Echoes of Ossian* and the folk tune 'Ramund var sig en bedre mand,' but concluded that the similar intervallic pattern of the two melodies was likely coincidental.[23] Indeed, the similarity was never recognized by audiences during Gade's lifetime, and the composer never mentioned 'Ramund var sig en bedre mand' in his composition diary and correspondence. Nonetheless, several twentieth-century scholars have insisted that Gade intentionally used the folk tune in an effort to create a national tone. They have portrayed *Echoes of Ossian* as a keystone of Danish nationalism, a symbol of Denmark's independence from German dominance.[24] Although this argument might be attractive to scholars in search of Danish identity, especially after the Danish-German conflict of World War II, it is misguided and, simply put, distorted by twentieth-century perceptions of national identity and cultural diversity. Gade did not write *Echoes of Ossian* for nationalistic reasons – such motivation would have been out of place in the politically-patriotic Denmark of the 1830s and early 40s. Instead, he designed his overture with an international, i.e. German, audience in mind. Indeed, when Gade composed the sequel to his Ossian Overture, a secular cantata entitled *Comala* in 1846, he fashioned it according to the tastes of Leipzig audiences. *Comala* was received enthusiastically in Germany and later won favor in England as well. But the cantata has never been embraced by Danish audiences. Because *Comala* was written during Gade's stay in Leipzig, it has consequently never been accepted as a nationalistic work, even though it was conceived as a companion piece to *Echoes of Ossian* and makes use of the same melodic material so often associated with the folk tune 'Ramund var sig en bedre mand.'

The reception history of Gade's first symphony is more straightforward. Gade's symphony was rejected by his Danish colleagues in 1842 for being 'too German.' Indeed, in Denmark the symphony did not receive a favorable following until after Gade's return to Denmark in 1848. In the 1850s and 60s, the symphony's primary theme, Gade's melody to 'Kong Valdemars Jagt,' became recognizable to a large segment of Denmark's population due to its inclusion in

---

[23] Spitta, 376.

[24] Mathiassen, 'Ossian Ouverture,' 67–77; Jensen, 'Niels W. Gade,' 244–45; Oechsle, *Symphonik nach Beethoven*, 135–47.

post-war songbooks. With each passing generation, Gade's melody became more deeply ingrained in Denmark's consciousness and more closely associated with cultural nationalism. By the beginning of the twentieth century, Gade's symphony had taken on a nationalistic meaning that the composer could have never predicted.

And so we are left with the question: Are Gade's early compositions nationalistic works? By his own intention – no. Through the transformations wrought by reception history – yes. The unpredictable twists of Denmark's political history in the nineteenth century and the reception of Gade's music by twentieth-century scholars has effectively transformed the perception of the young composer's original intentions. When Gade composed *Echoes of Ossian* and the C-Minor Symphony in the early 1840s, he was trying to appeal to an international, i.e. German, audience. This was recognized by his contemporaries and accepted without comment. But by 1864, writing for a specifically German audience had become an act of cultural treason. Consequently, in the later decades of the nineteenth century new interpretations concerning Gade's connection to musical nationalism arose, and his role as Denmark's leading composer took on new meanings. Young scholars, raised on Danish folk tunes and committed to cultural nationalism, reinterpreted Gade's early works. In the twentieth century this trend continued, when scholars affected by the conflicts of World War II perpetuated the nationalist perception of Gade's music and its 'separateness' from German traditions. Today, with the advantage of hindsight, we can see that the reception history of Gade's works has come to have a stronger effect on our perceptions of the music than the composer's original intentions. Indeed, Gade composed his early orchestral works as expressions of musical 'Poesie.' But history transformed them into symbols of national pride.

Bibliography

Dictionaries, Encyclopedias, and 19th-century Journals

Adresseavisen. Copenhagen. 1891–1909.
Allgemeine musikalische Zeitung. Leipzig. 1798–1848.
Berlinische Musikalische Zeitung. Berlin. 1805–06
Berlingske Tidende. Copenhagen. 1749 ff.
Cecilia. Et Følgeblad til Muth-Rasmussens Musikjournal. Christiana. 1838–39.
Corsaren. Copenhagen. 1840–55.
Danmarks historiens blå bog. Copenhagen: Kraks Legat. 1971.
Dansk Biografisk Leksikon. 3rd Edition. Ed. Svend Cedergreen Bech. 16 vols. Copenhagen. 1979–1984.
A Dictionary of Music and Musicians. Ed. Sir George Grove. 4 vols. London: Macmillan. 1878–90.
Fædrelandet. Copenhagen. 1834–82.
Illustreret Tidende. Copenhagen. 1859–1924.
Intelligensblade. Copenhagen. 1842–44.
Kjøbenhavn Skilderi. Copenhagen. 1786–89.
Kjøbenhavnsposten. Copenhagen. 1827–56.
Musikalsk Tidene. Copenhagen. 1836.
Die Musik in Geschichte und Gegenwart. Ed. Friedrich Blume. 17 vols. Kassel. 1949–86.
Neue Zeitschrift für Musik. Leipzig. 1834 ff.
The New Grove Dictionary of Music and Musicians. Ed. Stanley Sadie. 20 vols. Sixth Edition. London. 1980.
Ny Portefeuille. Copenhagen. 1843–44.
Signale für die musikalische Welt. Leipzig. 1842–1941.
Sohlmans musiklexikon. Ed. Hans Åstrand. 5 vols. Second ed. Stockholm: Sohlmans Förlag. 1975.

Books, Letters, and Articles in Journals

Abrahamsen, Erik. 'Carl Maria von Weber in Copenhagen.' *The Chesterian* (June 1926).
Allchin, A.M. *N.F.S. Grundtvig: An Introduction to his Life and Work*. Aarhus: Aarhus University Press. 1997.
Andersen, Hans Christian. *Agnete og Havmanden* in *H.C. Andersens Samlede Skrifter*. Vol. 11. Copenhagen: C.A Reitzels Forlag. 1878.
---------- *En Digters Bazar*. Copenhagen: Gyldendal. 1944.
---------- *Mit Livs Eventyr*. 2 vols. Copenhagen: C.A. Reitzels Forlag. 1855.
Andersen, Jørgen. 'Fra Homer til Ossian: en skotsk maler i Rom på Abildgaards tid.' *Kunstmuseets Årskrift MCMXC*. Copenhagen: Statens Museum for Kunst. (1990): 55–71.
Anderson, Benedict. *Imagined Communities*. London: Verso. Revised edition. 1991.
Ascani, Karen. 'Den Skandinaiske Forening i Rom.' *Nordisk tidsskrift* (1982): 69–77.
Baggesen, Jens. *Agnete fra Holmgaard*. Copenhagen. 1808.

Barret, Glynn R. 'The Melancholy and the Wild: A Notice on Macpherson's Russian Success.' *Studies in Eighteenth-Century Culture* (1973): 125–35.

Behrend, William. *Niels W. Gade.* Copenhagen: Schønbergske Forlag. 1917.

---------- *Minder om Niels W. Gade. Kendte Mænds og Kvinders Erindringer.* Copenhagen. 1930.

---------- 'Omkring Niels W. Gade.' *Aarbog for Musik* (1922): 55–72.

Bendix, Frits. *Af en Kapelmusikers Erindringer: Miniaturportrætter fra Paullis Tid.* Copenhagen: H. Hagerups Forlag. 1913.

Berg, Sigurd. 'Literatur omkring Niels W. Gade 1843–1950.' *Dansk Musiktidsskrift* 42 (1967): 16–18.

Berggreen, A.P. *C.E.F. Weyse's biographie.* Copenhagen. 1876.

---------- *Folke-Sange og Melodier, fædrelandske og fremmede. Udsatte for Pianoforte.* 4 vols. Copenhagen. 1842–55.

---------- *Samling af Melodier til de af Selskabet for Trykkefrihedens rette Brug udgivne fædrelandshistoriske Digte.* Copenhagen. 1840.

---------- *Sange til Skolebrug.* 5 vols. Copenhagen. 1844.

Blicher, Steen Steensen. *Ossians Digte.* Copenhagen: Reitz. 1807.

Boetticher, Wolfgang. *Briefe und Gedichte aus dem Album Robert und Clara Schumann.* Leipzig. 1979.

Böker, Uwe. 'The Marketing of Macpherson: The International Book Trade and the First Phase of German Ossian Reception.' *Ossian Revisited.* Ed. Howard Gaskill. Edinburgh: Edinburgh University Press. 1991. pp. 73–93.

Bondesen, J.D. *Fortegnelse over Niels W. Gades Kompositioner.* 1886.

Brandes, Georg. *Main Currents in Nineteenth-Century Literature.* (Originally published in Copenhagen (1872–90) under under the title *Hovedstrøinninger i det 19de aarhundredes litteratur.*) 6 vols. London: W. Heinemann. 1924

Bredsdorff, Thomas. 'Nogen skrev et sagn om *Agnete og Havmanden,* hvem, hvornår og hvorfor?' *Fund og Forskning* 30 (1991): 67–80.

Brix, Lothar. 'Niels W. Gade als Klavierkomponist.' *Die Musikforschung* 26 (1973): 22–36.

Brun, Kai Aage. *Dansk Musiks Historie fra Holberg-tiden til Carl Nielsen.* 3 vols. Copenhagen: J. Vintens Forlagsboghandel. 1969.

Bull, Francis. *Nordisk Kunstnerliv i Rom.* Copenhagen: Gylendal. 1960.

Busk, Gorm. *Friedrich Kuhlau.* Copenhagen. 1992.

----------*Kuhlau Breve.* Copenhagen: Engstrøm & Sødring. 1990.

Carpen, Richard. 'Introduction and Editor's Note.' *Niels W. Gade's String Quartet in F Major 'Wilkommen und Abschied.'* Copenhagen: Dan Fog. 1994.

Carpenter, Frederic I. 'The vogue of Ossian in America: A Study in Taste.' *American Literature* 2 (1931): 405–17.

Celenza, Anna Harwell. '*Efterklange af Ossian*: The Reception of James Macpherson's *Poems of Ossian* in Denmark's Literature, Art, and Music.' *Scandinavian Studies* 70 (1998): 359–96.

---------- *Niels W. Gade. St. Hans' Evening Play Overture.* Middleton, Wisconsin: A-R Editions. 2001.

---------- 'Niels W. Gade's "Agnete og Havmanden": Additional source material and a new hypothesis concerning its origin (Part I: The Overture).' *Årbog for Musikforskning* 21 (1994): 45–47.

---------- 'Niels W. Gade's "Agnete og Havmanden": Additional source material and a new hypothesis concerning its origin (Part II: From overture to symphony and dramatic poem).' *Årbog for Musikforskning* 22 (1995): 57–68.

---------- *Unsre Kunst heißt Poesie: The Early Works of Niels W. Gade* (1817–1890). Ph.D. diss. Duke University, 1996.

Christensen, Charlotte. 'Ossian-Illustrationer i Danmark.' *Fond og Forskning* 19 (1972): 7–32.

Christiansen, Asger Lund. 'Gades Strygekvartetter.' *Musik* 1 (1967): 7–9.

Clausen, Karl. 'Den unge Niels W. Gade.' *Dansk sang* 19 (1967): 28–39.

Daas, Q.W.J. *De Gezangen van Ossian in Nederland.* Nijmegen: Gebr. Janssen. 1961.

Dahlhaus, Carl. *Between Romanticism and Modernism.* Translated by Mary Whittall. Berkeley: University of California Press. 1980.

---------- *Foundations of Music History.* Translated by J. Bradford Robinson. Cambridge: Cambridge University Press. 1985.

----------- *Nineteenth-Century Music.* Translated by J. Bradford Robinson. Los Angeles: University of California Press. 1989.

Dal, E. *Nordisk folkeviseforskning siden 1800.* Copenhagen. 1956.

Danmarks gamle Folkeviser. 12 vols. Copenhagen: Akademisk Forlag. 1976

Daverio, John. *Robert Schumann: Herald of a 'New Poetic Age.'* New York: Oxford University Press. 1997.

DeGategno, Paul J. *James Macpherson.* Boston: Twayne Publishers. 1989.

Deicke, Günther ed. *Deutsches Gedichtbuch.* Berlin. 1959.

Denis, Michael. *Die Gedichten Ossians eines alten celtischen Dichters.* Vienna. 1768.

Dörffel, Alfred. *Geschichte der Gewandhausconzerte zu Leipzig vom 25. November 1781 bis 25. November 1881.* Leipzig, 1884. Photographic reproduction published by VEB Deutscher Verlag für Musik. Leipzig. 1980.

Driesen, O. *Der Ursprung des Harlekins.* Berlin. 1904.

Eaton, J.W. *The German Influence in Danish Literature in the 18th Century: The German Circle in Copenhagen 1750-1770.* Cambridge: Cambridge University Press. 1929.

Engelbrecht, Johann A. *Fragmente der alten Hochschottländischen Dichtkunst, nebst einigen andern Gedichten Ossians, eines Scottischen Barden.* Hamburg. 1764.

Evangelist-kristelig Psalmbog, til Brug ved Kirke og Huus-Andacht. Copenhagen: Carl Frid. Schubart. 1798.

Ewald, Johanes. *Ewalds Samlede Skrifter.* Copenhagen. 1919.

Fiske, Roger. *Scotland in Music: A European Enthusiasm.* Cambridge: Cambridge University Press. 1983.

Fog, Dan. *Kompositionen von C.E.F. Weyse: Thematisch-bibliographischer Katalog.* Copenhagen: Dan Fog. 1979.

---------- *Musikhandel og nodetryk i Danmark efter 1750.* Copenhagen: Dan Fog. 1984.

---------- *N.W. Gade – Katalog, En fortegnelse over Niels W. Gades Trykte Kompositioner.* Copenhagen: Dan Fog. 1986.

Foltmann, Niels Bo. 'Kildemateriel til Niels W. Gades Symphoniker. Historisk/Analytisk Gennemgang af Symfoni Nr. 4.' Masters Thesis. Copenhagen University. 1990.

Forner, Johannes. 'Mendelssohn's Mitstreiter am Leipziger Konservatoriums.' *Beiträge zur Musikwissenschaft* 14 (1972): 185–204.

Gade, Dagmar. *Niels W. Gade, Optegnelser og Breve.* Copenhagen: Gyldendalsk Boghandels Forlag. 1892.

Gade, Johannes W. *Omkring Niels W. Gade, Breve fra Fader og søn.* (Hasselbachs Kulturbibliotek nr. 265) Copenhagen: Steen Hasselbalchs. 1967.

Galschiøt, M. *Skandinaver i Rom.* Copenhagen. 1923.

Gaskill, Howard. 'German Ossianism: A Reappraisal?' *German Life and Letters* 42 (1989): 329–41.

---------- 'Introduction.' *Ossian Revisited.* Ed. Howard Gaskill. Edinburgh: Edinburgh University Press. 1991. 1–19.

---------- 'Ossian at Home and Abroad.' *Strathclyde Modern Language Studies* 8 (1988): 5-26.

Gerstenberg, Heinrich Wilhelm. *Briefe über Merkwürdigkeiten der Litteratur*. Schleswig und Leipzig. 1766.

Gillies, Alexander. *Herder und Ossian*. Berlin: Junker und Dünhaupt Verlag. 1933.

Hamburger Kunsthalle. *Ossian und die Kunst um 1800*. Munich: Prestel-Verlag. 1974.

Hammerich, Angul. *Musikforeningens Historie 1836-1886*. Volume II of *Festskrift i Anledning af Musikforeningens Halvhundredeaarsdag*. Copenhagen: Musikforeningen. 1886.

---------- 'Niels W. Gade.' *Die Musik*. III, Vol. 22 (1903/04): 290-301.

Hansen, Finn Egeland. 'Niels W. Gade samlede værker – det hidtil største danske nodeudgivsesprojekt.' *Magasin fra Det kongelige Bibliotek* 5 (1990): 5-18.

Hansen, Kathryn Shailer. 'Adam Oehlenschläger and Ludwig Tiek: A Study in Danish and German Romanticism.' Ph.D. Dissertation. Princeton University. 1978.

Hansen, P. *Den danske Skueplads, Illustreret Theaterhistorie*. 3 vols. Copenhagen: Ernst Bojesens Kunst-Forlag.

Harwell, Anna Hedrick. (See Celenza, Anna Harwell).

Haywood, Ian. *The Making of History: A Study of the Literary Forgeries of James Macpherson and Thomas Chatterton in Relation to Eighteenth-Century Ideas of History and Fiction*. Rutherford: Fairleigh Dickinson University Press. 1986.

H.C. Andersens brevveksling med Edvard Collin og Henriette Collin. Copenhagen: Levin & Munkgaards Forlag. 1933.

Hendricksen, Knud. *Fra Billedmagerens Kalejdoskop*. Copenhagen. 1954.

Herder, Johann Gottfried. 'Auszug aus einem Briefwechsal über Ossian und die Lieder alter Völker.' *Von Deutscher Art und Kunst*. Originally published 1772. Reprint edition, Oxford: Clarendon Press. 1924.

---------- *Herders sämmtliche Werke*. Ed. B. Suphan. Berlin. 1887.

Hertz, Henrik. *Samling af danske Sang. Udgivet af Selskabbet for Trykkefrihedens rette Brug*. Copenhagen: Qvist. 1836.

Hitzig, Wilhelm. *Katalog des Archives von Breitkopf & Härtel, Leipzig. I. Musik-Autographen*. Leipzig. 1925.

Hoffmann, O., Editor. *Herders Briefe an J.G. Hamann*. Berlin. 1889.

Horstmeyer, Rudolf. *Die Deutschen Ossianübersetzungen des XVIII. Jahrhunderts*. Griefswald: Emil Hartmann. 1926.

Ingerslev-Jensen, Povl. 'Et Ukendt Værk af Niels W. Gade.' *Dansk Musik Tidene* (1942): 138-42.

Ingemann, B.S. 'Kong Valdemars Jagt (Et sjællandsk Folkesagn).' *Julegave, en Samling Digte*. Copenhagen. 1816.

Jahrmäker, Manuela. *Ossian: Eine Figur und eine Idee des europäischen Musiktheaters um 1800*. Berliner Musik Studien 2. Cologne: Studio. 1993.

Jansen, F. J. Billeskov. *Den Danske Lyrik*. 2 vols. Copenhagen: Hans Reitzels Forlag. Third Edition. 1985.

Jensen, Niels Martin. *Den danske romance 1800-1850 og dens musikaliske forudsætninger*. Copenhagen: Gylendal. 1964.

---------- 'Dansk nationalromantik: Forsøg til en begreps-og indholdsbestemmelse.' *Musik og forskning* 13 (1987/88): 37-56.

---------- 'Niels W. Gade og den nationale tone.' *Dansk Identitetshistorie III, Folkets Danmark 1848-1940*. Ed. Ole Feldbæk. Copenhagen: C.A. Reitzel, 1992. pp. 188-336.

Johnsson, Bengt. 'Liszt i Danmark.' *Fyens Stiftstidendes Kronik* (26 July 1986).

---------- 'Liszt og Danmark I.' *Dansk Musiktidsskrift* (1962/63): 81.

---------- 'Niels W. Gades Klaviermusik.' *Norsk Musiktidskrift* 9 (1972): 92-100.

Kabell, Aage. 'Sankt Hansaften-Spil.' *Danske Studier* 76 (1981): 32-44.

Kirk, Margit. 'Ossian-Ouverturens Program.' *Dansk Musiktidsskrift* 1 (1940): 1–5.

Kjerulf, Charles. *Niels W. Gade: Til Belysning af Hans Liv og Kunst.* Copenhagen: Gyldendalske Boghandel. 1917.

Krabbe, Niels. 'The Reception of Beethoven in Copenhagen in the 19th Century.' *Music in Copenhagen: Studies in the Musical Life of Copenhagen in the 19th and 20th Centuries.* Ed. Niels Krabbe. Viborg: C.A. Reitzel. 1996.

Krummacher, Friedhelm. 'Gattung und Werk – Zu Streichquartetten von Gade und Berwald.' *Kieler Schriften zur Musikwissenschaft* 26 (Kassel 1982): 154–175.

---------- 'Niels W. Gade und die skandinavische Musik der Romantik.' *Christiana Albertina, Forschungsbericht und Halbjahresschrift der Universität Kiel* 16 (1982): 19–37.

La Pointe, Janice. 'Birth of a Ballet: August Bournonville's *A Folk Tale* 1854.' Ph.D. diss. Texas Women's University. 1980.

Lippstadt, Wilhelm Dietrich. *Oehlenschlägers 'Sankt Hansaftenspil' im Abhängigkeits-verhältnis zur deutschen Literatur.* Borna-Leipzig. 1916.

Litzmann, Berthold. *Clara Schumann. Ein Künstlerleben. Nach Tagebüchern und Briefen.* 2 vols. Leipzig: Breitkopf und Härtel. 1910.

Llobera, Josep R. *The God of Modernity: The Development of Nationalism in Western Europe.* Oxford: Berg. 1994.

Lund Christiansen, Asger. 'Gades strygekvartetter.' *Musik* 1 (1967): 7–9.

Marschner, Bo. 'Den danske symphonis historie 1830–1890.' M.A. Thesis. Århus Universtity. 1969.

Mathiassen, Finn. 'Agnete, Havmanden og Gades "Jugendträume": En indsigelse og et par supplerende bemærkninger.' *Årbog for Musikforskning* 23 (1996).

---------- 'Niels W. Gade og troldtøjet.' *Festskrift Søren Sørensen.* Copenhagen: Dan Fog. 1990.

---------- '*Unsre kunst heisst poessie*: om Niels W. Gades Ossians-ouverture.' *Svensk tidskrift för Musikforskning* 53 (1971): 67–77.

Meisling, Peter. *Agnetes Latter.* Copenhagen. 1988.

---------- 'De sympatiske Havmænd – En lille replik til Thomas Bredsdorff.' *Fund og Forskning* 30 (1991): 81–86.

Moestrup, Jørn and Esther Nyholm. *Italien og Danmark, 100 års inspiration.* Copenhagen: G.E.D. Gad. 1989.

Møller, Dorthe Falcon. *Danske Instrument byggere 1770–1850.* Copenhagen: G.E.D. Gad. 1983.

Der Musikverein Euterpe zu Leipzig 1824-1874. Ein Gedenkblatt. Leipzig: C.F. Kahnt. 1874.

Neiiendam, Robert. *Det Kgl. Theaters Historie.* 5 vols. Copenhagen: Jespersen og Pios Forlag. 1930.

---------- *Michael Wiehe og Frederik Høedt.* Copenhagen: B. Pios. 1920.

Nielsen, Alfred. 'Fortegnelse over Niels W. Gades utrykte Værker i Det kgl. Biblioteks Musiksamling.' *Musikhistorisk Arkiv* 1 (1931): 176–186.

---------- 'Fortegnelse over Niels W. Gades Værker.' *Årbog for Musik* (1924): 60–80.

Nielsen, Bendt Viinholdt. *Rued Langgaard: biografi.* Copenhagen: Engstrøm & Sødring. 1993.

---------- *Rued Langgaards kompositioner: annoteret værkfortegnelse.* Odense: Odense University Press. 1991.

Nutt, Alfred. *Ossian and the Ossianic Literature.* London: David Nutt. 1899.

Nystrøm, Eiler. *Offentlige Forlystelser i Frederik den Sjettes tid.* 2 vols. Copenhagen: Gyldendalske Boghandel. 1913.

Nørlyng, Ole. 'Tonende folkefantasier – biedermeier og folkevise i August Bournonvilles, Niels W. Gades og Johann Peter Emelius Hartmanns ballet *Et Folkesagn.*' *Musik og forskning* 9 (1983/84): 27–67.

Oechsle, Siegfried. 'Die Musik Dänemarks in der deutschen Kritik 1843–1890.' *Vor hundert Jahren: Dänemark und Deutschland 1864–1900.* (Exhibition catalogue 1981): 137–42.

---------- *Symphonik nach Beethoven: Studien zu Schubert, Schumann, Mendelssohn und Gade.* Kassel: Bärenreiter. 1992.

Oehlenschläger, Adam. *Sankt Hansaften-Spil* in *Digte af Adam Øhlenschlæger.* Copenhagen. 1803

---------- *En Skiærsommernats Drøm. Lystspil af Shakespeare.* Oversat af Adam Oehlenschläger. Copenhagen: Brünnich paa Oversætternes Forlag. 1816.

Okun, Henry. 'Ossian in Painting.' *Journal of the Warburg and Courtald Institutes* 30 (1967): 327–56.

Olwig, Kenneth. 'Place, Society and the Individual in the Authorship of St. St. Blicher.' *Omkring Blicher 1974.* Copenhagen: Gyldendal. 1974.

Østergaard, Uffe. 'Peasants and Danes: The Danish National Identity and Political Culture.' *Becoming National: A Reader.* Ed. Geoff Eley and Ronald Grigor Suny. New York: Oxford University Press. 1996.

Overskou, Th. *Den danske Skueplads i dens Historie fra de første Spor af danske Skuespil indtil vor Tid.* 7 vols. Copenhagen: Thieles Bogtrykkeri. 1864.

Pederson, Sanna Florence. 'Enlightened and Romantic German Music Criticism, 1800–1850.' Ph.D. diss. University of Pennsylvania. 1995.

Pelker, Bärbel. *Die deutsche Konzertouvertüre (1825–1865). Werkkatalog und Rezeptionsdokumente.* Frankfurt am Main: Europäische Hochschulschriften, 1993.

Plantinga, Leon. *Schumann as Critic.* New Haven: Yale University Press, 1967.

---------- 'Schumann's Critical Reaction to Mendelssohn.' *Mendelssohn and Schumann: Essays on Their Music and Its Context.* Ed. Jon W. Finson and R. Larry Todd. Durham: Duke University Press. 1984.

Piø, Iørn. *Nye veje til Folkevisen II: DgFT 38, Agnete og havmanden.* Stockholm. 1970.

Ravn, V.C. *Koncerter og musikalsk Selskaber i ældre tid.* Vol. 1 of *Festskrift i anledning af Musikforeningens Halvhundredsaarsdag.* Copenhagen: Musik-foreningen. 1886.

Rerup, Lorenz. 'N.F.S. Grundtvig's Position in Danish Nationalism.' *Heritage and Prophesy: Grundtvig and the English-Speaking World.* Allchin, A.M., D. Jasper, J.H. Schiørring, and K. Stevenson, ed. Norwich: The Canterbury Press. 1994.

Rönning, F. *Rationalismens Tidsalder. Sidste Halvdel af 18. århundrede.* Copenhagen: Schønberg. 1886.

Roos, Carl. 'Øhlenschlæger og Ossian: Et supplement.' *Danske Studier* (1952): 127–29.

Saunders, Bailey. *The Life and Letters of James Macpherson.* London. 1895.

Schiørring, Nils. 'H.S. Paulli og Dansk Musikliv i det 19. Aarhundrede.' *Fund og Forskning* 4 (1957): 98–119.

---------- *Musikkens Historie i Danmark.* 3 vols. Copenhagen: Politikens Forlag. 1978.

Schumann, Robert. *Gesammelte Schriften über Musik und Musiker.* Leipzig. 1854.

Schytte, H.V. 'Gades Ossian-ouverture.' *Programmet* (1902/03): 14.

Skou, C. *Andreas Peter Berggreen.* Copenhagen. 1895.

Spitta, Philipp. 'Niels W. Gade.' *Zur Musik* (1892): 355–83.

Sterk, Valerie Stegnik. 'Robert Schumann as Sonata Critic and Composer: The Sonata from Beethoven to 1844, as Reviewed by Schumann in the *Neue Zeitschrift für Musik.*' Ph.D. diss. Stanford University. 1992.

Søllinge, Jette D. and Niels Thomsen. *De danske Aviser 1634–1989.* 3 vols. Odense: Odensuniversitetsforlag. 1989.

Thrane, Carl. *Danske Komponister. Fire Skildringer.* Copenhagen. 1875.

---------- *Fra Hofviolonernes Tid: Skildringer af Det kongelige Kapels Historie 1648–1848.* Copenhagen: Schønberske Forlag. 1908.

Todd, R. Larry. 'Mendelssohn's Ossianic Manner, with a New Source – "On Lena's Gloomy Heath".' *Mendelssohn and Schumann: Essays on Their Music and Its Context.* Ed. Jon W. Finson and R. Larry Todd. Durham: Duke University Press. 1984.

---------- *Mendelssohn: 'The Hebrides' and Other Overtures.* Cambridge: Cambridge University Press. 1994.

---------- 'Of Seagulls and Counterpoint: The Early Versions of Mendelssohn's *Hebrides* Overture.' *19th Century Music* 2 (1979): 199–206.

---------- 'An Unfinished Symphony by Mendelssohn.' *Music and Letters* 61 (1980): 293–309.

Tombo, Rudolf. *Ossian in Germany.* New York: Columbia University Press. 1901.

Udvalgte danske Viser fra Middelalderen. 5 vols. Copenhagen: Abrahamson, Nyerup & Rahbek. 1812–1814.

van Tiegham, Paul. *Ossian en France.* 2 vols. Reprint Edition. Geneva: Slatkine reprints. 1967.

Warrack, John. *Carl Maria von Weber.* Cambridge: Cambridge University Press. 1976.

Wåhlin, Vagn. 'Denmark, Schleswig-Holstein and Grundtvig in the 19th Century.' *Heritage and Prophesy: Grundtvig and the English-Speaking World.* Allchin, A.M., D. Jasper, J.H. Schiørring, and K. Stevenson, ed. Norwich: The Canterbury Press. 1994.

Weitnauer, Karl. 'Ossian in der italienischen Litteratur bis etwa 1832, vorwiegend bei Monti.' *Zeitschrift für vergleichende Literaturgeschichte* Neue folge (1906): 251–322.

Wessel, Matthias. 'Der Homer des Nordens – Die Ossian-Dichtung in der musikalischen Komposition.' Ph.D. diss. Hochschule für Musik und Theater Hannover. 1992.

Winkel, Juddi. 'N.W. Gades og I.P.E. Hartmanns strygekvartetter set på baggrund af den romantiske strygekvartet i øvrigt, specielt hos Mendelssohn og Schumann.' M.A. Thesis. Copenhagen University. 1975.

Wirnsberg, Georg, ed. *Vom Reichtum der deutschen Seele.* Leipzig. 1928.

Appendix One

Transcription of Gade's Composition Diary

<u>den 31e Juli 1839</u>

<u>Trio for Viol Violonc: & Pianoforte.</u>   B Dur
1.) x Adagio (Introd?) <u>'Wir sitzen so traulich beysammen.'</u>–[1]
    Allegro.   Helten drage fra
1.) //[2] Allegro 4/4___3/4   sin Kjære – Kamp
                             med følelser, og Urog –
    Slut: 1ste deel // og F: Overtalelse og Beden –
                             (Viol: & Cello)
                   <u>Gemacht</u>
                             Standheftig Modstand –
    Slut: 2 Deel.   Farvel.–   han drager afsted

//   (Et Marchtempo toner undertiden iggen
                             men ganske svagt)

2.) Adagio (Des/Es-Dur)   <u>'Komm bald wieder zu uns.</u>
                             <u>Wir haben deiner so lieb.</u>'

2 3.) Scherzo. Capriciøs løbende i Klav: pp (b moll)
                'Es spukt in der Nacht' ///////'
//
Cell & V. //////////////////////////////
Natstykke med farzando. <u>'Wir sitzen</u>
<u>so allein und traumen.'</u> 'So ängtlich
<u>ist die Nacht und so lang, so lang.'</u>

3 4.) Rolig Allº. <u>Es sind so lieblich in</u>
<u>der Hütte.</u> <u>'In der Heimat ist's so</u>
<u>schön.'</u>

---

[1] Undoubtedly a reference to the first line in Wilhelm Müller's poem 'Thränenregen.'
[2] // indicates illegible, crossed-out text.

September 1839)   <u>Sonate for Piano. E moll.</u>

1) <u>E moll</u> (All°)   O Herz, sey endlich stille
                     Was schlägst du so unruh(e)voll?
                     Es ist ja des Himmels Wille,
                     daß ich sie lassen soll!

2) <u>E Dur</u> (Adagio)   Wir wollen es muthig ertragen,
                     So lang nur die Thräne noch rinnt,
                     Und träumen von schöneren Tagen
                     die lange vorüber sind.

3) E moll (Finale)   Kühne Wogen, wildes Leben.
                     Laß den Sturm nur immer brausen,
                     Frischen Sturm im Herzen sausen;-

Septbr. 1839   <u>Quartet: F Major</u>
(NB. June 1840)

  <u>1</u>. Es schlug mein Herz, geschwind zu Pferde!
      Es war gethan [sic.] fast eh' gedacht;
(F.)   – – – –
      die Nacht schuf tausend Ungeheuer;
      doch frisch und frölich [sic.] war mein Muth [sic.]:
      In meinen Adern welches Feuer!
      In meinem Herzen welche Glut!

  <u>2</u>. dich sah ich, und die milde Freude
      floß von dem süßen Blick auf mich;
      – – – –
(B.) Ein rosenfarbnes Frühlingswetter
      Umgab das liebliche Gesicht, –
      – – – –
      – , welch Glück geliebt zu sein werden!
      Und Lieben, Götter, welch ein Glück!

  <u>3</u>. doch ach! schon mit der Morgensonne
      Verengt der Abschied mir das Herz:
      – – – –
      Ich ging, du standst und sahst mir zur Erden,
      Und sahst mir nach mit naßem Blick. –

Octbr:
1839) Agnete og Havmanden (á A rhóll)
         Sinfonie .

  1.) Agnete Længsel ved Havet. (Moderato) C A

  2.) Havfruernes Sang. (Fis moll Andante med Chor af
         Fruentimmerstemmer.) 'Agnete.' Agnete kom! til
         Dur (3 Chor: forskjellige.) (I moll med violi & cello.)
         (Fis Dur – .)

  3.) Agnetes Bryllup. (Scherzo E Dur. 3/4.)

  4.) Vuggevise. (C Dur Moderato eller Andantino.)
         (Clarinetsolo.)   afbrydes af
         Choral, Hvo ikkun lader Herren raade[3] – eller I Jesu-
pp   Navn skal al vor Gjerning skee[4] – synges
         af MandfolkeChor ganske pianissimo –
         (Dies irae, dies illa solvet saecla in favilla).

---

[3] Chorale text from *Evangelisk=kristelig Psalmbog, til Brug ved Kirke og Huus=Andacht*,
Copenhagen: Carl Frid. Schubart, 1798, # 301, p. 167.
    [4] Ibid. #135, p. 81.

Allegro agitato og Rectativ (Clarinetsolo.) –
Fortsættelse af Choralen –

x   attacca
5.) Finale. <u>Agnetes Kirkegang og Død</u>. (a moll)

(Og alle de smaa Billeder, de vendte sig omkring –
 – C Dur. 'O Herre Jesu tilgiv du min Synd'–
 – Og Altertavlen vendte sig og Alteret med den –
 Og Alt med den –
 Sig vendte, hvor hun Øjet
 I Kirken vendte hen. –

 da brast den Armes Hjerte,
 da iisned hendes Blod. –)[5]

(?)Choral: A Dur. '<u>Men du o Forsoner Kjære</u>
       <u>Tilgiver hver angerfuld Synder</u>' –

x   <u>Fine</u>
5.) Finale.———
 Havfruernes Sang (Fruen[s]t:) og Choralsan-
 gen (Mandst:) kalder Agnete.

---

[5] These seven lines come from Jens Baggesen's *Agnete fra Holmegaard* (1808).

[small drawing of a crown]

Novembr
1840)   Ouverture (<u>a moll</u>) (Efter Ossian.)

       – Et Oldtids Quad! Fremfarne Dages Storvæerk! –
       O Lora, dine Bølgers Rislen gjenkalder Fortidens Min-
       de.– Tre gamle Graner hælde fra Højens Isse; grøn
       er den snævre Slette ved dens Fod. – To Stene halv
(<u>a</u>.)   sjunkne i Jorden, vise deres mosklædte Rygge. –
       Et Oldtids Quad! Fremfarne Dages Storværk! –
       – Saa vare Bardernes Ord. –[6]
       Fortids Minde kommer ofte liig Aftensolen, til
       min Sjæl.[7]--<u>Med eet frem</u>bryde vore
       Barders Sange <u>paa: Kæmperne</u> sloge deres Skjolde.–[8]

       – Vidt fremvælter Kampens rædsomme, buldrende
x   mørke Sky, liig Taage, der strømmer ud over
(<u>a</u>.)   Dalen, naar et Uveir indhyller Himmelens
(forte) tause Sol. <u>Foran fremskrider Hærføreren (Tromba</u>
       liig den vrede Aand foran Skyen. – Fjernt paa
       Heden lader Carril Stridshornet lyde. –[9]

       – Jeg laae i Borgen om Natten. – Halv tillukte vare mine
       Øine. Liflige Toner kom til mit Øre, liig de stigende
       Luftninger der flyve hen over den mørkskyggede Eng.
       Det var <u>Selma</u> der[10] istemte det natlige Quad; thi hun
(F.)   vidste, at min sjæl var en strøm, som flød ved lif-
       lige Toner.[11] – Syng du søde Stemme, for du est liflig
       og lader min Nat henrinde i Fryd.[12]

---

[6] The excerpts in Gade's Ossian program were taken from *Ossians Digte. Oversatte af Steen Steensen Blicher*. 2 vols. (Copenhagen, 1807–09). This excerpt comes from the opening of 'Carthon' vol. 2, 178–79.

[7] 'Conlath og Cuthona,' vol. 2, 158.

[8] 'Temora,' vol. 2, 142.

[9] 'Fingal,' vol. 1, 159.

[10] Original Blicher text has 'vilden Fuarfeds Møe; hun' instead of 'Selma der.'

[11] 'Oina=Morul,' vol. 1, 91.

[12] 'Cuchullins Død,' vol. 1, 255.

       – Aander flyve paa Skyer og ride paa Vinde.
       De hvile tilsammen i deres Huler, og tale om
       de dødlige. – [13]

x   – Atter fremvælter Kampens rædsomme, buldrende
(a.)   mørke Skye, liig Taage, der strømmer ud over
       Dalen ——— [14]

       – Mine Dage ere hos de henfarne Aander,[15] ingen
       Morgen skal fremskinne for mig. – De skulle søge
       mig i Temora, men de finde mig ikke. – Drag Pilen
       fra min Side, og læg Cuchullin under hin Eeg; – [16]
       Nattens Skyer komme rullende ned, og hvile paa
(a.)   Cromlas mørkbrune Fjeld. – I Skoven suser den fjerne
( )   Vind, men taus og mørk er Dødens Slette. – End
(Ap.)   lyder Selmas[17] liflige Røst i mit Øre paa Lenas Hede. – [18]

       d. 30te Marz: 1841 fandtes foregaaend
       Ouverture (efter Spohr og Schneiders be-
       dømmelse) at være værdig den med
       Koncurencen udsette Pris.

      Saa, saa heri det ønskede Wink. <u>Deo gloria</u>

August   Ouverture efter 'St. Hans-
1841.)   aftenspil' af Øhlenschläger
        ferdig i September. –

/////
////// 1841. componerede '6 Danske Sange'
       tilegnede prof. Weyse. Trykte hos Olsen.
       udkom 8. Septr: 1841. Samme Tid compon
       4 Digte af Uhland.

---

[13] 'Fingal,' vol. 1, 155.
[14] Ibid., 159.
[15] Original Blicher text has 'Aar og' instead of 'Aander.'
[16] 'Cuchullins Død,' vol. 1, 265.
[17] Original Blicher text has 'Carrils' instead of 'Selmas.'
[18] 'Fingal,' vol. 1, 225.

October
1841)   Sinfonie (Efter Kjæmpeviser)
             c moll

    1.   <u>Introduction</u> (Indledning)

    2. <u>Allo</u>   De vare syv og syvsindstyve
                 Der de droge ud fra Hald,
                 Og der de komme til Brattingsborg
                 Der sloge de deres Tjald
                 Det donner under Ros, de danske Hofmænd
                     der de udride.[19]

x
(*)(3)   Hr Oluf han rider saa vide.
   (C Dur)   Alt til sit Bryllup at byde.
              Der dandse fire, og der dandse fem
  (As Dur) Elvekongens Datter rækker Haanden frem.[20]

x
(2)(3) Andantino. (Es Dur)
              Svend Vonved
              – Han slaaer Guldharpen prude
  Omqvæd: Den Sommer og den Eng saa vel
              kunde sammen.[21]

(Viol. med Omqvæd)   Jeg gik mig ud en Sommerdag at høre
Duet mellem Fl. og   Fuglesang, som Hjertet monne røre,
Cl. med Harpe   I de dybe Dale,
Accomp. Blæsinst: Blandt de Nattergale.
i Chorrefrain

———————

        Da nu min Hjertenskjæreste var funden
        Sang og blomstrede det rundt i Lunden
        Baade dybe Dale
        Og de Nattergale.[22] (<u>Legende</u>)

———————

---

[19] First strophe from *Udv. da. Vi.* #1, *Turneringen* (*DgF* #7 F).

[20] First and second strophes from *Udv. da. Vi.* # 35 *Elveskud* (*DgF* # 47B).

[21] Part of first strophe from *Udv. da. Vi.* # 10, *Svend Vonved* (*DgF* # 18D), chorus taken from *Udv. da. Vi.* # 66, *Asbjørn Snares Frieri til Kongens Datter* (*DgF* # 131E).

[22] The first and last strophes of Henrik Hertz's 'Jeg gik mig ud en Sommerdag at høre,' from *Samling af danske Sange. Udgivet af Selskabet for Trykkefrihedens rette Brug. Samlet og ordnet af Henrik Hertz*, vol. 1 (Copenhagen, 1836), 143.

Appendix Two

Personalia of Danish Figures

Various sources were consulted for this appendix: Frits Bendix's *Af en Kapelmusikers Erindringer*, Dorthe Falcon Møller's *Danske Instrumentbyggere 1770–1850*, Carl Thrane's *Fra Hofviolonernes Tid, Danmarks historiens blå bog, Dansk Biografisk Leksikon, The New Grove Dictionary of Music and Musicians*, and *Sohlmans musiklexikon*.

Cross references are indicated with an asterisk (*).

ANDERSEN, Hans Christian. (1805–75). Author. Although best known for his fairy tales, Andersen created works in various genres: poetry, novels, plays, librettos, etc. Born in Odense, Andersen came to Copenhagen in 1819 to pursue a theatrical career, studying voice with the singing master Siboni and then dance at the Royal Theater's ballet school. When his voice changed in 1822, he was dismissed from his studies. At this time he began to write plays and poetry. His first poems were published in 1827, and in 1831 he traveled abroad for the first time. He received a travel grant from the foundation *Ad usus publicos* in 1833, and spent the next two years in Italy. In 1835 he published his first novel, *Improvisatoren*, as well as his first volume of fairy tales. From 1840 until his death, Andersen continued to publish and travel extensively. Although Denmark was reluctant to recognize Andersen's talent in the early years of his career, his fame in Germany, England and France eventually convinced his countrymen of his genius. Today he is regarded as Denmark's most famous author.

BAGGESEN, Jens. (1764–1826). Poet. A student of J.H. Wessel and C.M. Wieland, Baggesen was greatly influenced by late eighteenth-century German literature. He gained an international reputation quite early in life, writing poems in Danish, German and French, and he traveled extensively. In 1789, Baggesen wrote the libretto *Holger Danske*, which, although criticized by his contemporaries, has stood the test of time. In 1790 he became a professor at the University of Copenhagen, and in 1798 a co-director of the Royal Theater. Although he showed an interest in Nordic mythology early in his career, he later abandoned such topics, leaving them to *Oehlenschläger and *Grundtvig. A feud with Oehlenschläger plagued Baggesen's final years.

BAY, Rudolph. (1791–1856). Ambassador, composer and performer. Well-known for his tenor voice and guitar playing, Bay was sought-after in Copenhagen's salon milieu. He became a volunteer in the foreign ministry in 1815 and was made secretary consulate in 1816 in Algiers, where he remained until 1831. He traveled to Italy in 1819/20 where he studied music. Bay returned to Copenhagen in 1831 and gained a position in the Royal Chapel the following year.

He was made a professor in 1834, and in 1838 he became Cantor at the Holmen Church in Copenhagen.

BECHMANN, Andreas. (1779–1838). Piano manufacturer active in Copenhagen from 1813 until 1838. After studying abroad (probably in Germany) Bechmann moved to Copenhagen in 1813 and established a business with *H.F. Richter.

BERGGREEN, Andreas Peter. (1801–80). Folklorist, teacher and composer. Influenced by *C.E.F Weyse, Berggreen first gained attention as a composer in 1823 with his cantata for the 200th anniversary of Regensen, a well-known student college in Copenhagen. During the next few years he composed several more cantatas and incidental music for the Royal Theater. In 1838 he became organist for Copenhagen's Trinity Church, and in 1843 the singing master at the Metropolitan School. He edited numerous collections of part-songs for schools (for example, *Sange til Skolebrug*, 1837), compiled an important collection of Danish and foreign folksongs and melodies (*Folke-Sange og Melodier*, 1842-1855), and published two periodicals: *Musikalsk Tidene* and *Heimdal*. In addition, he was revered as a distinguished teacher of music theory: in 1858 he was appointed honorary professor, and in 1878 he was granted an honorary doctorate from the University of Copenhagen.

BLICHER, Steen Steensen. (1782–1884). Poet, teacher, minister. One of the first spokesmen for Pan-Scandinavianism, Blicher wrote articles on various political issues and organized the first 'folkmøde' (folk gathering) on Himmelbjerget on August 1, 1839. Blicher's first publication was a two-volume translation of *The Poems of Ossian* (1807–09). This was followed by several poetry collections (1814, 1826, 1835, and 1840) and a travelogue of Jutland. (1817). In addition, Blicher published a series of stories based on old Nordic myths and folk tales. From 1827 until 1829 he published the periodical *Nordlyset*. He often used local dialect in his works and was praised for his vivid descriptions of Denmark's stark, rugged landscapes.

BOURNONVILLE, August. (1805–79). Balletmaster and choreographer. Bournonville studied in France and then returned to Copenhagen to become the Royal Theater's ballet master. He produced more than fifty ballets and a large number of divertissements and opera numbers on a variety of themes, from idyllic ballets (*Livjægerne paa Amager*, 1871; *Fjernt fra Danmark*, 1860) to ballets based on folk-life images (*Kermessen i Brügge*, 1851), Nordic sagas (*Thrymskviden*, 1868), and contemporary themes (*Konservatoriet* and *Et Avisfrieri*, 1849). But his main interest was romantic ballet, which combined dance and pantomime (*Napoli*, *Sylphiden* and *Blomsterfesten i Genzano*).

BREDAL, Ivar. (1800–64). Composer and violist. Bredal entered the Royal Chapel Violin School in 1816; one year later he was granted a position as violist in the Royal Chapel. He became concertmaster in 1835, and in 1836 served as conductor for the Musikforenigen in Copenhagen. In 1849 he was granted the position of choral director at the Royal Theater. As a composer Bredal was greatly influenced by *Friedrich Kuhlau (Bredel's Singspiel *Bride of Lammermoor* used Kuhlau's *Elverhøi* as a model).

COLLIN, Edvard. (1808–86). Danish under-secretary. In 1832 Collin became secretary for the Foundation *Ad usus publicos* where he remained until the foundation was dissolved in 1842. He was a founding member of the Music Society in 1836, and he served as a member of that society's board of administrators from 1836 to 1876. Collin's greatest interest was Danish literature, and he took great pride in building a private collection of more than 25,000 volumes. Collin was a close friend of *H.C. Andersen, and in 1882 he published an account of his family's relationship with the great author entitled *H.C. Andersen og det collinske Huus*.

FERSLEW, Christian. (1817–83). Opera singer. Ferslew attended the Latin school in Aalborg where the composer, *R. Bay, first noticed his musical talents and recommended that he move to Copenhagen. In Copenhagen, Ferslew studied with the singing master Siboni, making his debut at the Royal Theater on 12 May 1837. During the next decade, Ferslew struggled, but finally, in 1845, was given an official position at the Theater. Known for his rich bass voice, Ferslew starred in a number of operas over the next few decades: i.e. Walter Fürst in *Wilhelm Tell*, Arovist in *Norma*, Sarastro in *The Magic Flute*, and the commandant in *Don Juan*.

FRØHLICH, Johannes Frederik. (1806–60). Composer, violinist and conductor. As a child, Frøhlich studied piano, violin and flute. In 1812 he made his debut as a performer. He was engaged as a violinist by the Royal Theater in 1821, becoming choirmaster in 1827. In 1834 Frøhlich was hired as one of three conductors for the Royal Theater; in later years he became responsible for opera performances. Frøhlich was one of the Music Society's founding members, and he served as the society's director from 1836 until 1841. In 1838 he traveled to Italy for health reasons. Upon his return he wrote music for several of *Bournonville's ballets. But ill health still plagued him, and in 1844 he was forced to resign his post at the theater. Frøhlich's works are chiefly instrumental and his style was strongly indebted to Mozart, Rossini, *Weyse and *Kuhlau. An autograph, chronological list of his works now found in DkB (Ny kgl. Saml. 3258 A 4°) was sent to Bournonville in 1866 by Kuhlau's niece. This list shows that about one third of Kuhlau's compositions are now lost.

GADE, Axel. (1860–1921). Violinist and composer. Second son of Niels W. Gade, Axel wrote a biographical account of his father which was published, posthumously, in Wilhelm Behrend's *Minder om Niels W. Gade. Kendte Mænds og Kvinders Erindringer* (1830).

GADE, Dagmar. (1863–1952). Only daughter of Niels W. Gade. She published a biography about her father in 1892 entitled *Niels W. Gade, Optegnelser og Breve* wherein she presented a great deal of Gade's correspondence with family and colleagues.

GADE, Felix. (1855–1928). First son of Niels W. Gade. Like his brother, *Axel, and sister, *Dagmar, Felix wrote a biographical account of his father, but this work was never published. The manuscript is now held in DkB: Ny kgl. Saml. 1716, Gade's efterladte papirer.

GERSON, George. (1790–1825). Amateur composer and violinist. As a child Gerson studied violin in Copenhagen with *Tiemroth. He later moved to Hamburg to study business. While there he learned to play the piano and soon became an active member of that city's musical circles. Upon his return to Copenhagen in 1812, Gerson was employed by the merchant, Joseph Hambro. In 1819 he became a partner in Hambro's business. Throughout his life, Gerson maintained an interest in music, and he played an active role in Copenhagen's musical life, both as a violinist and as an organizer of musical events. Very few of Gerson's musical compositions (mainly piano pieces and songs) have been published. His musical style shows the influence of Haydn, Romberg and Mozart. A manuscript copy of his collected works (in five autograph volumes) can be found in DkB.

GLÆSER, Franz. (1798–1861). Bohemian composer and conductor. After composing farces and parodies in Vienna, Glæser went to Berlin, and composed more serious works: *Aurora, Die Brautschau auf Kronstein* and *Des Adlers Horst*. Glæser moved to Copenhagen in 1842, and in 1845 was appointed court conductor. Apart from occasional pieces, he composed only three major works during his Copenhagen years: the operas *The Wedding by Lake Como*, *The Water Spirits* and *The Golden Swan* (*H.C. Andersen wrote the librettos for the first two). Glæser's works are now held by DkB, Deutsche Staatsbibliotek Berlin and Gesellschaft der Musikfreude in Vienna.

GRUNDTVIG, Nicolai Frederik Severin. (1783–1872). Pastor, poet, and historian. After serving as a tutor and school teacher, Grundtvig studied religion and became an ordained minister. He reformed, almost single-handedly, the Danish church. Grundtvig was dedicated to his belief that the way to salvation lay in loyalty to God and the homeland, and he often expressed this belief through poems and historical studies. Looking at Grundtvig's poetry one observes that while his earliest works were concerned with heroic figures from the past, praise for Denmark's nature and people became the dominant topic after 1815. Denmark's native language became an important theme in the 1830s, and in 1848, the beginning of the Schleswig-Holstein troubles sparked a long series of national/political folksongs. In his Christian psalms and texts Grundtvig brought to life stories from the Old and New Testaments: *Kong Pharao var en ugudelig Krop* and *Et Barn er født i Bethlehem*. In addition to his work as minister and poet, Grundtvig also took an active role in reforming Denmark's educational system.

HANSEN, Christian Julius. (1814–75). Composer. After failing to attain a career as a professional singer, Hansen began to study composition. Both *C.E.F. Weyse and *J.P.E. Hartmann showed much interest in his work. In 1840 he entered the Musikforenigen's overture competition, and his Overture in E major received honorable mention (Gade's *Echoes of Ossian* took first prize). Hansen's overture was performed by the Music Society on 6 April 1842 and published, posthumously, in 1875. In 1845 Hansen became organist at Copenhagen's Garrison's Church. From his early years until his death Hansen directed various singing and student societies – the majority of his most well-known compositions were written for these groups.

HARTMANN, Johann Peter Emilius. (1805–1900). Composer and organist. As a child Hartmann studied music theory, organ, piano and violin with his father, Johann Ernst Hartmann. He made his debut as a violinist at age fifteen with his life-long friend and colleague *August Bournonville. At age nineteen he succeeded his father as organist at Copenhagen's Garnison Church. After studying law at the University of Copenhagen (he graduated in 1828), Hartmann was given a position in government. Although Hartmann remained active in government throughout his life, he nonetheless was able to pursue a full career as composer, organist, conductor and music educator. He made his debut as a composer in 1826 with a concert of his own works, including a cantata to a text by *A. Oehlenschläger, and in 1827 began to teach at Siboni's music school. In 1843 he succeeded *C.E.F Weyse as organist at Frue Kirke and in 1867 was appointed joint director, along with N.W. Gade and *H.S. Paulli, of the newly founded Copenhagen conservatory. Hartmann was one of the founders of Copenhagen's Music Society, and he served as its president for fifty-three years. He was made professor in 1847, and in 1874 he received an honorary doctorate from Copenhagen University. During his lifetime Hartmann was viewed as one of Denmark's greatest musicians, yet audiences outside his homeland knew little of his work. Hans von Bülow commented on Hartmann's fate in 1882: 'Hartmann remained rather foreign to us Germans. He is simply by preference a national composer ... but for imagination, skill and taste he should be equally renowned with the international Gade.'

HEIBERG, Johan Ludvig. (1791–1860). Author. Best known for his comedic theatrical works, Heiberg introduced the vaudeville genre to Danish audiences, and his study, *Om Vaudevillen som dramatisk Digtart og om dens Betydning paa den danske Skueplads*, lay the groundwork for other Danish authors, namely *Oehlenschläger, *Henrik Hertz and *H.C. Andersen. Intrigued by German idealism and Hegel's ideas, Heiberg wrote a number of philosophical works. In addition he published several artistic journals: *Kjøbenhavns flyvende Post* (1827–30), *Perseus, Journal for den spekulative Idé* (1837–38), and *Intelligensblade* (1842–44). In 1828 he was hired as a writer for the Royal Theater, and in 1839 he was given the position of censor. He was named titular professor in 1829 and in 1830 became an associate professor in logic, aesthetics and Danish literature.

HEIBERG, Johanne Luise. (1812–90). Actress. Undoubtedly the most prominent actress in nineteenth-century Denmark, Heiberg starred in hundreds of performances at the Royal Theater in Copenhagen. She began her studies at the Royal Theater's ballet school, but soon became enthralled with the dramatic arts. In 1831 she married *Johan Ludvig Heiberg.

HELSTED, Carl. (1818–1904). Composer and voice pedagogue. Helsted learned to play flute and cello at an early age, and in 1837 he was given a position in the Royal Chapel orchestra. Helsted was noted for his comely tenor voice, and he was one of the first Danes to awaken interest in Schubert's lieder. In 1840 he traveled abroad and made the acquaintance of Europe's most prominent figures, i.e., Mendelssohn, Schumann and Berlioz. In 1841 he received honorable mention in the Music Society's Overture competition. He also wrote numerous songs, a symphony, a piano quartet and *Liden Kirsten* for soprano, women's choir and orchestra. After studying voice with Manuel Garcia in Paris, Helsted returned to Copenhagen in 1843 and concentrated on a career in voice pedagogy.

HELSTED, Edvard. (1816–1900). Composer and piano pedagogue. Helsted studied violin with *C. Schall and became a member of the Royal Chapel Orchestra in 1838. In 1840 he was asked to compose the music to *Bournonville's ballet *Toreadoren*. Other collaborations with Bournonville included *Napoli* (first act only) and *Blomsterfesten in Genzano*. In 1863 he became the conductor for all vaudevilles and ballets at the Royal Theater, and in 1869 he obtained a teaching position at the newly-founded Copenhagen Conservatory.

HERTZ, Henrik. (ca. 1797–1870). Poet. The best of Hertz's early poetry is characterized by a romantic eroticism; his later works contain naturalistic descriptions. Known for delicate reworkings of folk ballads, Hertz quickly gained a reputation as a master of genre poetry. In addition he wrote several works, mostly vaudeville, for the Royal Theater.

HOLM, Vilhelm. (1820–60). Viola player. Holm studied violin with *Wexschall at the Royal Chapel's violin school. From 1847 until his death he served as a viola player in the Royal Chapel. Holm was an avid chamber music performer and served as a vital member of Copenhagen's Chamber Music Society. As a composer, he concentrated primarily on ballet music: *Pontemolle* (1866), *Livjægerne paa Amager* (1871), *Et Eventyr i Billeder* (1871), *Mandarinens Døtre* 1873 and *Weyses Minde* (1874). In 1869 he succeeded *E. Helsted as conductor of vaudeville and ballet at the Royal Theater.

HOLST, Wilhelm. (1807–98). Actor. Admired for his clear voice, Holst enjoyed a relatively successful career at the Royal Theater, where he performed over 400 roles. With the onset of the Schleswig-Holstein War in 1848, Holst took a leave from the theater and volunteered for the front line. He later published his battle experiences in a series of popular articles and books.

HOPPE, Ferdinand. (1815–90). Solo dancer. Hoppe became a student at the ballet school in 1827 and in 1834 made his professional debut at the Royal Theater in a performance of *Den Stumme i Portici* (Auber's *La Muetta a Portici*). Hoppe's remarkable technical ability distinguished him at an early age, but his fragile frame often excluded him from dancing the roles of heroes and lovers. Consequently he became a *demi-caractère-danser*. He performed in Stockholm, Berlin, Vienna, Paris and Milan. From 1863 until 1883 Hoppe served as a dance instructor at the Royal Theater.

HØEDT, Frederik. (1820–85). Theatrical director and actor. From an early age Høedt showed an interest in philosophy, aesthetics and dramaturgy. As a young man he was a prominent member of Copenhagen's salon society. Høedt was an excellent interpreter of contemporary literature and often presented recitations for private audiences. When his father died he became independently wealthy, and he traveled to Paris to observe the newest trends in the theatrical arts. In 1851 Høedt presented a new interpretation of Shakespeare's *Hamlet*, which ensured Høedt's career as a respected actor. He was named the Royal Theater's stage director for plays in 1858, and stage director for all opera performances in 1861. In 1861 Høedt was passed over for the lead in a revival of *Hamlet*. Infuriated, he left the Theater, and with him went *M. Wiehe, *N.P. Nielsen, and *A. Bournonville. From 1856 until his death Høedt served as a drama instructor, and his authority greatly influenced the following generation of Danish theater.

INGEMANN, B.S. (1789–1862). Poet. The best of Ingemann's numerous poems from the first decade of the nineteenth century present a soft, refined sentimentality. In the decades that followed, he wrote patriotic songs. His lyrics from the 1820s are dominated by devotional poetry for use in schools and at home. In the following decade this interest gave way to simple, intimate children's lyrics. From this period also come the poetry cycles based on Holger Danske (a shoemaker in Jerusalem), Solomon and Sulamith. Between 1840 and 1850 Ingemann dedicated much of his time to writing psalm tones, which secured his reputation as a funereal poet.

KOCH, PETER CHRISTIAN (1807–80). Journalist. One of the leading Danish activists in Schleswig until he moved to Copenhagen in 1856. His weekly *Dannevirke*, which he published in Haderslev from 1838 until 1855, was an important forum for Danish Nationalism.

KROSSING, Peter Casper. (1793–1838). Composer. Student of *F.L.Æ. Kunzen. Krossing became organist at Frederik's German Church in Christianshavn in 1816 and singing master at the Royal Theater in 1820. His works, now largely forgotten, display a range of genres: cantata, piano quintet, symphony, and song. His most famous work includes a number of folksong-like melodies written to poems by *B.S. Ingemann (*15 Sange af B.S. Ingemann satte i Musik med Pianoforte eller Guitarre Accompagnement* and *Smaasange med Accompagnement af Piano-Forte*).

KUHLAU, Friedrich. (1786–1832). Composer and Pianist. Together with *C.E.F. Weyse, Kuhlau is considered the foremost representative of the late Classical period in Denmark. Born in Germany, Kuhlau studied theory and composition in Hamburg, but fled to Copenhagen in 1810 when Napoleon invaded Germany. He gave his first public concert in 1811 at the Royal Theater and in 1813 was given a position in the Royal Chapel. He served as chorus-master at the Royal Theater in 1816 and 1817. Throughout his life Kuhlau was praised for his fine piano playing. He traveled to Vienna, where he met Beethoven, in 1821 and 1825. In 1828 he was made honorary professor in Copenhagen. Unfortunately little of Kuhlau's work survives outside his published compositions – in 1832 a fire swept through his home, destroying all his sketches and unpublished manuscripts.

KUNZEN, Ludwig Æmilius. (1761–1817). Composer. Born in Lübeck (then part of Denmark), Kunzen came to Copenhagen in 1824 under the recommendation of J.A.P. Schultz and succeeded as a keyboard performer and composer (the opera *Arion's Lyre* was his greatest success). After the failure of his opera *Holger Danske*, however, he moved to Berlin, where he opened a music shop and edited the journal *Musikalisches Wochenblatt*. In 1792 Kunzen became

Kapellmeister at a theater in Frankfurt am Main, and in 1794 he took up a similar post in Prague. He returned to Copenhagen in 1795 as Schulz's successor at the Royal Chapel and remained there for the rest of his life. As a composer, Kunzen was particularly influenced by Schulz (instrumental works and songs) and Mozart (opera).

LANGGAARD, Rued Immanuel. (1893–1952). Composer and organist. Praised as a child prodigy, Langgaard gained much attention in his youth as a composer and organist. His early works, before 1918, show the influence of Bruckner, Liszt, Wagner and Mahler. In later years, however, his style became more adventurous. Influenced by Carl Nielsen, he developed an atonal polyphonic style (perhaps most clearly represented in his Symphony No. 6, written in 1919) which appears to foreshadow Hindemith's work of the early 1920s. On the whole, Langgaard's early works are characterized by a symbolist aesthetic and deep religious feelings, and this attitude brought him into conflict with the mainstream of European thought after World War I. Opposed to the anti-metaphysical objectivity of neo-classicism, Langgaard replaced his more experimental writing with a Romantic style based on the music of N.W. Gade (the Seventh Symphony, 1925–6, in particular echoes Gade's style).

MARSCHALL, Andreas. (1783–1842). Piano manufacturer active in Copenhagen from 1812 until 1842. Born in Tirnau, Hungary. After working for various piano manufacturers in Germany, Marschall came to Copenhagen in 1810 as a carpenter. He worked briefly for *P.C. Uldahl before setting up his own business in 1812; he was the biggest producer of pianos in Copenhagen (shipping one third of his production abroad) until a fire destroyed his business in 1838.

MARSTRAND, Wilhelm. (1810–73). Painter. Marstrand studied at the Academy of Art in Copenhagen, and in 1836 traveled to Italy on a fellowship from the foundation *Ad usus publicos*. He was made a professor in Copenhagen in 1848, and in 1853 he became director of the Academy of Art – a position he held 1853–57 and 1863–73. Marstrand was generally regarded as an average talent by his contemporaries. Nonetheless, he managed to lead a successful career as a portrait and genre painter. Marstrand was second only to *Thorvaldsen in terms of foreign recognition.

MATTHISON-HANSEN, Hans. (1807–90). Organist and composer. At an early age Matthison-Hansen showed an interest in both drawing and music. In 1829 he entered the Royal Academy of Art in Copenhagen. Living in the home of his teacher, C.W. Eckersberg, Matthison-Hansen began to study various string instruments. Encouraged by *C.E.F. Weyse, Matthison-Hansen accepted the position as organist at Roskilde Cathedral in 1832 and remained there until his death. He gave concerts throughout Northern Germany and Scandinavia, and was responsible for the introduction of J.S. Bach's organ works to Denmark. Although Matthison-Hansen composed several chamber works for strings in his early years, he is primarily remembered as a composer of church music. On the whole, his music is characterized by a smooth, melodious style influenced by Bach and C.E.F Weyse.

NIELSEN, Anna. (1803–56). Actress. Second only to *Johanne Luise Heiberg, Nielsen was Denmark's most beloved actress in the first half of the nineteenth century. Tall and blonde, Nielsen represented the ideal, Nordic beauty. Nielsen was best known for her dramatic roles as a wife and mother, and she was the actress most preferred by *A. Oehlenschläger. In 1823 she married the concertmaster *Fr. Wexschall, but the marriage ended in bitter divorce in 1831. In 1834 she married the actor *N.P. Nielsen.

NIELSEN, Nicolai Peter. (1795–1860). Actor. Nielsen entered the Royal Theater in 1820. He was often chosen to play the role of Nordic heroes. In later years, Nielsen also gained a reputation as a comedic actor. Nielsen remained at the Royal Theater until 1855; he was also an avid amateur musician – he played the French horn and his compositions include: a rondo called *Souvenir de Bergen* and music to *Majgildet*.

OEHLENSCHLÄGER, Adam. (1779–1850). Poet. Oehlenschläger worked as an actor at the Royal Theater from 1797 until 1799. In 1803, he made his breakthrough as a professional poet with *Guldhornene* and *St. Hansaften-Spil*. These works, and his early tragedies, ushered the Romantic style into Danish literature and established Oehlenschläger's reputation. In the 1820s and 30s, however, the tide quickly turned. Oehlenschläger's works received unjustly harsh reviews from critics such as *J.L. Heiberg, causing Danish audiences to lose interest. (Notwithstanding these reviews, in Norway and Sweden Oehlenschläger was still considered the 'Poetry King.') In the 1840s he regained his status in Denmark as one of the country's greatest poets. In his later years, his plays were successfully presented at the Royal Theater, including *Knud den Store*, *Dina*, *Amleth*, and *Kjartan og Gudrinil*.

PAULLI, Holger Simon. (1810–91). Conductor, composer and violinist. Paulli studied violin with *Claus Schall and *F.T. Wexschall, becoming an assistant in the Royal Chapel Orchestra in 1822 and a member in 1828. From 1835 he conducted the Royal Chapel orchestra's ballet music rehearsals, and in 1849 he succeeded Wexschall as primary conductor. He collaborated with the ballet-master *August Bournonville and wrote music for more than ten of his ballets (e.g. *Napoli* 1842 – composed with *E. Helsted, N. Gade and H.C. Lumbye; *Conservatoriet* 1849;

Kermessen i Brügge 1851; *Blomster-festen i Genzano* 1858). In addition to his ballets, Paulli composed two singspiels, a concert overture, several violin pieces and songs. From 1863 until 1883 he was conductor of the Royal Chapel's Orchestra and in charge of all opera performances, and in this capacity he introduced Denmark to operas by Verdi and Wagner. Upon the founding of the Copenhagen Music Conservatory in 1866 he was appointed joint director with N.W. Gade and *J.P.E. Hartmann.

PETERSEN, Niels. (ca. 1801–51). Flautist, also known for his singing and keyboard playing. He studied with P.C. Bruun. In 1818 he became a member of the Royal Chapel. In 1824 he visited Stockholm, Oslo, Leipzig and Berlin. He was an organist for six years at St. Ansgar's Church in Copenhagen.

PHISTER, Ludwig. (1807–96). Actor. Phister joined the Royal Theater in 1830. Best known for his comedic performances, he often mimicked well-known Copenhagen figures in his various stage roles. Phister was the star of Holberg's comedies for fifty-two years. In all, he performed 649 different roles at the Royal Theater.

RASMUSSEN, Poul Edvard. (1776–1860). Judge and amateur musician. Composer of the melody to the well-known folksong: 'Danmark, dejligst Vang og Vænge,' Rasmussen helped to compile the first comprehensive collection of Danish folk melodies: *Danske Viser fra Middelalderen*, 5 vols. (1812–14), and edited *Udvalg af Danske Viser*, 2 vols. (1821). Toward the end of his life he worked in Farum, a small Danish town, as a music teacher. His unpublished memoirs are housed in DkB.

RICHTER, Hans Friderich. (ca. 1778–1851). Piano manufacturer and music dealer. Born in Friderichstad in Schleswig, Richter was active in Copenhagen from 1813 until 1847. He worked with *Andreas Bechman from 1813 until 1832 as a partner in the firm Richter & Bechman.

SCHALL, Claus Nielsen. (1757–1835). Composer, dancer, and violinist. Schall joined the Royal Theater in 1772 as a dancer and in 1775 became a member of the Royal Chapel. He was appointed répétiteur and director of the ballet at the Royal Theater in 1776, and he began to take an interest in composition, writing music for many of the ballets. In the late 1780s Schall made an extensive tour of Paris, Dresden, Berlin and Prague. He returned to Copenhagen in 1792 and became Concertmaster at the Opera. In 1795 Schall was hired as composer of the Royal Ballet, and in 1818 he became the music director at the opera, where he conducted the premiere of Weber's *Der Freischutz* overture in 1820. As a composer Schall collaborated with the choreographer Vincenzo Galeotti – Schall wrote music to approximately twenty of Galleotti's ballets, which range from light divertimentos to full-length tragedies. Schall's models were Mozart and Gluck. His other music includes Singspiele, songs, and instrumental chamber music.

SCHALL, Peder. (1762–1820). Younger brother of *Claus Schall. Cellist in the Royal Chapel, guitarist and composer of popular vocal works with guitar accompaniment.

SCHRAM, Fritz. (1818–87). Violinist. After studying with *Wexschall at the Royal Chapel's violin school, Schram was hired as a violinist in the Royal Chapel orchestra. In 1831 he was given the position of solo violinist. In addition to his work at the Royal Chapel, Schram was a sought-after quartet player and teacher. For many years he performed jointly with the pianist Princess Anna of Hessen.

SCHRAM, Peter. (1819–95). Opera singer and actor. In 1831 Schram became a student at Siboni's music school, which was connected with the Royal Theater, and in 1834 he made his debut. He studied music theory with *J.P.E. Hartmann, and voice with Manuel Garcia in Paris. Schram was hired as a permanent member of the Royal Theater in 1845, and he remained there until his death, performing in no less than sixty-three seasons. Praised for his tenor voice and stage presence, Schram was considered a leading theatrical figure in nineteenth-century Denmark.

v. STAFELDT, Adolf Wilhelm Schack. (1769–1826). Author and county administrator. Orphaned at age eleven, v. Stafeldt was enrolled in military school. He became a lieutenant in 1788 and a first lieutenant in 1791. From 1791 to 1793 he studied archeology in Göttingen, and from 1795 to 1800 he traveled to Germany, Austria, Italy, and France. Inspired by German literature and philosophy (i.e. Herder, Schiller, and Schelling), Stafeldt was one of the first poets to introduce a romantic style in Denmark. But unlike *A. Oehlenschläger and *N.F.S. Grundtvig – who introduced Northern mythology into Danish poetry – Stafeldt continued to use figures from Greek mythology, presenting them in a new, romantic style.

THORVALDSEN, Bertel. (1770–1844). Sculptor. Considered Denmark's most famous artist, Thorvaldsen received international acclaim in the nineteenth century for his monumental neo-classical sculptures. He began his studies at the Academy of Art in Copenhagen in 1781 and moved to the model school in 1786. In 1793 he won the Academy's gold medal, and in 1796 he was awarded a large travel grant. Thorvaldsen moved to Rome in 1797, and except for a short trip to Denmark in the mid 1830s, remained there until 1838. His studio in Rome was the center of a large circle of artists, and in the first decades of the nineteenth century many Danish artists traveled to Rome to work with Thorvaldsen. When

Thorvaldsen returned to Copenhagen in 1838, he was greeted as a hero. A flotilla of boats filled with cheering citizens sailed out to meet his ship, and a museum designed especially for the exhibition of his works was built in the city's center.

TIEMROTH, Christian. (1766–1840). Violinist. Born in Germany, Tiemroth studied in Vienna where he was admired by W.A. Mozart. After coming to Copenhagen in 1785, he entered the Royal Chapel in 1786 and became concertmaster in 1809. He was the musical leader of the Copenhagen club *Det harmoniske Selskab* and a noted violin teacher. His prominent students included *G. Gerson, *Fr. Wexschall, and *C.E.F. Weyse.

ULDAHL, Peter Christian. (1778–1820). Piano manufacturer active in Copenhagen from 1809 until 1820.

WAAGEPETERSEN, Christian. (1787–1840). Wine merchant. One of Copenhagen's most successful businessmen, Waagepetersen was also a great lover and sponsor of the arts. His home was a popular meeting place for the city's elite, and musical performances were the common entertainment. Waagepetersen was a generous sponsor who supported a number of Denmark's finest musicians.

WEIS, Carl Mettus. (1809–72). Under secretary in the Danish ministry. He was an amateur active in Danish chamber music performances in the mid-nineteenth century.

WEIS, Ernst Marcus. (1807–73). Titular councillor of state and chief senior deputy judge. Like his brother, *Carl, Ernst Weis was an amateur active in Danish chamber music performances in the mid-nineteenth century.

WEXSCHALL, Friderich. (1798–1845). Violinist. Recognized by his contemporaries as one of Denmark's finest musicians, Wexschall enjoyed a long career at the Royal Chapel in Copenhagen. He eventually earned the position of concertmaster and in 1835 was made director of the Chapel's Violin School. Wexschall was a dynamic soloist, and he played a vital role in the history of Danish chamber music.

WEYSE, Christoph Ernst Friedrich. (1774–1842). Composer and organist. Arriving in Copenhagen in 1789 to study with J.A.P. Schultz, Weyse soon became noted for his performances of Mozart's piano concertos. He became organist at Copenhagen's Reformed Church in 1792, and moved to the Cathedral in 1805, where he remained until his death. From 1819 Weyse held the position of court composer. He was made titular professor at the University of Copenhagen in 1816 and received an honorary doctorate from the same institution in 1842. In his later years, Weyse's authority in Copenhagen's musical life was virtually uncontested. By nature a conservative, Weyse was rooted in eighteenth-century musical ideas. He composed in several genres, but only his piano works received international attention. Today, however, Weyse is best remembered for his production of songs (romances and folksongs) which still appear in modern collections. Throughout his life Weyse was an avid collector of music. At his death this collection was left to DkB.

WIEHE, Michael. (1820–64). Actor. Wiehe's big break at the Royal Theater came in 1842 when he starred in *Aladdin*. In 1844 he co-starred with *Johanne Luise Heiberg in *Henrik Hertz's *Amanda*. Wiehe went on to play roles such as Shakespeare's Romeo and Schiller's Mortimer, and he enjoyed a long, successful career at the Royal Theater. In 1861, however, he resigned when his close friend, *F. Høedt, quarreled with the Theater's director, *J.L. Heiberg. Wiehe was active in Copenhagen's musical circles and was a life-long friend of N.W. Gade.

ZINCK, Ludvig. (1776–1851). Composer. Zinck was associated with the Royal Theater for more than fifty years: he entered as a student in 1790, was made a prompter in 1802, and served as a singing master from 1806 until 1842. Two of his most famous students were *Anna Nielsen and *Ludvig Phister. In 1807 Zinck became court organist, a position he held until his death. Zinck composed and arranged music for approximately seventy productions at the Royal Theater, the most famous being vaudevilles by *J.L. Heiberg.

ZINN, Johann Friedrich. (1779–1838). Wholesale merchant. Zinn inherited a prosperous business from his father and by 1809 made it the second-most profitable firm in Copenhagen. Zinn was a generous supporter of the arts, and in the early decades of the nineteenth century his home was a popular meeting place for Copenhagen musicians.

Appendix Three

Transcriptions of Danish Texts

Autobiographical Fragment by Niels W. Gade
Fredensborg, 16 August 1885
Published in Dagmar Gade, *Niels W. Gade*, 3–7.

Den 17de April 1812 blev en ung Snedkermester og hans unge Brud ægteviede i Trinitatis Kirke. Han hed Søren Nielsen Gade, var 22 Aar og nedstammede fra jydske Bønder, som havde optaget Navnet Gade efter en lille By mellem Kolding og Frederits. Hendes Navn var Marie Sophie Hansdatter Arentzen, 20 Aar, hendes Forfædre havde havt Hjem paa Bornholm. Tiden omkring og efter 1812 var meget stormfuld og kun lidet egnet til at frede om Huslivets stille Idyl. Evropas Fredsforstyrrer Napoleon var vel Betvungen; men der herskede Nød og Ufred i de fleste Lande. For Danmarks Vedkommende var denne Tid en af de mest bedrøvelige: Norge var afstaaet, Pengevæsenet i den største Forvirring, overalt Trang, Mismod, Standsning i Handel og Vandel. Alt dette havde kuet Befolkningen og bragt et filisteragtigt Skjær over det Hele. Man levede blot for det daglige og meget tarvelige Brød.

Dog, det unge Ægtepars beskedne Hjem var en Idyl, belyst af Kjærlighedens Solskin, derfor hørte de ikke Tidens Storme udenfor, og deres tarvelige Kost blev til den herligste Ret.

I dette stille Hjem saa jeg første Gang Lyset den 22nde Februar 1817 og fik i Daaben Navnen: Niels Wilhelm Gade. Jeg var det eneste Barn, og da jeg havde ladet vente paa mig i 5 Aar, blev jeg naturligvis modtaget med saameget større Glæde og plejet med den kjærligste Omhu af Forældrene.

Til min tidligste Erindringer fra Barnealderen regner jeg en lille Begivenhed fra mit 4de Aar. En Sommeraften havde jeg af Forældrene faaet nogle Skillinger til at kjøbe Kager for hos Konditoren lige overfor. Med glade Forhaabninger gik jeg over Gaden og naaede lykkelig og vel ind i Boutiken og fik mit Kræmmerhuset med Kager; men paa Tilbagevejen var jeg ikke saa heldig, jeg snublede og faldt, og Kræmmerhuset trillede ned i Rendestenen. Jeg blev meget forskrækket over den uventede og bratte Forandring af Situationen, brast i en hæftig Graad og løb ilsomt hjem, hvor baade Moder og Fader trøstede mig over Uheldet, men forgjæves, jeg kunde ikke standse min Hulken. Jeg maatte bringes til Sengs, og jeg kan endnu tydelig huske Stemningen, jeg var i, – det var, som al mit Livs Lykke – ved egen Skyld – var sjunken ned i Lethes mørke Vande og for bestandig holdtes fangen der, uden Haab om nogensinde at gjense Lyset.

Omtrent ved den Tid havde min Fader med sin ældre, eneste Broder, Jens Nielsen Gade, lagt sig efter Instrumentmageriet, og de havde sammen etableret en Handel med musikalske Instrumenter, fornemlig Guitar og Violin. Denne Handel gik ganske vel, og Brødrene bleve enige om at udvide Forretningen ved at etablere en Boutik hver for sig. Min Fader flyttede derfor fra den fælles Bolig i Borgergaden længere bort, midt ind i Byen, paa Hjørnet af Nygade og Skoubogade. Jeg erindrer tydelig mig selv siddende paa gulvet i Hjørnestuen i den ny Bolig, legende med 'Adresseavisen,' medens Solen skinnede ind ad Vinduerne og dannede lyse Firkanter paa Gulv og Vægge, som udbredte et hyggeligt Velvære. Jeg var omtrent 6 Aar gammel, og her begyndte mine første musikalske Øvelser; – min Fader havde nemlig foræret mig en lille Barneguitar, som jeg klimprede paa, – omtrent samtidig studerede jeg A. B. C. Bogen under min Moders Vejledning. Den Gang var Guitar, Fløjte og til Dels Harpe de af Dilettanter mest yndede Instrumenter. Herrer og Damer sang sværmeriske og sentimentale Romanzer af Rudolph Bay, Plantade o.s.v. til Accompagnement af Guitaren, som hang i et lyseblaat Baand om Skulderen, – saaledes var Moden i Begyndelsen af Tyverne. Min Fader havde et vist Ry for at Forfærdige velklingende og veludseende Guitarer efter spansk Façon, og hans Handel var den Gang meget indbringende. Senere fortrængtes Guitaren af Pianofortet; han var ikke saa heldig i Fabrikationen af dette Instrument, der opstod ogsaa flere Fabrikanter (Richter, Uldahl, Bechmann, Marschall o.a.), hvorfor hans forretning gik noget tilbage, – Alligvel vedblev huslig Tilfredshed og Glæde at blomstre i Fædrehjemmet, min Faders sangvinske Temperament og joviale Indfald bragte altid Solskin og godt Humeur tilveje, naar min Moders sværmeriske og dybere Natur saa mørke Skyer trække op paa Fremtidens Himmel. Begge havde de Sands for Poesi og for Læsning, og i Tyverne blomstrede Digtningen i Danmark, da Oehlenschläger, Heiberg, Grundtvig, Schack-Staffeldt og Ingemann levede og skrev deres bedste Værker. Min Fader havde musikalsk Talent, og skjøndt han aldrig havde lært noget Instrument, kunde han spille lidt paa næsten alle Instrumenter. Min Moder holdt ogsaa af Musik, men hendes Hovedpassion var dog Theatret og især Tragedien, hvori den Gang Talenter af første Rang glimrede. Helten og den nordiske Mø i Oehlenschlägers Tragedier udførtes fortræffeligt af Nielsen og Mad. Wexschall (senere Mad. Nielsen). Dr. Ryge var uovertræffelig i Roller som Hakon Jarl, Palnatoke o.s.v. – De komiske Roller udførtes ligledes af fortrinlige Kunstnere, Frydendahl, Lindgreen, Stage og flere. Det var, som om disse mange ypperlige Digtere og dramatiske Kunstnere vare givne os som Vederlag for vor politiske Lidenhed, ja, vi havde jo kunstneriske og videnskabelige Størrelser som Thorvaldsen og H.C. Ørsted, der vakte hele Evropas Opmærksomhed og kastede Glands tilbage over det lille Danmark. – Befolkningens Interesse droges derved til Digtningens Verden, til Kunst og Theater, for Politik var Sandsen meget ringe.

Letter from Niels W. Gade to Edvard Helsted
Copenhagen. 1836
Published in Dagmar Gade, *Niels W. Gade*, 20–23.

Til Ven Helsted! Motto: 'Ensom er jeg dog ej ene.'
… Kjære Ven, jeg savner Dig meget; vore behagelige Aftentoure savner jeg ogsaa.
Her er ret kjedsommeligt i denne Tid, da Carl er reist til Kjøge, og jeg altsaa er
ganske ene i denne store By, ingen Musik nogetsteds, som er ordentlig, en
skrækkelig Hede, ingen musikalske Venner at tale med, og Du veed jo nok, at intet
i Grunden ret interesserer mig uden dette ene. Paa Grund af denne Mangel paa
gjensidig Meddelelse har jeg forsøgt paa at opskrive nogle Tanker, som jeg ogsaa
vil betro Dig og dette Brev. I Fald Du skriver mig til, skriv mig da, hvad Du synes
om nedenstaaende, eller i saa Fald Dine Modbemærkninger.

Tanker, da mine Venner vare bortreiste.
– – – – – – min Trøst i denne min Enlighed er som altid, i Tilbedelse og
Hengivenhed nu og da at modtage blide Kys af min Elskede. Det er den evigunge,
aldrig forgaaende, der ikke skues med jordiske Øine, men som svæver for vor
Fantasi i himmelblaat Gevandt og bærer alle Dyder i sig, hende der leder os i hin
højere Verden og selv drager Forhænget til Side og lader os paa sig skue
Gjenskinnet af et Glimt af Guds Herlighed – Engles Harmonier – – –
Dog blot et Nu, – og Beskueren taber Bevidstheden og daler atter til Jorden.
– Dog den Ejegode lader ham ikke blive i intet. Hun vækker ham og lader ham i
et Speil skue Herligheden. – *Kunst* er det velgjørende Reflex. – – Jo længere han
seer, desto mere bemestres han af en uforklarlig Følelse, han beaandes (begejstres)
af hende, *Idealet*, det højeste Maal af alt skjønt, godt og dydigt, hans Tanke og
Aand udvides, han vil i maalløs Henrykkelse kaste sig for sin Skabers Trone. – Han
var paa det højeste Trin af den Himmelstige, som Mennesket kan betræde, men nu
stiger han med Rolighed ned igjen og gjemmer bestandig Erindringen om de
skjønne Øieblikke, han nød; naar Fristelser og slemme Laster vil rokke ham, da
genkalder han sig sit Ideal, og bort, langt bort fly de, lige som naar Solen i sin
Majestæt og Klarhed kaster Taagen til alle Sider.
Overvældes han af en ubenævnelig Længsel efter at udgyde sit Hjerte i
Lovsang, da løser hun hans Tunge ved et flygtigt Kys, og han selv bliver Skaber
til et jordisk-aandigt Værk, som udspringer af hans Indre og er en Gnist af hin
himmelske *Kunst*, hvoraf han er besjælet.
– – – Det Hele maa Du ansee for en uudført Skizze. Flere Udtryk ere ogsaa
som Følge af en uøvet Pen ikke de bedste, men jeg tror dog at kunne faa noget ud
deraf; i det mindste i min Tanke er det mig klart, hvad jeg vil sige, men maaske jeg
ikke er saa heldig i at udtale det. Læs det og tænk over det…. Dersom (naar Du
en Aften spadserer) Vinden blæser fra Sjælland, og den tilfældigvis skulde kaste
Dig et Blad af Træerne paa Næsen, da skal Du ikke blive vred, men smukt følge

Din Indbildning og antage det for en Hilsen fra Din Ven

N. W. GADE.

Letter from A.P. Berggreen to Niels W. Gade
Copenhagen, 30 August 1838
DkB: Ny kongelige Samling 1716, 2to.

Min kjære Ven og Discipel!
Benyttende mig af Deres Faders Tilbud sender jeg Dem denne Hilsen for at sige
Dem, hvor meget det har glædet mig af Deres Brev til Deres Forældre at erfare,
at De befinder Dem saa vel; jeg tænker omtrent som en Fugl, der er sluppen ud af
sit Buur, og nu flyver omkring i Guds frie Natur. Ved dette Buur meener jeg dog
ikke Deres Hjem, ved hvilket ethvert godt Menneske (naar han, som De har et
godt Hjem) hænger med sin hele Sjæl, men det Fangebuur, hvori Dem forhadte
Forhold holdt Dem fast. Saa kjært som Hjemmet imidlertid er os, saa ville vi dog
gjerne i vor Ungdom ud i Verden, for at samle Forraad af Erfaringer,
Forestillinger, Tanker, Billeder, hvormed vi i en sildigere Alder kunne beskjæftige
os. Jeg misunder Dem sandelig ikke Deres Lykke, men skulde jeg ganske opgive
Haabet om at see noget Mere af Verden, end jeg hidtil har seet, da vilde det vist
betage mig en stor Deel af min Livsglæde. – – Min Melodisamling til de
fædrelandshistoriske Digte er snart færdig. Da De ikke vilde ud med Deres
Composition til 'Absalon,' har jeg componeret en Melodie til dette Digt. Jeg
spillede Deres andre Melodier for Deres Fader forleden Dag, og han glædede sig
med mig ret inderlig over dem og Dem.
     Jeg savner Dem meget. Det forekommer mig som var De Kjød af mit Kjød, og
Blod af mit Blod. Som min musikalske Søn maa De i det Mindste tillade at jeg
betragter Dem. Det er ikke Forfængelighed, der lader mig see Dem i dette Forhold
til mig, men min Følelse for Dem har i den lange Tid, vi haver havt med hinanden
at gjøre, hævet sig til en Kjærlighed, der er sig sin Reenhed Bevidst, idet jeg med
en Faders, en Broders, en Vens Øine vil følge Dem paa Deres Vei. Lad mig derfor
ikke, min kjæreste og egentlig eeneste Discipel! forgjæves vente Underretning fra
Dem; men lad mig høre ret ofte fra Dem! Jeg har nu egentlig Ingen, med hvem jeg
saaledes kan underholde mig om Musik, som med Dem! Vi forstode hinanden!
– Glem ikke Fjeldmelodierne! og dersom De kunde overkomme nogle Samlinger
svenske Sange (Romancer), da vilde De bevise mig en stor Tjeneste med at kjøbe
dem for mig. I Stockholm ere udkomne Nogle af en Lindblad og Geier (Digteren),
hvoribland staaer 'Soslargevisen' af Atterbom (saa vid jeg veed efter en
Folkesang). – Klokken lidt over 3 gik jeg, den Dag De reist, hjem til Dem, for at
følge Dem ombord, men borte var De! Jeg blev da og snakked Deres Moder lidt
til rette. Fader og Moder længes jo efter Dem, men de vil at undvære den glæde

at se Dem om sig, naar Deres Lykke fordrer denne Opoffrelse. ... – Lev nu vel, min kjære Gade! Reis lykkelig! De Gode har ingen Nød! Glem mig ikke!

Deres Ven,
A.P. Berggreen

Letter from Niels W. Gade to A.P. Berggreen
Gothenborg, 24 September 1838
Published in C. Skou: *A.P. Berggreen*, (Copenhagen 1895), 55–58.

Min kjære Lærer og Ven!
De har beæret mig med Navnet 'Ven'! – jeg er stolt af dette Navn, som Deres Godhed har tillagt mig, og som gjør mig uendelig lykkelig. Men hvorledes og med hvilken Følelse maa da jeg kalde den min Ven, til hvem jeg ikke alene bindes med Kjærligheds, men tillige med saa stærke Taknemmelighedsbaand. – Ja Dem, kjære Ven, skylder jeg meget, meget – De har skuet i mit Indre, Deres skarpsindige Blik har opdaget den Lænke, som fængslede min Fod og standsede, eller vilde have standset den regelmæssige Gang, De brød den, og fri, fri aander atter Fuglen under Himlens Blaa.

Jeg føler først nu mit eget Jeg – dog misforstaa mig ej og tro mig ikke en indbilsk Taabe, som, følgende Solens Glans, flyver i Flammen – opvaagnet, som naar en Drivhusplante fra Nordens kunstige Solvarme hensættes under Sydens Azur. Hele mit indre Gjenfødelse; mit forrige Liv ligger som et Chaos, uformeligt og livløst i Baggrunden, hvoraf Skaberlivet kalder det haarde og Bløde, det Tunge og Lette at forene sig. De mange herlige og store Natursituationer, mit legemlige Øje har havt Lejlighed til at skue, have i det Aandelig vakt nye følelser, nye Tanker og givet den aandelige Virken Stof og Næring for lang tid. Dog mangler jeg en Ven, en Medhjælper i min Nærhed, med hvem jeg kan bearbejde dette Stof, med hvem jeg kan vexle Tanker og Anskuelser, en Broder, en Selskaber, som ret er efter mit Sind, – 'Kjød af mit Kjød, Blod af mit Blod,' en – Dem.

I denne min Nød, manglende mine venner, paaberaabte jeg Aanderiget om Hjælp og Lindring; og saa! – jeg blev bønhørt. En Aand, saa stor og mægtig som ingen, lod mig læse sin Fryd og Smerte, fortalte mig Historien om Prins Hamlets Tungsind, om Romeos Kjærlighed og Othellos Skinsyge – Shakespeare er hans Navn, den store Aand med det store, altomfattende Hjerte, hvis Varme og Begeistring henrev mig og ligesom opfriskede og modnede en Plan, som alt i længere Tid har spøget i min Hjerne. – Jeg vil meddele Dem denne og ved Lejlighed høre Deres Betænkning derom, – Eventyret om Agnete og Havmanden har altid forekommet mig at være et meget musikalsk Sujet, og uden egentlig at have lagt nogen Plan til dets videre Udarbejdelse som Musikstykke har det dog bestandigen foresvævet mig. ('Vogt Dem vel for den skjønne Melusine, Hr. Gade!

en farlig Skjønhed og en ikke mindre farlig Rivalinde.' 'Jeg veed det, jeg veed det meget vel, min Herre, og tillader paa ingen Maade nogen Sammenligning mellem Jomfru Agnet og skjøn Melusine; men skulde en Maler for en underskjøn Gjenboerskes Skyld lægge Hænderne i Skjødet og ikke turde forsøge at male et Dameportrait? Nej! jeg veed det vist, der er Plads for os alle, om ikke i Hovedgaden, saa dog i en beskeden lille Sidegade.')

Nu har jeg altsaa lagt Haand paa Værket og givet det Form af Ouverture. Jeg har tænkt mig Agnetes Længsel ved Strandbredden efter en hende ubekjendt Gjenstand som Hovedmomentet i dette Stykke. Som to hinanden modstridende Principper optræder Havmandes Elskovsklage og hendes egen Samvittigheds Røst (idet hun ved at elske Havmanden tror at beggaa noget Ondt). Denne Kamp mellem et God og Ondt udgjør Middelpunktet, indtil hun mod Slutningen overgiver sig paa Naade og Unaade i Havmandens Favn. Med den musikalske Udarbejdelse er jeg omtrent halvvejs og saa temmeligen til min egen Tilfredshed. Jeg arbejder flittigt, og det gaaer godt fra Haande.

Jeg vilde endnu skrive en Del; men jeg seer Papiret lidt efter lidt svinde bort under min Haand, saa at jeg nu maa til at tænke paa de mange Hilsener, der ligge mig paa Hjertet. Mine kjære Forældre, dernæst De og Deres Familie, dernæst – ja, De veed nok selv, hvem jeg vil bede at modtage mine hjerteligste Hilsener og varmeste ønsker om deres bestandige Velgaaende. – Onsdag eller Torsdag rejser jeg til Stockholm. – Jeg venter snart lidt fra Deres Haand. Hvorledes gaar det med Operaen? Jeg veed ikke ret, hvorledes jeg skal kalde mig, Deres hengivne, eller – jeg vil kalde mig

Deres
Niels W. Gade

Letter From Felix Mendelssohn to Niels W. Gade
Leipzig, 13 January 1843
Published in Dagmar Gade, *Niels W. Gade*, 27–28.

Hochgeehrter Herr!

Wir haben gestern die erste Probe Ihrer Symphonie in C moll gehabt, und wenn auch Ihnen persönlich ganz unbekannt, kann ich doch dem Wunsche nicht wiederstehen Sie anzureden, um Ihnen zu sagen, welche ausserordentliche Freude Sie mir durch Ihr vortreffliches Werk gemacht haben, und wie von Herzen dankbar ich Ihnen für den großen Genuß bin, den es mir gewährt. Seit langer Zeit hat mir kein Stück einen lebhafteren, schöneren Eindruck gemacht, und wie ich mich mit jedem Tact darin mehr verwunderte, und dennoch mehr zu Hause fühlte, so war mir es heute ein Bedürfniß, Ihnen meinen Dank für so viel Freude auszudrücken, Ihnen zu sagen, wie hoch ich Ihr herrliches Talent stelle, wie mich diese Symphonie, das Einzige, was ich bis jetzt von Ihnen kenne, auf alles Frühere und

Später begierig macht! Und da ich höre, daß Sie noch so jung sind, so ist es eben das Spätere auf das ich mich freuen kann, zu dem ich in einem so schönen Werke die festen Hoffnungen begrüße, für das ich Ihnen jetzt schon danke, wie für den Genuß, den ich gestern gehabt habe!

Wir werden noch mehrere Proben von der Symphonie machen, und erst in 3–4 Wochen dieselbe zur Aufführung bringen. .... Herr Raymund Härtel sagte mir, es sei davon die Rede, daß Sie selbst im Laufe des Winters herkämen. Wäre das doch der Fall, und könnte ich Ihnen dann meine Dankbarkeit und meine hohe Achtung mündlich besser und deutlicher ausdrücken oder beweisen, als es die leeren schriftlichen Worte thun! Wir mögen uns nun aber jetzt kennen lernen oder nicht, so bitte ich Sie mich immer für einen solchen anzusehen, der all Ihren Werken mit Liebe und Theilnahme folgen wird, und dem die Begegnung mit einem Künstler, wie Sie, und einem Kunstwerke wie Ihre C moll Symphonie jederzeit die größte, herzlichste Freude sein wird. So empfangen Sie denn nochmals meinen Dank, und genehmigen Sie die vollkommene Hochachtung, mit welcher ich bin

Ihr ergebener
Felix Mendelssohn Bartholdy

Letter from Niels W. Gade to Felix Mendelssohn
Copenhagen, 28 January 1843
Published in Dagmar Gade, *Niels W. Gade*, 29–30.

Mit welcher ausserordentlichen Freude, mit welchem innigen lebhaften Dank, mit welcher tiefgefühlten Bewunderung habe ich Ihren theuren Brief gelesen. Freude über das Glück einem Meister gefallen zu haben, Dank für die seltene Güte, mit der dieser Meister einen unbekannten Jüngling geschrieben hat, und Bewunderung für den Mann, der ein ebenso großer Mensch als Künstler ist. Wenn ich Ihnen den ganzen Umfang meiner Dankbarkeit beschreiben sollte, müßte ich Ihnen auch die ganze Bedeutung Ihres Briefes für mich schildern.

Ich brauche Ihnen aber nicht zu sagen, daß meine Kräfte und mein Vertrauen auf mich selbst durch eine solche – vielleicht allzurühmliche – Anerkennung wunderbar gestärkt werden mußten; und Sie müssen auch gewiss selbst geahnt haben, daß ein Brief von Ihnen nicht unbekannt verbleiben könnte und daß Alle der Stimme des Meisters folgen würden.

In der That ist es so geschehen. Sie haben mir eine Wohlthat erwiesen für die ich Ihnen ewig danken werde. Ich fühle mich so stark und freudig, wie ich mich noch nie gefühlt habe und das Publikum ist mir ebenso gut geworden, als begeistert für einen Mann, der so schön, so künstlerisch und menschlich fühlt.

Möchte ich doch bald nach Leipzig kommen, um Ihnen, was ich hier geschrieben habe, noch weit inniger und besser zu sagen. Leider kann ich Ihnen meinen Dank niemals so zeigen, wie ich es gern wollte. Um Ihnen einen schwachen

Beweis davon zu geben, habe ich mir jedoch erlaubt, Ihnen meine Sinfonie, die mir durch Ihre Güte einen Werth bekommen hat, zu widmen. Es ist nur ein wenig, aber das Beste, was ich habe. Binnen kürzer Zeit werde ich mir die Freiheit nehmen, Ihnen meine übrigen Sachen zu schicken. Sie werden diesen eine wohlwollende Aufnahme schenken. Ich bringe Ihnen nochmals meinen innigsten Dank für einen Brief, der mir eine so seltene Freude verschafft hat, und dabei das Glück einem Meister, von dem ich so vieles gelernt habe, meine tiefste Bewunderung und Liebe bezeugen zu dürfen.

N. W. GADE

Letter to Niels W. Gade from Felix Mendelssohn
Leipzig, 2 March 1843
Published in Dagmar Gade, *Niels W. Gade*, 30–33.

Hochgeehrter Herr!

Gestern in unserm 18. Abonnements-Concerte wurde Ihre C moll Symphonie zu ersten Male aufgeführt, zur lebhaften, ungetheilten Freude des ganzen Publicums, das nach jedem der 4 Sätze in den lautesten Applaus ausbrach. Nach dem Scherzo war eine wahre Aufregung unter den Leuten, und der Jubel und das Händeklatschen wollten gar kein Ende nehmen, – ebenso nach dem Adagio. Ebenso nach dem letzten, – und nach dem ersten – nach alle eben! Die Musiker so einstimmig zu sehen, das Publicum so entzückt, die Aufführung so gelungen – das war mir eine Freude, als hätte ich das Werk selbst gemacht! Oder noch eine größere; denn im Eigenen sieht man immer die Fehler und das Nicht-Gelungene am deutlichsten, während ich in Ihrem Werke noch gar nichts empfinde, als Freude über alle herrlichen Schönheiten. Durch den gestrigen Abend haben Sie sich das ganze Leipziger Publicum, das wirklich Musik liebt, zu dauernden Freund gemacht; keiner wird von jetzt an von Ihrem Namen und Ihrem Werke anders als mit der herzlichsten Hochachtung und Liebe sprechen, und jedes Ihrer künftigen Werke wird mit offenen Armen empfangen, sogleich mit der äußersten Sorgfalt einstudirt und freudig von allen hiesigen Musikfreunden begrüßt werden. 'Wer die letzte Hälfte des Scherzo geschrieben hat, das ist ein vortrefflicher Meister, und von dem haben wir das Recht die größten und herrlichsten Werke zu erwarten.' Das war die allgemeine Stimme gestern Abend auf unserm Orchester, im ganzen Saal – und veränderlich sind wir hier nicht. So haben Sie sich durch Ihr Werk eine große Menge Freunde für's Leben erworben; erfüllen Sie unsere Wünsche und Hoffnungen, indem Sie viele, viele Werke in derselben Art, von derselben Schönheit schreiben, und indem Sie unsere geliebte Kunst neu beleben helfen, wozu Ihnen der Himmel alles gegeben hat, was er geben kann. …

Haben Sie noch Dank für Ihren lieben Brief, und die freundliche Absicht, die Sie mir darin zu erkennen geben. Haben Sie aber noch mehr dank für die Freude, die Sie mir durch das Werk selbst gemacht haben, und glauben Sie, daß niemand Ihre Laufbahn mit mehr Theilnahme verfolgen, Ihren ferneren Arbeiten mit mehr Hoffnungen und mit größerer Liebe entgegensehen kann, als

Ihr hochachtungsvoll ergebener
Felix Mendelssohn Bartholdy

Appendix Four

Transcriptions of Mendelssohn's Letters to Copenhagen's Music Society

Leipzig d. 3ten April 1840

Der verehrten Administration des Musikvereins zu Copenhagen,
     bin ich für Ihr so eben empfangenes Schreiben vom 28ten v. M. und alles
Ehrenvolle welches darin für mich enthalten ist, aufs Dankbarste verpflichtet.
Obwohl ich mir sonst zur Annahme eines Antrags wie die Ihrige nicht die
erforderliche Autorität des Urtheils zutrauen möchte, und eine Aufgabe zu
übernehmen fürchten müßte, die meine Kräfte übersteigt: so ist mir doch anderseits
Ihr Zutrauen, und die Mitwirkung mit zwei so ausgezeichneten Künstlern wie
Spohr und *Schneider* allzu ehrenvoll, als daß ich einem weitern Bedenken Raum
gäbe, und ich nehme daher das mir ertheilte Schiedsrichteramt mit Vergnügen an,
und sehe Ihren näheren Bestimmungen darüber entgegen.   Mit vollkommer
Hochachtung

ergebenst
Felix Mendelssohn Bartholdy

Leipzig d. 30sten Dec. 1840

Hochgeehrter Herr [J.P.E. Hartmann]
     Vor geraumer Zeit erwies mir der Musikverein zu Kopenhagen die Ehre mich
zu einem der Richter in einer Preisbewertung zu ernennen, die, wenn ich nicht irre
die beste Ouvertüre betraf; u. ich nahm damals das mir zuertheilte Amt an, da
meine Zeit mir erlaubte, mich demselben mit der Gewissenhaftigkeit zu
unterziehen, welche es erfordert.   Da sich nun aber seitdem meine Arbeiten in
solchem Maaße vermehrt haben, daß ich beim besten Willen nicht neue dazu
übernehmen kann, u. da bis jetzt sich der Ausführung der damaligen Absicht auch
bei Ihnen Schwierigkeiten entgegengestellt zu heben scheinen, so muß ich Sie zu
meinem aufrichtigen Bedauern bitten, mich der übernommenen Verpflichtung
gütigst zu überheben, da in diesem Augenblick meine Zeit mir nicht gestatten
würde, die Compositionen so genau und so wiederholt zu prüfen, wie ich es vor
meinem eignen Gewissen für nötig ertachte.   Darf ich Sie bitten, in meinem Namen
dem Vereine zu sagen, wie leid es mir thut auf die mir gütigst übersandten Auftrag
Verzicht leisten zu müssen, und wie dankbar ich für das mir erwiesene, so
erhrenvolle Vertrauen bin.

Mit vollkommer Hochachtung ergebenst
Felix Mendelssohn Bartholdy

Leipzig d. 24 Jan. 1841

Euer hochverehrten Administration des Musikvereins

geehrtes Schreiben vom 16ten empfange ich so eben, und würde gern mich entschliessen haben das mir übertragne Preisrichter-Amt fortzuführen um Ihnen die Unannehmlichkeiten einer nochmaligen Wahl dadurch zu ersparen, und Ihnen zu bewiesen, wie aufrichtig ich die Ehre zu schätzen weiß, die mir durch Ihr Vertrauen erzeigt worden ist – aber glauben Sie mir, daß ich nicht ohne wichtige Gründe einer solchen Ehre entsagen konnte, und daß ich wirklich nicht im Stande bin, so sehr ich es auch wünschen mag, für jetzt die nöthige Zeit zu finden um solch ein Amt mit der erforderlichen Gewissenhaftigkeit zu versehen. Ich beabsichtige bald wieder eine Reise anzutreten, u. muß vorher so vielerlei Arbeiten und Geschäfte in Ordnung haben, daß es mir schwer wird allem zu genügen; als ich Ihre schmeichelhafte Aufforderung annahm hatte ich freie Zeit und glaubte Ihrer Sendungen in der Zeit von einigen Wochen oder Monaten entgegensehen zu dürfen. Da dies Ihnen durch die Umstände unmöglich gemacht worden ist, so würden die Sachen nun wieder bei mir Monate lang liegen müssen, ja ich wüßte Ihnen für den Lauf des Frühjahrs und Sommers noch gar nicht einmal eine bestimmte Adresse anzubringen, wo ich zu treffen wäre, da mich meine Reise vielleicht bis Italien führen wird, und um nicht Ihren Zwecken mehr zu schaden als zu nützen, u. die Sache entweder zu sehr in die Bänge zu ziehen oder oberflächlich zu behandeln, was ich mir beides nicht erlauben darf, bleibt mir nichts übrig als Sie nochmals um Entschuldigung zu bitten, daß ich das mir zugedachter Ehre für jetzt entsagen muß. Genehmigen Sie meine aufrichtigen ergebenen Dank dafür, u. die Versicherung der vollkommensten Hochachtung mit welcher ich bin

Ihr ergebenster
Felix Mendelssohn Bartholdy

Appendix Five

Edition of the
Rejected Second Movement of
Gade's Piano Sonata, Op. 28

Andantino

Index